INSIDE OUT

Worship
in an Age of
Mission

Thomas H. Schattauer, General Editor

FORTRESS PRESS | MINNEAPOLIS

Designed by Richard Krogstad.

*Library of Congress
Cataloging-in-Publication Data*
Inside out : worship in an age of mission /
Thomas H. Schattauer, general editor.
p.   cm.
Includes bibliographical references and index.
ISBN 0-8006-3156-0 (alk. paper)
1. Worship.
2. Missions—Theory.
3. Lutheran Church—Liturgy.
I. Schattauer, Thomas H.
BV10.2.I57   1999
264'.041—dc21   99-052336
CIP

The paper used in this publication
meets the minimum requirements
of American National Standard
for Information Sciences—
Permanence of Paper
for Printed Library Materials,
ANSI Z329.48-1984.

Manufactured in the U.S.A.
AF 1-3156

03   02   01   00   2   3   4   5   6

For our students —
past, present, and future

CONTENTS

PREFACE

This book began as a conversation among colleagues. In spring 1997, the professors of worship at the seminaries of the Evangelical Lutheran Church in America gathered in Chicago at the invitation of the ELCA worship staff for what has become an annual meeting. In the course of a discussion about the future of worship in our church, we identified a number of urgent matters affecting the liturgical life of North American congregations, among them the relationship between worship and mission in our own cultural context. As we talked, we began to consider how we might together address this issue from our perspective as those who study and teach liturgy. These chapters, authored by all nine ELCA seminary professors of worship and one colleague from the Evangelical Lutheran Church in Canada, are the result of that initial conversation and a sign of our partnership.

Although there are differences in approach and even disagreement among us, we share this point of view: the assembly for worship is intrinsically connected to the mission of God in Christ for the sake of the whole world (missio Dei), and consequently worship is integrally related to every form of the church's mission of witness and service. It is no accident that the concluding section of the ELCA's recent statement on the practice of word and sacrament concerns the means of grace and mission. There we find this encouragement: "In the teaching and practice of congregations, the *missional intention* of the means of grace needs to be recalled. By God's gift, the Word and sacraments are set *in the midst of the world, for the life of the world.*"[1] The chapters in this volume seek to interpret what that might mean, and it is our hope that they do so in a way that contributes to a larger ecumenical discussion about liturgy and mission.

Now we invite the reader into this conversation. The first and last chapters serve as introduction and conclusion to the body of eight chapters, which focus on particular liturgical topics—proclamation, baptism, holy communion, church year, liturgical space, music, ritual, and occasional services—in relation to mission. The chapters are interrelated but not dependent on one another, so the reader may take them up in any order.

Special thanks are due to Paul Nelson, ELCA Director for Worship, for hosting that first conversation and to Frank Stoldt at Augsburg Fortress, Publishers, for his support from the outset. Each chapter has benefitted from the keen eye of Beth Gaede, and Dennis Bushkofsky and Eric Vollen have patiently guided this book through the editorial process at the publishing house; to them we are most grateful. As the general editor, it has been my great privilege to work with each of the authors and to shepherd the project through its various stages. One could not hope for a more stimulating and supportive group of colleagues. My thanks to them for their commitment to the project and their persistence in bringing it to completion. May our work serve the missio Dei in local liturgical assemblies and further the faithful stewardship of the mysteries of God in our own time and place.

Thomas H. Schattauer

NOTES

1. *The Use of the Means of Grace: A Statement on the Practice of Word and Sacrament* (Evangelical Lutheran Church in America, 1997), application 51B, emphasis mine.

Liturgical Assembly as Locus of Mission

Thomas H. Schattauer

Over thirty years ago, J. G. Davies wrote a little book entitled *Worship and Mission*. At the outset, he noted the lack of contemporary reflection on the relationship between the church's worship and its mission:

> Those who make worship the object of their specialized study scarcely ever mention mission—not even in a footnote; while those who are concerned to develop the theology of mission seem in general to have little time for cultic acts. So worship and mission are treated as two totally distinct objects of theological investigation; they are placed in isolated compartments without the possibility of cross-fertilization and without the question of their unity being raised at all.[1]

Indeed, an examination of the work of liturgiologists and missiologists, according to Davies, might raise questions about the "complete dichotomy and even incompatibility" of worship and mission.[2]

It would not take too long to demonstrate that this disinterest in or aversion to considering the relationship between worship and mission no longer characterizes the work of those concerned primarily with either the church's mission or its worship. Much recent reflection about liturgy and mission has been motivated by questions about inculturation or contextualization in those parts of the world that have received patterns of worship from European and North American missionaries.[3] The advent of a post-Christian era in the West has encouraged significant reflection about the forms of worship appropriate to this new missional situation.[4]

The question remains whether we have reached any clarity about the relationship between liturgy and mission. There are, it seems to me, at least three approaches to the relationship: "inside and out" (conventional), "outside in" (contemporary), and "inside out" (radically traditional).

In the first approach, liturgy is understood and practiced as the quintessential activity for those inside the church community. Mission is what takes place on the outside when the gospel is proclaimed to those who have not heard or received it or, to broaden the notion of mission, when the neighbor is served in acts of love and justice. The relationship between the inside activity of worship and the outside activity of mission is portrayed thus: worship nurtures the individual and sustains the community in its life before God and in its life together, and from where Christians go out to serve the church's mission as proclaimers and doers of the gospel. They return to worship, perhaps with a few more folk gathered by this witness, and the cycle begins again. In this model, worship spiritually empowers those inside the church who take up the church's mission in the outside world. Note that this process describes an indirectly instrumental relationship between worship and mission. Worship serves the purpose of mission, not because it directly accomplishes the tasks of evangelical proclamation and diaconal service but because it offers access to the means of grace that propel the individual and the community as a whole into such activity. Worship and mission, however, remain distinct activities within clearly demarcated spheres of the church's life—inside and out.

Although this conventional approach to the relationship between worship and mission upholds the autonomy of the church's liturgical life, the strict demarcation between the church's internal activity (worship) on behalf of its members and the church's external activity (mission) for the sake of the world bifurcates our understanding of Christian life and finally fails to grasp adequately their unity. A contemporary response to the conventional model has been to bring the "outside" activities of mission directly into the context of worship. The sacred precinct of the liturgy becomes one of two things—either a stage from which to present the gospel and reach out to the unchurched and irreligious, or a platform from which to issue the call to serve the neighbor and rally commitment for social and political action. The first represents the outside-in strategies of the church growth movement, which promotes what is called contemporary worship, most noticeably in the suburban megachurches but also in the many congregations seeking to imitate them. The second represents the outside-in strategies of both liberal and conservative Christians who seek to orient worship to specific social and political goals. Note that in either strategy, the relationship between worship and mission is understood instrumentally but more directly than in the conventional inside-and-out approach. The church's worship is reshaped to take up the tasks of the church's mission, construed as evangelical outreach, social transformation, or both. The tasks of mission become the principal purpose of the church's worship—outside in.

There is a third way—inside out. This approach locates the liturgical assembly itself within the arena of the missio Dei. The focus is on God's mission toward the world, to which the church witnesses and into which it is drawn, rather than on specific activities of the church undertaken in response to the divine saving initiative. The missio Dei is God's own movement outward in relation to the world—in creation and the covenant with Israel, and culminating in Jesus Christ and the community gathered in him. This community is created by the Spirit to witness to the ultimate purposes of God, to reconcile the world to God's own self (2 Cor. 5:18-19). The gathering of a people to witness to and participate in this reconciling movement of God toward the world is an integral part of God's mission. The visible act of assembly (in Christ by the power of the Spirit) and the forms of this assembly—what we call liturgy—enact and signify this mission. From this perspective, there is no separation between liturgy and mission. The liturgical assembly of God's people in the midst of the world enacts and signifies the outward movement of God for the life of the world. Note that in this approach, the relationship between worship and mission is not instrumental, either directly or indirectly, but rather the assembly for worship *is* mission. The liturgical assembly is the visible locus of God's reconciling mission toward the world. The seemingly most internal of activities, the church's worship, is ultimately directed outward to the world. The judgment and mercy of God enacted within the liturgical assembly signify God's ultimate judgment and mercy for the world. Like a reversible jacket, the liturgy can be turned and worn inside out, and by so doing we see the relationship between worship and mission—inside out.[5]

∾

INSIDE OUT

It is this third approach—inside out—to the relationship between worship and mission that I want to explore further. It is both thoroughly contemporary and radically traditional, and it moves us beyond the conventionally traditional inside-and-out as well as the radically contemporary outside-in approaches. This is the approach Davies himself adopted in his explication of worship and mission:

> In the past the theological understanding of worship has been developed mainly in one direction, i.e., *inwardly:* for example, it has been interpreted as that which builds up the Body of Christ.... I think the time has come when we must adopt another approach, which is complementary rather than an alternative; we must seek to understand worship *outwardly* in terms of mission.[6]

In some recent attempts to articulate the shape of the church's mission in the North American context, we can discern a similar inside-out approach to the church's worship. In *Missional Church*, the product of a team of North American Protestant (Reformed, Methodist, Baptist, and Mennonite) theologians, worship is described as central to a "missional ecclesiology for North America":[7]

> Our postmodern society has come to regard worship as the private, internal, and often arcane activity of religionists who retreat from the world to practice their mystical rites. By definition, however, the *ekklesia* is a public assembly, and its worship is its first form of mission.... The reality of God that is proclaimed in worship is to be announced to and for the entire world.[8]

In his reflections on the church as a distinctive culture within post-Christian society, Rodney Clapp, an Episcopalian with strong ties to American evangelicals writes:

> I reject the terms of those who think the church at its worship is necessarily inward focused and removed from the "public" world. I want Christians to stop thinking in the essentially modern and liberal categories that cut up our lives as "private" and "public," "inward" and "outward."... Liturgy is the public work par excellence of the church—something that, if omitted, would mean the church was no longer the church. Far from being a retreat from the real world, worship enables Christians to see what the real world is and equips them to live in it. Liturgy also implies and enacts mission....
> ...All liturgy is related to mission.... The church exists for the sake of the world.... Worship teaches and forms us to live by the Jesus story so that others—the entire world, the church prays—will learn to live according to reality and wholeness. The people, the culture, that is now the church is joyful that God has already drawn it together, but it lives in hope of a greater joy, a joy that achieves fullness only in the kingdom's fullness.[9]

Some Lutherans have also taken up the inside-out approach. Bruce Marshall, for example, has argued for the central significance of

the church's eucharistic worship for the way that God is encountered in the midst of the world, within as well as outside the
church:

> On the one hand,...the church's unifying participation in God's own
> life happens, not primarily in the minds and hearts of individuals
> (though it does, of course, happen there), but in the public eucharis-
> tic celebration by which Christ joins individuals to himself and so
> makes them his own community. On the other hand, the eucharistic
> fellowship of the church, in which human beings are joined to Christ,
> and so to the Father, by the Spirit, is the particular way in which the
> triune God visibly exhibits to and in the world his own single and
> eternal life.[10]

Frank Senn's book *The Witness of the Worshiping Community* is an
extended explication of the claim that "worship is itself an aspect of
the mission of God."[11] Or listen to Gordon Lathrop:

> The local assembly...is itself the full presence, in this place, of all that
> Christians have to say about the ordering of place, time, and society.
> Christian liturgy means to invite people to discover the wide applica-
> bility—we may call it, poetically and religiously, the universal
> meaning—of what is done in the assembly....
> The world that is thereby suggested is not the status quo, but an
> alternative vision that waits for God, hopes for a wider order than has
> yet been achieved or than any ritual can embody, but still embraces the
> present environment of our experience.[12]

Certain statements in the Evangelical Lutheran Church in
America's statement on liturgical practice, *The Use of the Means of
Grace,* also evidence the inside-out approach to understanding the
relationship between worship and mission:

> In every celebration of the means of grace, God acts to show forth
> both the need of the world and the truth of the Gospel.... Jesus Christ,
> who is God's living bread come down from heaven, has given his flesh
> to be the life of the world. This very flesh, given for all, is encountered
> in the Word and sacraments.
> ...In the teaching and practice of congregations, the missional in-
> tention for the means of grace needs to be recalled. By God's gift, the
> Word and the sacraments are set in the midst of the world, for the life
> of the world.[13]

Statements like these, however, stand next to statements that continue to reflect the inside-and-out approach with its instrumental
view of worship:

In every gathering of Christians around the proclaimed Word and the holy sacraments, God acts to empower the Church for mission.[14]

The conventional distinction between worship on the inside and mission on the outside has not fully given way to a more radical understanding of their deep unity. Nonetheless, the inside-out impulse has gained a foothold.

~

Eucharistic piety

The inside-out approach to the relationship between worship and mission bears with it concrete implications for the shape and content of the church's liturgical life and the piety of Christian people. Allow me to illustrate this with some reflection on my own liturgical genealogy.

Sunday services in the church of my youth invariably began with the confession of sins. I remember vividly the words from the *Service Book and Hymnal* (1958) that the pastor (who was also my father—liturgical genealogy is inevitably intertwined with family genealogy) spoke before the prayer of general confession:

> Almighty God, our Maker and Redeemer, we poor sinners confess unto thee, that we are by nature sinful and unclean, and that we have sinned against thee by thought, word, and deed. Wherefore we flee for refuge to thine infinite mercy, seeking and imploring thy grace, for the sake our Lord Jesus Christ.[15]

I know that those beautiful and gracious words about fleeing for refuge to God's infinite mercy sunk deeply into my being. I also know that I spent a great deal of my spiritual energy reflecting about how I was "by nature sinful and unclean" and precisely how I had sinned against God "by thought, word, and deed," so that I could flee to God's mercy. Paul's contorted speech in Romans 7 about the good that I would but cannot do because of the "sin that dwells within me," including its note of thanksgiving to God through Christ for deliverance from "this body of death," provided a touchstone in my devotional life between Sundays.

Holy communion was celebrated monthly, and receiving Christ's body and blood was for me an even more intense and personal confrontation with my own sinfulness and the promise of forgiveness. I remember the impression of the proper prefaces that wonderfully linked our thanksgiving to Christ in the unfolding feasts and seasons of the church year. The words of institution, however, made the deepest impact: "my body, which is given for you…my blood, which is shed for you, and for many, for the remission of sins; this do…in remembrance of me."[16] My first communion took place on Maundy Thursday following confirmation on Palm Sunday of my ninth-grade year. This conjunction of first communion with the Holy Week commemoration of our Lord's last supper with his disciples provides an emblem for a significant piece of my Lord's supper piety. The mental picture that I brought to the reception of communion transported me back to the upper room on the night of our Lord's betrayal, and there I took my place at table among the Lord's disciples.

These recollections of the practice of confession and communion and how they shaped my own piety are by no means the whole picture of my early liturgical formation. That larger view would have to take account of many things: the impact of the preaching that shaped every service; the joy I always found hearing my voice joined with others in the song of liturgy and hymns and choir anthems; the impression of a spatial environment that visually gathered us around table, pulpit, and font;[17] and much more. It would also have to take account of the turmoil I was experiencing outside the church and my own struggle to understand it in relation to what I did inside on Sunday morning: black Americans marching, suffering, dying for fundamental civil rights; the specter of environmental degradation and nuclear war; protests against the Vietnam War and the draft; apocalyptic predictions about overpopulation and hunger; the voices of women raised for equal rights; and the youth culture itself, with its hair and jeans and music and sex and drugs; and again much more.

This liturgical genealogy is my own, and at certain points it may even be idiosyncratic. Let me suggest, however, that the two reflections about confession and communion point to a pervasive liturgical piety characterized by the following abstractions. It was penitential, individual, retrospective, and institutional. It was about sin and forgiveness; it was about a personal relationship to God and to other people; it was focused on past events, especially Jesus' life, death, and resurrection; and it was about the administration of grace in the church through the means of word and sacrament. It corresponded to the conventional inside-and-out approach to worship and mission.

It would be difficult to identify the point where my own liturgical piety began to shift. As I have indicated, traces of something else were already present in my early liturgical formation. The Contemporary Worship series,[18] the trial materials that prepared the way for the publication of *Lutheran Book of Worship*[19] in 1978, in conjunction with my own seminary studies in Bible, theology, liturgy, and Christian art and architecture were especially formative. In the new liturgical rites, I noted and welcomed the absence of the words "by nature sinful and unclean" in the order of confession and forgiveness that preceded the service of Holy Communion. Instead, we confessed that "we are in bondage to sin and cannot free ourselves."[20] And it was even possible to begin a Sunday service without the preparatory confession. *LBW* also promoted attention to the eucharistic center of Christian worship and exposed me to eucharistic praying that set the celebration of the Lord's supper (and my last supper piety) within the sweep of God's activity from the creation of the world to the consummation of all things in the Lord's "coming in power to share with us the great and promised feast" (Eucharistic prayer I).[21]

There was a moment, however, when I began to articulate the movement that was taking place in my liturgical piety. In February 1977, Wolfhart Pannenberg gave some lectures at Yale Divinity School entitled "Theological Issues in Christian Spirituality," since published in the volume *Christian Spirituality*.[22] The first two lectures traced the shift from the penitential piety that has dominated Western Christianity since the Middle Ages to a eucharistic piety emerging in our own time.

Pannenberg described the development of a Protestant pietism that focused "on the awareness of sin and guilt as a condition for genuine faith. One could be certain of salvation precisely to the extent that one identified oneself as a sinner completely dependent on the grace of God."[23] And further, he said:

> The strength of penitential pietism consisted in its support of those who felt themselves planted in the unshakable ground of the divine promise in Jesus Christ. But the price of this strength was self-aggression.... Another limitation has been its virtual individualism.... [A]n authentic conception of the Christian church was hard to develop on this basis,...for the body of Christ is more than an association of independent individuals.[24]

According to Pannenberg, there were signs that this penitential piety was giving way to a new type of piety, which he called eucharistic. Whereas the old piety had its origin in the medieval practice of penance, this new piety had its source in a renewed practice of the eucharist. "The rediscovery of the Eucharist may prove to be the most important event in Christian spirituality of our time, of more revolutionary importance than even the liturgical renewal may realize."[25] In Pannenberg's view, the symbolism of the eucharist in its communal, sacrificial, and eschatological dimensions represented a reorientation of Christian piety away from a narrow focus on the individual entangled in sin and toward the church as a communion of those united to Christ, toward the world as the object of God's reconciling mission in the death of Jesus, and toward the kingdom of God as the ultimate "social destiny of all human life."[26] For Pannenberg, worship is at the center of the church's mission in relation to God's own ultimate purposes for the world:

> There is no reason for the existence of the church except to symbolize the future of the divine kingdom that Jesus came to proclaim. This explains in what specific sense worship is in the center of life of the church: The worship of the Christian community anticipates and symbolically celebrates the praise of God's glory that will be consummated in the eschatological renewal of all creation in the new Jerusalem.[27]

I listened attentively to all of this twenty-some years ago and realized that Pannenberg's description of an epochal shift in Christian piety summed up the reorientation of my own liturgical piety. His provocative reflections in those two essays have been a touchstone for my thinking about worship ever since. The focus of worship shifted from matters of personal salvation and devotion to matters of the liturgical assembly's significance "for the life of the world," to use the Johannine phrase (John 6:51—ὑπὲρ τῆς τοῦ κόσμου ζωῆς) found in the Byzantine anaphora of St. Basil[28] and popularized by the Russian Orthodox theologian Alexander Schmemann.[29] The liturgy, most especially the eucharist, enacted God's world-redeeming and world-reconciling purpose in Christ, and it constituted a people to witness to that eschatological reality in every dimension of its life. The community of the church and its liturgical assembly was from this perspective the visible locus of the missio Dei, the symbolic enactment of God's eschatological purposes for the world in the midst of the world. Whereas my former liturgical piety was penitential, individual, retrospective, and institutional, the newly emerging piety was eucharistic, communal, prospective, and symbolic. It corresponded to the radically traditional inside-out approach to worship and mission.

For each of these adjectival abstractions about the contemporary liturgical assembly—eucharistic, communal, prospective, and symbolic—we can point to particular liturgical patterns and practices that constitute what it means to celebrate the liturgy of the church in its local assembly (inside) as a liturgy for a church in mission (out)—inside out. The "missional intention for the means of grace," "the Word and the sacraments...set in the midst of the world, for the life of the world" *(The Use of the Means of Grace)* are much more than newfangled ideas about worship meant to uphold the relevance of liturgy for a missional church. On the contrary, they represent the deepest movements of historic liturgical practice. What follows sketches some concrete examples of the inside-out approach to the liturgical practice of a missional church.

Liturgical Assembly as Eucharistic
The principal form of Christian prayer is *eucharistia* or "thanksgiving." The central prayer of the liturgy is a great thanksgiving, restored to its fullness in Lutheran liturgical books first in the American Lutheran *Service Book and Hymnal* (1958) and now in *Lutheran Book of Worship* (1978). Its deepest roots are to be found in forms of Jewish prayer called *berakoth* (blessings) and Jewish sacrifice, especially the *zebach todah* or sacrifice of thanksgiving, as well as in the pattern of Jesus' own meal fellowship, especially on the night in which he was given up to death on a cross for sake of this world's life. Christian *eucharistia* gives thanks over the bread and wine of that same meal fellowship but now with the risen Lord. In its thanksgiving, the Christian assembly remembers its crucified and risen Lord. It also acknowledges the work of a gracious God in creating the world, calling out a people Israel, and gathering a new people as witness to the gospel of Jesus' death and resurrection. Moreover, the assembly that prays this prayer anticipates the fulfillment of God's promises and supplicates the Holy One for its own unity in the Spirit, which signifies already the promised unity of all tribes and nations in the kingdom of God.

Between its thankful remembrance and its hope-filled supplication, the church in its liturgical assembly carries out its eucharistic mission to witness to God's liberating judgment of the world and the world-encompassing mercy of God in the cross of Jesus Christ. The horizon of this great prayer of thanksgiving is always the world and the world's future in the unfolding of God's plan of salvation. Such a prayer celebrates *koinonia*, the reconciled communion with God that is already possible through Christ in the community of the church and yet remains a hope for the world and all its people, indeed, for the whole created order. In this way, the liturgical assembly in its *eucharistia* witnesses to and participates in the missio Dei. The liturgical assembly centered on such fervent praying in thanks for what God has done and in confident supplication for the world is a far remove from one oriented around the prayer of the penitent and the Lord's supper celebrated only as a promise of forgiveness, both of which focus on the self and its deliverance from sin.[30]

Liturgical Assembly as Communal

THOMAS H. SCHATTAUER

In liturgical formularies, the assembly itself is often designated by the term *people* (in Greek, λάος; in Latin, *populus*), and this usage is preserved, for example, in the English translation of the *Roman Sacramentary* and the American *Book of Common Prayer*. The reference of the term, it seems to me, is multiple—"this people" here gathered, that is, the local assembly; "a people," that is, the church as the visible people of God in the world; and even "the people," that is, the totality of all people. In the liturgy, all three of these meanings stand in relationship to one another. This local assembly is the church catholic in a particular place; it is also in communion with other local assemblies and as such represents the whole people of God; and this people finally also stands for all people, for in the liturgy, this people "does the world" as God would have it.[31]

All these meanings suggest the deeply communal character of Christianity. According to the Russian Orthodox theologian Georges Florovsky,

> Christianity entered history as a new social order, or rather a new social dimension. From the very beginning Christianity was not primarily a "doctrine," but exactly a "community." There was not only a "Message" to be proclaimed and delivered, and "Good News" to be declared. There was precisely a New Community, distinct and peculiar, in the process of growth and formation, to which members were called and recruited. Indeed, "fellowship" *(koinonia)* was the basic category of Christian existence.[32]

At the center of the gospel stand two things together, the message of salvation for the ungodly—for all—in Jesus Christ, embodied in an assembly for all, an assembly defined not by the markers of difference—age, race, gender, wealth, or status—but by baptism into Christ. In this way, the *koinonia* of the church, constituted and manifest in its liturgical assembly, is the missio Dei, as it happens now and in anticipation of the fullness of this communion in the kingdom of God. More than a collection of individuals with concern for personal salvation, the liturgical assembly enacts the communion that is the church, in the hope of that wider communion that is God's ultimate purpose.

Liturgical Assembly as Prospective

Much of Christian liturgical celebration appears to be about past events. At Christmas, we remember the birth of Jesus; at Epiphany, the visit of the magi; on Good Friday, Jesus' death on the cross, and at Easter, his resurrection; on Ascension Day, Jesus' going to the Father; and at Pentecost, the outpouring of the Spirit on the disciples. Whenever the Lord's supper is celebrated, it is Jesus' last supper with his disciples or the crucifixion with Jesus' body given and blood poured out. The liturgy, from this perspective, becomes a ritual "bridging of the gap" between these events and our present, a ritual mechanism either to make the past somehow present to us or to make us somehow present to the past. This focus on the liturgical representation of the past, however, seems to miss the point that the liturgy is about a relationship with the risen Lord, who lives and reigns with the Father and the Holy Spirit, and to whom this past belongs. Moreover—and this is the critical point—the Risen One is himself the first fruits of the kingdom that lies before us, and consequently the remembrance of him always orients us to that future. Liturgical *anamnesis* is as much about the present and the future as it is about the past. Let us say it this way: Through the *memory* of Jesus Christ—his coming in the flesh, his life, death, and resurrection—our lives are directed in *hope* to the kingdom of God that Jesus proclaimed and to God's ultimate purposes for us and our world, just as we enjoy even now Christ's life-giving *presence* in the assembly of the faithful through word and sacrament by the power of the Holy Spirit.

As a community with prospective vision, the church in every present moment lives toward the reign of God inaugurated in Jesus Christ. The eschatological perspective permeates the liturgical assembly, because in Christ this community enacts the hope of the world for its ultimate reconciliation to God in a fellowship of love, peace, and justice. The missio Dei is nothing other than what the church as an eschatological community enacts in its liturgical assembly and in which it participates precisely by this enactment. Such an assembly is anything but focused on the past but lives in the present toward the future God has promised in Jesus Christ.

Liturgical Assembly as Symbolic

At the Vigil of Easter, there is an ancient and lengthy prayer, the Easter proclamation, that sings the meaning of that night in the light of the paschal candle. The proclamation begins with an extended invitation summoning the whole created order into the praise of God for the deliverance and restoration the Almighty One has wrought in Christ:

> Rejoice, now,
>> all heavenly choirs of angels....
> Exult, also, O earth,
>> enlightened with such radiance....

Be glad also, O mother Church,…
and let this house resound
with the triumphant voices
of the peoples.
Wherefore, dearly beloved,
who stand in the clarity
of this bright and holy light.…[33]

This arena is a highly symbolic one in which the gathering of a local company of the faithful around a flickering flame in the middle of the night is set in relation to choirs of angels, the earth, and the whole church encompassing the peoples, all joined in a joyful eruption of cosmic praise. The liturgical assembly is never just what it appears to be. It always points to the eschatological reality beyond itself, to the purpose of God in Christ for the world and its peoples, for the whole created order. This is what it means to call the liturgical assembly symbolic.

The liturgical assembly is suffused with symbolic language and symbolic acts precisely because the church itself is a symbolic community.[34] The purpose of the church is essentially symbolic: in its very existence as a community in Christ, the church points to the kingdom of God as the ultimate shape of reality. The gathering of people into this symbolic representation of God's purposes for the world is the church's part in the missio Dei, all of which underscores the fundamental connection between the symbolic character of the liturgical assembly and the church's mission. More than a place for individuals to encounter word and sacrament as institutions of grace, the church in its assembly around word and sacrament enacts a ritual symbol of God's gracious purpose for the world and so participates in God's world-encompassing mission.

~

ENGAGING THE CULTURE

The next step is to show how this inside-out approach to the relationship between the church's worship and its mission resonates in response to the greatest aspirations and the deepest needs at work in the contemporary cultural context. How do the eucharistic, communal, prospective, and symbolic dimensions of the liturgical assembly engage the vitality and delights, the lacks and longing of the contemporary moment in North American culture? How does the eucharistic gathering of God's people in a particular place as a sign of God's purposes for the world—as a visible enactment of the missio Dei—engage us as people shaped by the forces of life in the modern or postmodern world? These are large questions that ask us to ponder the intersection of the liturgical assembly and contemporary life and to articulate how the contours of this gathering are precisely about God's mission among us and in our world today. What follows is the beginning of such a reflection.

God at the Center

If the liturgical assembly is indeed pervasively eucharistic—consummately enacted in the great thanksgiving and the reception of communion—what does such thanksgiving to God mean for people today? How might such thanksgiving shape the experience of contemporary life in North America? First, it orients us to the source of all things, to the almighty and everlasting God, who has created and continually sustains the world and everything in it. Such a recognition is diminished, if not altogether eliminated, in the scientific rationality that permeates the daily existence of most people. The modern worldview gives place to God, if at all, at the margins of life and confines the divine to what is private and personal. The God of Christian *eucharistia*, however, stands at the center of all things and is not limited to any sphere of life. The practice of thanksgiving at the heart of Christian worship embodies the doxological foundation of human existence. As Nathan Mitchell writes,

> To be is to worship; human existence is inescapably liturgical, doxological. Doxology...is "ontologically constitutive"; it is what makes our existence as human subjects possible.... Quite simply, we become ourselves only in the act of praising God.[35]

Furthermore, the *eucharistia* of the liturgical assembly offers a distinct alternative to the way of life shaped by modern consumer culture. The market economy is a dynamic, creative, and dominant force in contemporary life. It offers the promise of prosperity, freedom, and choice to large segments of North American society. At the same time, substantial numbers of people do not participate in this promise and struggle with poverty in the midst of affluence. Such an economy depends on consumption—on consumers who acquire things and enjoy them. Acquisition and enjoyment give shape to life in a consumer culture. The eucharistic gathering of Christians, however, "proclaim[s] the Lord's death until he comes" (1 Cor. 11:26; also eucharistic prayer I in *LBW*[36]) and seeks to shape our lives in relation to the cross of Christ. Instead of defining human existence in terms of the acquisition and enjoyment of things, the thanksgiving to God for Jesus' passion, death, and resurrection at the center of Christian worship defines the fullness of life in terms of the gift of communion with God and its corollary, the possibility of freedom to live for others according to God's purposes for the world.

Christian *eucharistia* in the contemporary North American liturgical assembly is about the mission of God in a time and place where there is forgetfulness about God and a compulsion to satisfy ourselves through the accumulation of many possessions. It redirects us to the living God, to our communion with this God through Christ, and to a life for others. Finally, this *eucharistia* is deeply connected to the fervent supplication that these blessings from God will extend beyond the assembly itself and encompass all who know this same forgetfulness and compulsion.

A Distinctive Community

The communal dimension of the liturgical assembly also meets the present moment in a very particular way. Many commentators have noted the radical individualism that characterizes the contemporary American way of life, including its religious life. If, however, the liturgical assembly is about "the people" in every sense of that word—the locally gathered people, the people of God throughout the world, and all people everywhere—then the matter of Christian worship is about something other than confirming us in our individual ways. It shapes a common life, a life decidedly with others. "Behold the church!" declared the nineteenth-century German Lutheran pastor and theologian Wilhelm Loehe. "It is the very opposite of loneliness—blessed fellowship!"[37] The fellowship of the church satisfies "the desire for fellowship...born in us," just as it directs us to the "real fellowship desired by God, a fellowship created by God for eternity."[38] The act of assembly for worship at the center of Christian life and practice enacts this fellowship, establishing the place of the individual in community. "There is no solitary earth and no solitary heaven,"[39] to again use Loehe's words. Because it enacts the essentially communal nature of human existence and human destiny, the liturgical assembly counters the distortions of contemporary individualism.

The communal vision at the heart of the church and its worship, however, also counters the distortions of communal claims and arrangements that destroy the dignity of the individual. Alongside the impetus to individualism, the modern period is replete with nationalistic impulses, ideological movements, and utopian programs that seek to shape human communities and command the allegiance of individuals. In their extreme forms, such movements are coercive and exclusionary, and they often operate out of an understanding of human nature that fails to grasp fully the human capacity for evil. The inevitable result is a disregard for the individual and a lack of concern for the well-being of each person. It is important to acknowledge that such disregard can also infect the church as a community. Nonetheless, the kind of community to which the church is committed—especially in its worship—is not determined by territory, ideology, or fantasy. It is a place where each individual stands equally before God's judgment and mercy and where the well-being of the least cannot be ignored.

The communal character of the liturgical assembly is a critical aspect of the mission of God in contemporary circumstances. On the one hand, it critiques every notion of the autonomous individual and affirms the fundamentally social nature of human existence. On the other hand, it critiques every form of human community that disregards the dignity and well-being of the individual, including the structures and practices of churchly life itself. This critique takes place because the church, constituted in its liturgical assembly, is a distinctive community amid the plurality of human communities, the one community that refers us ultimately to the fellowship that God establishes and promises to be the destiny of human existence.

God's Future

Because the community of the church refers beyond itself to the fellowship of all people in the kingdom of God, its assembly for worship has a prospective character, as we have seen. This theological orientation to the future provides a connection to the contemporary focus on the future. One characteristic of the modern sensibility is to cast off the weight of the past and to look forward with confidence in human progress. The meaning of things is in what lies ahead of us, and this is where our cultural energy is directed. The Christian eschatology that shapes the prospective dimension of the liturgical assembly is similar to this outlook but with two important qualifications. First, the past is understood more positively. It is not just a limit to be surpassed. Rather, through the activity of God in human history, the past bears relation to the future—especially in the life, death, and resurrection of Jesus, which contain the meaning of the future. Second, the future that concerns the liturgical assembly is a particular future. It is God's future, a future beyond all human projection and imagining. So the prospective orientation is finally trust in God, to whom the future belongs, not a misplaced confidence in human progress.

Indeed, there are many who do not share the modern confidence about the future. Nurtured by postmodern disillusionment about human progress, they are skeptical, even despairing, about the future. What remains is the present, a present dissociated from the past and the future. Robert Jenson has addressed the difficulty of having no future orientation:

> It is the whole vision of an Eschaton that is now missing outside the church. The assembly of believers must therefore itself be the event in which we may behold what is to come....
>
> If, in the *post*-modern world, a congregation or whatever wants to be "relevant," its assemblies must be unabashedly events of shared apocalyptic vision. "Going to church" must be a journey to the place where we will behold our destiny, where we will see what is to come of us.[40]

The prospective vision of the Christian liturgical assembly shapes a context in which people isolated in the present moment are broken open to the testimony of God's activity in human history and to the hope for a future determined by God's purposes for the world. Such a response to contemporary cynicism offers a framework for living that upholds connections to the past and the future while acknowledging the complexities and limitations of human existence.

Once again the church in its assembly for worship is about the mission of God in the present as that assembly engages contemporary perspectives on the world's future (and its past). Where there is unlimited confidence about the human ability to understand and shape the future, the prospective dimension of the liturgical assembly directs that confidence instead to the future that God promises. Where there is doubt about the future, it constructs a framework of hope in God's purposes for the world.

Engaging the Culture's Images

We come finally to the symbolic dimension of the liturgical assembly and its intersection with contemporary life. One clear point of intersection is the role that visual images play both in the symbolic environment of the liturgy and in the electronic media. Present-day North Americans are awash in a sea of images emanating from the television and increasingly from the computer. Whereas words—spoken, written, and printed—have been the dominant form of human communication, the visual image has emerged as a powerful force in contemporary mass communication. The visual image is also critical to the liturgy's ritual and symbolic communication, and indeed the importance of the visual image in contemporary culture has helped to heighten sensitivity to the visual experience of worship and to what is imaged in the ritual activity of worshiping assemblies.

Attending to the visual image in Christian worship becomes all the more important when we look further into the messages communicated by the electronic media. In her study of the impact of television images, Gregor Goethals has labeled television "the electronic golden calf," suggesting a correspondence between America's worship at this video altar and Israel's idolatrous worship of the golden calf at the foot of Mount Sinai (Exod. 32).[41] She convincingly interprets the constant flow of images from the television, which saturates our experience, as an "expression of an encompassing faith in the American way of life."[42] These electronic images construct a "symbolic canopy" that shapes a way of life, particularly in relation to the values of individualism and consumerism:

> "Choice" is…the most magical word in American culture…. The steady hum over radio and television about the choices we have is a litany to liberty, to the freedom to choose one product over another, and above all to define one's individuality through one's choices.[43]

She concludes that "unless we recognize the power of the media to construct symbolic worlds, we will not even grasp the range of mediated values or recognize the real choices to be made. Nor will we understand the need for a daring iconoclasm."[44]

The images at work within the church's own symbolic life, especially its liturgical assembly, are potentially the Christian community's most powerful force for engaging and critiquing the electronic images of contemporary life and breaking the idolatrous images that contend for our worship. The ritual images of worship—derived from scripture and enacted in the reading of the word and its proclamation, in the gathering at the font, and in the eating and drinking at the table of thanksgiving—all relate to the saving death of Jesus and to the hope found there for the whole world. This symbolic canopy mediates God's judgment and God's generosity. It is not so much about choice as it is about being chosen "in Christ before the foundation of the world" (Eph. 1:4); it is not so much about individuality as it is about being part of "a chosen race, a royal priesthood, a holy nation, God's own people" (1 Peter 2:9). Those who participate in the liturgical assembly are encompassed by its images and in that symbolic canopy themselves become the image of God's purposes for the world. The liturgical assembly is about the missio Dei in the midst of the symbolic world of contemporary popular culture.

∼

LITURGY FOR A CHURCH IN MISSION

These embryonic reflections are intended to show that the liturgical assembly is where God's mission takes place—a locus of mission—not merely in the abstraction of theological ideas but in the concrete reality of North American cultural circumstances. In its eucharistic, communal, prospective, and symbolic dimensions, that local gathering of God's people does engage the vitality and delights, the lacks and longing of this time and place. The words of Wilhelm Loehe, whose own pastoral work over a century ago demonstrated the deep connections of liturgy and mission, offer us a fitting conclusion: "The church has put together according to holy orders...services of various kinds and esteems them to be understood by all the faithful as the highest harmony of earthly life and not only to be sung and spoken but to be lived."[45] The liturgy sung, spoken, *and lived* is liturgy for a church in mission—inside out.

NOTES

The bulk of this essay was initially prepared for the author's inaugural lecture at Wartburg Seminary, Dubuque, Iowa, on May 5, 1999.

1. J.G. Davies, *Worship and Mission* (London: SCM Press, 1966), 9.

2. Ibid., 10.

3. For an introduction, see the chapter "Inculturation" in John Fenwick and Bryan Spinks, *Worship in Transition: The Liturgical Movement in the Twentieth Century* (New York: Continuum, 1995), 157–66. The Lutheran World Federation study on worship and culture has generated a significant body of literature on these issues in its Cartigny, Nairobi, and Chicago statements, together with their supporting papers and bibliographies; see S. Anita Stauffer, ed., *Worship and Culture in Dialogue* (Geneva: Lutheran World Federation, 1994); *Christian Worship: Unity in Cultural Diversity* (Geneva: Lutheran World Federation, 1996); and *Baptism, Rites of Passage, and Culture* (Geneva: Lutheran World Federation, 1999).

4. In North America, this includes the debate surrounding so-called contemporary and traditional forms of worship as well as efforts to contextualize worship in the diverse cultures of North America. On the contemporary versus traditional discussion, compare, for example, Kennon L. Callahan, *Dynamic Worship: Mission, Grace, Praise, and Power* (San Francisco: HarperSanFrancisco, 1994) and Timothy Wright, *A Community of Joy: How to Create Contemporary Worship* (Nashville: Abingdon Press, 1994) to Frank C. Senn, *The Witness of the Worshiping Community: Liturgy and the Practice of Evangelism* (New York: Paulist Press, 1993) and the series Open Questions in Worship, ed. Gordon W. Lathrop, 8 vols. (Augsburg Fortress, 1994–96), especially vol. 1, *What Are the Essentials of Christian Worship?* vol. 2, *What Is "Contemporary" Worship?* vol. 3, *How Does Worship Evangelize?* and vol. 6, *What Are the Ethical Implications of Worship?* On the matter of worship and the cultures of North America, see, for example, vol. 7 in the Open Questions series, *What Does "Multicultural" Worship Look Like?* See also the new ethnic liturgical resources prepared by the Evangelical Lutheran Church in America: the Spanish-language worship

book *Libro de Liturgia y Cántico* (Minneapolis: Augsburg Fortress, 1998) and *This Far by Faith: An African American Resource for Worship* (Minneapolis: Augsburg Fortress, 1999).

5. These schematic descriptions of what I have termed the conventional, contemporary, and radically traditional approaches to the relationship between worship and mission risk reducing some rather complex realities of church life and forcing them into clearly delineated models. Nonetheless, there is heuristic value—that is, we can learn something—in such descriptions, as long as we are clear that the understanding and practice of worship in relation to mission in its concrete actuality in congregational life will not conform neatly to any proposed model.

6. Davies, *Worship and Mission,* 7.

7. Darrell L. Guder, ed., *Missional Church: A Vision for the Sending of the Church in North America* (Grand Rapids, Mich.: Wm. B. Eerdmans, 1998), 242.

8. Ibid., 243.

9. Rodney Clapp, *A Peculiar People: The Church as Culture in a Post-Christian Society* (Downers Grove, Ill.: InterVarsity, 1996), 114–15.

10. Bruce D. Marshall, "The Disunity of the Church and the Credibility of the Gospel," *Theology Today* 50, no. 1 (April 1993): 81–82.

11. Senn, *The Witness of the Worshiping Community,* 5.

12. Lathrop, *Holy Things: A Liturgical Theology* (Minneapolis: Fortress Press, 1993), 207–10.

13. *The Use of the Means of Grace: A Statement on the Practice of Word and Sacrament* (Evangelical Lutheran Church in America, 1997), principle 51 and application 51B.

14. Ibid., principle 51; the heading for principle 51 itself underscores the instrumental view—"The Means of Grace Lead the Church to Mission."

15. *Service Book and Hymnal* (Minneapolis: Augsburg Publishing House; Philadelphia: Board of Publication, Lutheran Church in America, 1958), 1.

16. Ibid., 12.

17. The space was one designed by Sovik, Mathre, and Madson, Northfield, Minnesota, for Bethesda Lutheran Church, Ames, Iowa, and dedicated in 1964.

18. Contemporary Worship, 10 vols. (Minneapolis: Augsburg Publishing House; Philadelphia: Board of Publication, Lutheran Church in America; St. Louis: Concordia Publishing House, 1969–76).

19. *Lutheran Book of Worship* (Minneapolis: Augsburg Publishing House; Philadelphia: Board of Publication, Lutheran Church in America, 1978).

20. Ibid., 56.

21. Ibid., 70.

22. Wolfhart Pannenberg, *Christian Spirituality* (Philadelphia: Westminster, 1983).

23. Ibid., 17.

24. Ibid., 31–32.

25. Ibid., 31.

26. Ibid., 46.

27. Ibid., 36.

28. See R.C.D. Jasper and G.J. Cuming, *Prayers of the Eucharist: Early and Reformed,* 3rd ed. (New York: Pueblo Publishing, 1987), 119.

29. Alexander Schmemann, *For the Life of the World: Sacraments and Orthodoxy* (Crestwood, N.Y.: St. Vladimir's Seminary Press, 1973).

30. It is worth noting that prior to his polemical writings about the mass, which presented the Lord's supper as a testament or promise of forgiveness, Luther's theology of the Lord's supper gave great weight to *koinonia* as the significance of the sacrament; see "The Blessed Sacrament of the Holy and True Body of

Christ, and the Brotherhoods, 1519," in *Luther's Works,* ed. Helmut T. Lehmann (Philadelphia: Fortress Press, 1960), 35:50–60. Although the centrality of this conception of the sacrament recedes in Luther's struggle against the sacrifice of the mass, it is never abandoned and should remain a part of any full account of Luther's understanding of the Lord's supper. One could explore, for example, the connections of the communion concept of the sacrament to Luther's strong defense of the real presence against the views of other reformers; see "The Adoration of the Sacrament, 1523" in *Luther's Works,* ed. Lehmann (Philadelphia: Fortress Press, 1959), 36:286–87; in "The Sacrament of the Body and Blood of Christ—Against the Fanatics, 1526" in *Luther's Works,* ed. Lehmann (Philadelphia: Fortress Press, 1959), 36:352–53; and "Against the Heavenly Prophets in the Matter of Images and Sacraments, 1525" in *Luther's Works,* ed. Lehmann (Philadelphia: Fortress Press, 1958), 40:178. See Yngve Brilioth, *Eucharistic Faith and Practice: Evangelical and Catholic,* trans. A.G. Hebert (London: SPCK, 1961), 95–98, 133–35; Pannenberg, *Christian Spirituality,* 38–41; and Thomas H. Schattauer, "The Reconstruction of Rite: The Liturgical Legacy of Wilhelm Löhe," in *Rule of Prayer, Rule of Faith: Essays in Honor of Aidan Kavanagh, O.S.B.,* ed. Nathan Mitchell and John F. Baldovin, S.J. (Collegeville, Minn.: Liturgical Press, 1996), 275–76.

31. The reference is to Aidan Kavanagh, *On Liturgical Theology* (New York: Pueblo Publishing, 1984); see esp. chap. 4, "Doing the World," 52–69.

32. Georges Florovsky, *Empire and Desert: Antinomies of Christian History,* as quoted in Clapp, *A Peculiar People,* flyleaf.

33. *Lutheran Book of Worship* Ministers Edition (Minneapolis: Augsburg Publishing House; Philadelphia: Board of Publication, Lutheran Church in America, 1978), 144.

34. See Pannenberg, *Christian Spirituality,* 35–38.

35. Nathan Mitchell, "The Amen Corner: 'Worship as Music,'" *Worship* 73, no. 4 (July 1999): 254. Mitchell is reflecting on and quoting from Catherine Pickstock, *After Writing: On the Liturgical Consummation of Philosophy* (Oxford: Blackwell, 1998), 196.

36. *LBW,* 70.

37. Wilhelm Loehe, *Three Books about the Church,* trans. and ed. James L. Schaaf (Philadelphia: Fortress Press, 1969), 51.

38. Ibid., 50.

39. Ibid., 49.

40. Robert Jenson, "How the World Lost Its Story," *First Things,* no. 36 (October 1993): 24.

41. Gregor T. Goethals, *The Electronic Golden Calf: Images, Religion, and the Making of Meaning* (Cambridge, Mass.: Cowley, 1990). Today her study would need to include the impact of the computer and the dissemination of images through the Internet.

42. Ibid., 145.

43. Ibid., 150–51. The term "symbolic canopy" appears on p. 163.

44. Ibid., 156.

45. Wilhelm Löhe, "Von den heiligen Personen, der heiligen Zeit, der heiligen Weise und dem heiligen Orte" (1859), in *Gesammelte Werke,* vol. 3/1 (Neuendettelsau: Freimund, 1951), 570.

Proclamation: Mercy for the World

Jann E. Boyd Fullenwieder

How do scripture and proclamation relate to God's mission and the Christian assembly? We cannot answer this question without addressing two prior questions: What is God up to in the world? And what is God up to in the Christian assembly? Once we respond to these questions, we can explore what specifically scripture and proclamation have to do with the worshiping community, those united with Christ through the waters of baptism, and God's mysterious ways with us. Then we will be able to examine some of the urgent and even ancient concerns about our current gospel proclamation.

∾

WHAT IS GOD UP TO IN THE WORLD?
God meets us in the midst of history and in the universe of God's creation. It is there that God simultaneously shows and tells us who God is. By blessing creation as the arena of God's speech, God identifies the source of life. God speaks purposefully, even speaking as a triune reality from everlasting to everlasting. God speaks, thus beginning the grand, far-flung generative dialogue of creation. God speaks promise, choosing Israel as a sign of God's covenant to be with us always. God speaks the Word, Jesus, who reveals God to the world, promising and providing abundant life. Through the incarnation of God in the son of Mary, God chose to become human, to be bound by time and culture and to a particular language. God chose what is weak, broken, prone to decay: a gendered, historied body born into a particular tradition of symbols, signs, and rituals

communicated through a nonuniversal language. Yet God's good news to us is that this Word of God "became flesh and lived among us, full of grace and truth" (John 1:14).

Jesus—growing within his mother's womb, being born, living, serving, dying, and being raised to preside "at the right hand of God"—is God's proclamation, revealing who we are not and who God created us to be, disclosing God's unquenchable love for the whole creation. Through the activity of the Holy Spirit and the ministry of Jesus, God creates a people in every time and place to speak for God in the world. The church, created by God's word, is God's "mouth house," as Martin Luther quipped, a sign of God's holy will to hear the cry of the whole creation—and to heal, making all things new.

God continually initiates dialogue in history. In Jesus' life, God's dialogue with the world takes concrete, historic, and visible shape. In Jesus, God images who God is for the world: the One who fulfills, heals, and endures all things, even death, and who ultimately overturns death. From the beginning, God calls humanity to be partners, to keep and prosper what God gives. In Jesus-for-us, God shows us the goal of all God's dreams for humanity, dreams for life beyond brokenness and despair, beyond death.

～

How do we hear God speaking to us?

We hear God in the common garb of ordinary, human speech. Through ordinary people called to faith and to prophetic preaching, the God of Israel speaks, sharing the divine imagination and will. The focus of this divine proclamation is Jesus, the embodiment of God's desire for creation: that all creation be in faithful relationship with our creator God. Through Jesus, in the activity of the Holy Spirit, God's living word is spoken to us. Where God's word is heard, faith is created, and the church comes into being.

In this meeting of ordinary people attending to those things God gives us to do in word and sacrament, God proclaims the one who was and is and is to come; the one who is always for us; the one who is doing for us what we cannot do for ourselves—bringing life out of death. God is specifically involved with people through the tongues and ordinary activities by which we make sense of daily life. In every generation—from Abraham and Sarah, Mary and Joseph, Ambrose and Monica, Heloise and Abelard, Anne Askew and Hugh Latimer, Sarah Osborne and Rasmus Jensen, Dorothy Day and Oscar Romero, to Desmond Tutu and Mother Theresa, the disappeared and generations yet to be born—God speaks in the peoples' own tongues.

JANN E. BOYD
FULLENWIEDER

Mortal Language

Jesus is God's preacher. Jesus is the Word, the one who came preaching and the one who, being preached, revealed God. Yet Jesus was a Jew from Nazareth who spoke a particular language, in a particular religious context, to an ancient people. What do we make of the multilingual nature of human societies, this babel of tongues and variety of cultural frames of reference when we seek to speak Christ in words so that faith may spring forth and water creation?

The place where Christ and multilingual signs meet is the Sunday assembly. Frail flesh and words—forced to carry more than we can imagine—meet in the ancient shape of the gathering *in and for* the Word. In that assembly, the Word is brought to expression in the preaching that moves us to confess, and in authentic prayer that moves us to give thanks at the table from which we are sent away filled, formed to love creation. In this meeting, among the people assembled for the sake of Christ, grace is poured out, love is eaten, God greets us in truth we may trust. This meeting—like God's dialogue with the world—is always public (although words might be spoken within this dialogue between God and one person), and freely expressed words are heard, seen, signed, and symbolic.

God's availability to people in the simple stuff of language displays the humility of the God who chooses to be God by becoming incarnate. Languages, whether expressed in words or gestures, are found everywhere among humans and their societies. Our capacity to develop linguistic patterns through the use of images and symbols shapes human cultures. Thus, languages are limited and mutable mediators of knowledge. They shift over time and identify peoples of particular places as each civilization expresses itself. Nonetheless, God uses human communication to summon people of faith, so that God's will may be made known and life may abound.

∼

WHAT IS GOD UP TO IN THE CHRISTIAN ASSEMBLY?
In the Christian assembly, God's body takes form in our hearing, in our taking and eating, and in our going forth in grace. So the meeting is proclamatory, composed of a pattern of events, all signing that God is present. Here Jesus' preaching continues: it calls

everyone to the bath and the teaching, initiating them into the community of God's plentiful life. Here, through preaching, God speaks to those who follow, seek, and are curious. The preaching is always missionary, proclaiming the news that the dominion of God is being ushered in by one who is risen from the dead, opening for examination the promises of God, calling people to turn to God and see life, welcoming home the prodigal who has squandered the riches, searching for language that calls to the center those yearning ones who are scattered at the fringes and wandering on the byways.

In the meeting, God also places a water hole for all creation, a water hole large enough to drench any desert in history, deep enough to survive any drought, wide enough that all might gather to drink, wade in the waters, be pulled under and brought to the surface, revived from the heat of any day. Moreover, through the clear and strong witness of the proclamatory action of Sunday's gathering, God springs forth with fresh waters. The fountainhead for these waters without price is the gathering itself. It is to these waters that the church in every age calls others, crying throughout the marketplaces and village streets—Wisdom vending grace. Here is freedom. Here is a way to pray that will not falter. Here is a Spirit we do not make ourselves and that does not perish. Here is meaning that does not disintegrate amid the toxins of our lives. Here is one who meets us by the waters when we arrive thirsty or curious or ready to draw for ourselves. Here is one who knows us and teaches us to worship in truth. Here is one who teaches us new meanings to old words, as if we were the ancient Samaritan woman coming to draw what we think we understand, only to be surprised.

As the body God chooses here and now, as the water hole in this place, God makes the assembly multivalent and uses the event to call all creation home. The elder brothers and sisters who have been in the church all their lives; the hungry people dragged in from everywhere—smelly, suffering from incurable diseases, broken in spirit, full of errors and self-deceits, bellowing blindly for help, snaking up tree trunks to scope out Jesus; and the polite newcomers trying to see what is happening—Jesus calls all these folk through the preaching of the assembly. So God continues calling all the generations into the freedom of God, a freedom determined not by what has been but by what will be.

Full of God's active Spirit, the words of scripture opened through preaching and the use of sacramental signs equip the church for its calling to show forth Christ. The words of the meeting declare that our lives and struggles rest in Jesus, who is

raised beyond death and is fulfilling all God's promises. These are
the words of eternal life; they alone are worth echoing, translating, illustrating, imagining, and enacting.

The words that speak the eternal life of God are not calling people into an ideology or methodology. The meeting with Christ is lively communion with one another. It is an event making all things new, a declaration of a will that cannot be broken. When we who are baptized take up our birthright to meet and to hear the scriptures, to recall or enact the visible words of washing, to eat and drink in accordance with the words of Holy Scripture, and to be sent forth to bear and do the words of eternal life, we are rehearsing a particular mind that is ours in Christ Jesus. Taking up the preaching and meal-keeping of Jesus, the assembly participates in Jesus by the power of the Holy Spirit active in these events. This whole event is primary proclamation, primary witness.

~

WHAT DO SCRIPTURE AND PROCLAMATION HAVE TO DO WITH GOD'S PROJECT?

Preaching is central to God's activity in the meeting. Jesus came out to preach (Mark 1:33-39) and called both seekers and the unsuspecting, crying out for them to come, follow, and enter into the joy of God. Jesus sent out others to spread this word (Acts 2). Jesus saw this preaching within the context of the teaching and practice that makes disciples (Matt. 28:19). Jesus himself was washed and practiced table fellowship. Jesus himself took up the Hebrew Scriptures as the word of God, juxtaposing them with his life and death to reveal the fullness of their meanings.

Likewise, the church takes up its sacred scriptures and opens them by way of the cross. This proclamatory act of interpreting the gospel for a particular company of hearers anchors, identifies, directs, and orients the baptized to the world in the way of Jesus. The offerings of hearers and tellers are made coherent by the Spirit praying through the encounter in sighs too deep for words. Approaching, adoring, and being called into the word, the church is then called out to serve Christ in the neighbor, the stranger, and the one in need who is before us. Being steeped in the word is being steeped in passion for the other. Preaching Christ is preaching mission to the world that Christ redeemed.

Reading the Bible is central to encountering Jesus Christ, through whom, in the activity of the Spirit, we see and worship God. The scriptures anchor the proclamatory event of worship.

They bear witness that Jesus, risen from the dead, interprets the sacred texts and is recognized in the breaking of the blessed bread (Luke 24:30-31). Jesus promises to be present in the midst of those preaching and teaching around the bath (Matt. 28:20) and in the shared eucharistic meal (Mark 14:22), and he promises that the scriptures will testify to him (John 5:39). We discover ourselves as disciples when we seek Jesus in these events. These actions of the assembly in accordance with scripture are where God greets us in peace and gives us the words of eternal life. These promises do not mean that God is not free to speak to God's creatures in any way God chooses. Rather, they mean that in these central events Jesus ushers us into the presence of God to hear and see who we are as partners in Christ's ministry. By these events, we are also clothed with power from on high to become bearers of this word into the darkness of the world.

Scriptures' Relevance to Life

The scriptures are relevant to us because there we meet God in Christ Jesus. Our world is overwhelmed by what is conveyed to us through the scriptures, the naming of God and God's promises. The scriptures are not relevant because they can be directly applied to our lives or used to guide our choices in every circumstance. The scriptures are not relevant because they immediately make sense to readers in every time and place. The scriptures are not relevant because they are reliably consistent and monolithic in their witness to God or because through them we can directly assimilate the mind of God and so redeem ourselves. Nor are the scriptures relevant because they offer a guide to self-care and self-help. The scriptures are not relevant because they are beautiful and fascinating sources for literary and historical pursuits. The scriptures *are* relevant because they belong to all the people of God who feed on them by faith with thanksgiving. Opened in the name of Jesus, we see in the scriptures God with people in every time and every place.

Unfolding God's story and promises—preaching the meaning of the prophetic and good news of God—is part of what reading the scriptures means. As in any meeting, whether between strangers or lifelong companions, the meeting between God and God's people around the text answers some questions and raises others, clarifies some aspects of identity and obscures others, confirms some understanding and opens us to surprise and ineffable mystery. Familiarity develops over time, for the meeting creates a history between the parties. Yet an essential mystery and surprise permeate the relationship. Often serious questions remain among faithful peoples about

how to interpret the things that proclaim God. Nonetheless, we JANN E. BOYD
FULLENWIEDER
share those things.

Encountering Christ in the Proclaimed Scriptures

Scripture reading is central in most Christian worship gatherings as a sacred witness to what the baptized have received and handed on. The received canon—the readings that make up the Bible—emerged out of an ancient and ecumenical consensus about what was authorized for reading in the assembly of the baptized. From the beginning, Christian use of the scriptures—first, the Hebrew Scriptures, and then, the records of the apostles—has been based on communal discernment, not on personal, individual tastes. Great traditions within the body of Christ do use different lists of texts. Roman Catholics and Orthodox Christians include in their canon the deuterocanonical books of the Old Testament (that is, the Apocrypha). Episcopalians and some Lutherans embrace the reading of these texts but eschew them for the elucidation of doctrine. Many Protestants do not read them at all. Nonetheless, the ecumenical agreement on the great core of biblical texts mirrors the ecumenical faith that Jesus comes to us in the public reading of scripture.

The driving hope behind reading the scriptures to one another in worship is that Jesus Christ will be encountered in our hearing of these words. We do not read the Bible to find scientific or historical evidence or ethical prescriptions. We do not read the Bible to entertain ourselves with antique curiosities, rituals, atrocities, and love poems. Like Zacchaeus of old, we climb up into the scriptures, a great tree of life grafted to the Crucified One's cross, that we might see Jesus. There we discover that we, too, are seen, named, invited, and welcomed to share the life of God, whom we spy through the branches and leaves of scripture, even as Christ has already spied us.

Because we pray to encounter God in the readings, rarely would we read just one portion of scripture, somehow equating one text with God. Rather, we read several texts and are gathered through them into God's presence. Some scholars have proposed that synagogue practice in Jesus' day involved a cycle of readings that included a selection from the first five books of the Bible coupled with a thematically related selection from other portions of the Hebrew Scriptures. These readings were then preached (Luke 4:21). In Christian communities from as early as A.D. 150 (as Justin Martyr records the events of the Lord's day[1]), selections from the writings of the apostles or the prophets were read, and the presider preached to the assembly, inviting listeners into the pattern of these readings.

This historic habit of appointing cycles of readings for the Sunday assembly, and later for the prayer offices, undergirds the several contemporary variants of a three-year lectionary that includes three readings and a psalm for each Sunday and festival day. The readings are drawn from the gospels, the Hebrew Scriptures, and the letters to the New Testament churches. The gospel reading is the capstone and the last to be read. The first reading, usually from the Hebrew Scriptures, often anticipates matters brought up in the gospel. The psalm is prayed through a variety of forms—perhaps through song—as a meditative response to the first reading. The second reading relates to the life of Christian community through the context of New Testament churches.[2]

Though reading the Bible itself is an essential element of Christian worship, following a lectionary is not. The practice of using a lectionary nevertheless does embody several essential understandings about the use of the Bible in worship. First, it fosters unity among Christians. Although there is already unity in the shared use of the Bible, this unity is emphasized further by the ecumenical practice of following a shared pattern of reading from the Bible. A lectionary manifests a consensus among churches about reading the same selections on Sundays and at other times. The use of a lectionary signals that Christians are called in all our diversity to hear God's word. Moreover, the reality that we are addressed by and receive God's word from outside ourselves is signaled by taking up a pattern of readings that has been given to us together. Other habits—the preacher's choosing texts according to personal or pastoral concerns, interest groups selecting texts that "go along with" particular political agendas or social projects, or denominations reading only those texts that clearly underscore their traditional theologies—obscure the radical nature of the Bible as a word addressed *to* us. The use of a lectionary addresses us beyond our own predilections and idiosyncracies, as God does.

A lectionary can also enable people to contemplate and study in advance the readings to be proclaimed on Sundays. Such use of the lectionary emphasizes that the scriptures are the property of the entire people, not just its preachers. Publishing the lectionary citations to facilitate this engagement with the texts suggests that the preacher is called forth out of the whole priesthood of the assembly to preach from the inheritance of all the baptized.

A lectionary must remain open to critical examination, ecumenical reflection, and adjustments. Careful review as part of the ongoing stewardship of the Sunday assembly's shared reading practices attends to human bias and myopia. A lectionary is, after all, a culturally influenced creation and must be understood as a communal editing of the Bible for the purposes of public worship. Like the canon itself, a lectionary is the result of choices about what to include, what to leave out, and how to arrange the readings.

Contemporary preachers and assemblies should ask how much and which parts of the Bible have been given to us to read in the three-year ecumenical lectionary. What is not included in these selected readings? By what principle of interpretation have certain narratives and figures been omitted from public hearing? Who benefits from the inclusions, and who benefits from the exclusions? Do the texts maintain the raw, confrontational oddness of the varied texts through which God speaks? Or is the colorful, cursing and blessing, embarrassing, scandalous activity of God and God's people tailored to please us? Is there an authentic representation of the tremendous cultural diversity through which the word of God comes to us in the Bible?

Because reading scripture is central to the proclamation of the living Word of God, great care must be given to the public, oral reading of the texts for the assembly. The gospel is a word to hear. Let it be heard. Let it be translated into the best language of the people gathered. Let the translation address the brokenness of human language and be shaped as evangelically as language permits. Let the readers read as if they offer the only words that give eternal life. Let them read clearly, with care, and with expression appropriate to the text and not to their self-display. Let the readers understand that they carry Christ swaddled in the ordinary wrappings of mere words. Let the assembly recognize the gifts a variety of people bring to reading the scriptures.

In an assembly so deeply formed by words and the visible words of the sacraments, by ritual gesture and other artifacts of human expression, let there be little naivety regarding the power of language and images. Let wisdom and discernment be reflected in the language and images around the readings, and in the preaching, praying, singing, and gathering around the table. Can the eucharistic prayers, the hymns, and the portions of liturgy cobbled together out of scripture and historical materials be clearly seen to mirror the Christ of the text and reflect the Holy Trinity? Is the language strong enough for public use or is it too small, too tailored to fit our agendas? Is the language varied enough, with images for all sorts and conditions of people?

Preaching: the availability of the living voice

We can say that the mind of Jesus Christ is the same yesterday, today, and tomorrow, but we cannot say that same thing about the minds of those to whom Jesus comes in and through the scriptures. The Christ of these texts needs to be made clear to us in our hearing. We also need to leave room for Christ to work beyond the texts. In the scriptures, the mind of Christ confronts our minds, made up as they are by experience, history, and culture. Increasingly our minds are molded by the powerful forces of technology and world markets. We bombard ourselves with information from across the universe, yet ironically, we seem to hold fewer things in common with others around the globe. We need proclamation that calls us face to face with the God of the good news. With the apostle Paul, our assemblies must learn to speak the gospel clearly to our need of God. With the apostle Mary Magdalene and the other women, our assemblies must also learn to speak the gospel even though some people will consider it silly—the "idle tale" told at dawn on the eighth day, when the tomb was found broken and empty.

Preaching must proclaim Christ Jesus, God-with-us, in terms particular to people in a specific time and place. So the art and language of preaching is necessarily ephemeral and deeply human, which is to say, limited. Nonetheless, God chooses to pour out grace for our need; "in our own languages we hear them speaking about God's deeds of power" (Acts 2:11). The gospel must be spoken to actual hearers, addressing actual fears, concerns, and dreams in language that communicates meaning and hope to the hearers. We need only skim through an anthology of great sermons to see that whole languages and metaphors have been constructed and razed from epoch to epoch in the project of communicating the gospel in the vernacular of a particular day.

The preachers' words, unfurling the gifts of scripture and the sacraments so that the people may see and hear them as words for "us," not just words for "me," must help listeners encounter God in utter trust. Preaching announces to all present that creation is redeemed totally by the mercy made visible in Jesus' living and dying and his being raised to usher in God's dominion of peace. God's work in Christ frees the baptized to be initiated into this Jesus Christ now, to truly praise God and be conformed to the mind of the crucified, who enacted God's total commitment to loving the whole creation and the neighbor as God's very self. Preaching Christ as the story of God for the world is preaching that makes Jesus

available to all who crowd roadsides, city streets, marketplaces,
sacred spaces, porticos, inner rooms, village wells, tops of trees, and
bedsides of the dying; in short, to all who cross the byways of life in
hope of touching life and health and, if it can be true, God—for us,
with us, now.

Our offerings are human. Our best language is broken. Our
best translations are approximations. Our best readings are deeply
personal aural constructions. Our preaching is a friable form.
Nonetheless, we endeavor to be transparent and authentic in relation to the Risen One. We trust the activity of the Spirit in our midst
to heal and transform our speech into the living voice of God.

God takes up the offering of words alongside our acts to proclaim God. The grammar of this speech is cruciform and its core
terms are given: the texts are from the Bible, and the signs are
washing, the shared meal, and people called forth. In simple, human
proclamation, we interpret ourselves, our lives, and all of creation
according to the identity and purposes of God's Word, Jesus. So
God grants health, life, and entry into the everlasting peace of God.

Because God's water hole is for all creation, because God's
sermon is for the entire world, preaching toward the waters of our
baptism into the reign of God is always political and ecumenical.
The water-soaked words are not sealed up and set aside for some
other life, but are poured out here, now, from one who lived and
suffered in the world. Thus, preaching and enacting the gospel is
doing something about how the church *is:* living out our unity with
all our splendid diversity, honoring the mystery of God working in
us in different ways, and witnessing to the world as united partners
who bring good news. Preaching and enacting the gospel is also
doing something about the way the world *is:* equipping people to
see their lives and the works of their hands in relation to a world
where all is God's; living in partnership with one whose peace and
justice outdo any human imagination. Preaching must not be about
right thinking regarding social agendas and politics, as if creating
and following such agendas were the only viable way to go about
actually doing something to prosper the world. Preaching must not
be about only what people see, as if God can be demonstrated
through a proof. Preaching must be about what is unseen, what lies
within the actions and ministries of the assembly—a hope at work
in the world, hidden yet triumphant.

To Whom Do We Preach?

If preaching the gospel is a continuation of the preaching of Jesus,
then it is preaching at once to every one who shows up and to those

who are far off. It is preaching to those who think they know Jesus and the God of Israel, and to those who just want health or help. It is preaching for the whole world to be converted to the mercy and welcome of God. It is preaching to those who are hemorrhaging, scarred, lost, unbelieving, hungry, or possessed—to all who need to be plunged under the trinitarian waters. It is preaching for the world God so loves, for those in need of a physician. It is preaching for faith in any season: joy, defeat, betrayal, dying, and the emptiness of death. It is preaching for a sure and certain hope in God who makes all things new and brings life out of death and light out of darkness.

Sorrow and frailty, yearning for gladness, and divine weakness meet in the assembly of human hearts on either side of the ambo. Yet these hopes and fears are shaped in terms of personal and social histories and languages. So preaching must acknowledge the world of hearers in specific terms that mirror to them their need of God and pour out the plenitude of God who supplies their lack. So also preaching must hold the circumstances of their world against the horizon of the present activity of God. This means that mere repetition of biblical passages, words, or formulas will not answer the questions that haunt, drive, inspire, or move people.

Preaching to "make known the name of Christ and the Father's mercy promised in Christ"[3] is making known one who goes by many names: Abba, Jesus Christ, Paraclete, Elohim, Adonai, I AM, Vine, Lamb, Gate, Shepherd, Comforter, Advocate, Wisdom, and many more. But making known means something more than naming. In our North American culture, and perhaps worldwide, the name of Jesus is widely recognized, but this familiarity in no way indicates that Jesus is being made known.

We preach to announce the activity of God for the world, call for the reorientation of our whole lives, gather one another into the mercy of God, and equip ourselves for witnessing to the hope that is within us in this hungry and anxious world. Clearly we do not preach that we may be comfortable but that the world and we may be comforted. Comfort means something quite different in the mind at work in scripture. Comfort comes to the exile who never lives to see the return as well as to the exile who does. Comfort comes both to the thief who dies crucified and to the child raised from the dead.

We preach to call people to the trinitarian bath to be initiated into the countercultural body of Christ and daily to live deeply into the meaning of the identity they have received in the bath. Such preaching means preaching people upside down, shaken up, inside out of their current lives, and rehearsing the peace of God now present in a world that knows no peace. There is nothing entertaining, pleasant, dispassionate, spectatorial, or democratic about this kind of confrontation, anymore than there is about discovering you are the center of the action in a shock-trauma unit.

Perhaps it is time for North American assemblies to admit to ourselves that preaching is more like awakening in a shock-trauma unit than it is like being lulled in a swinging cradle. We make our familiar contented proposals about God and fail to hear the voice that rebuked Peter in love so long ago, "Get behind me, Satan" (Matt. 16:23). Because the language of our society is so deeply ingrained in us, we have trouble with the demanding, rude, unapologetic claims of the biblical God, and we unwittingly steam up "the mirror of our existence" and render grace unnecessary and unreceived.[4]

Apostolic preaching urgently announces that something life-giving and everlasting is at work in calling people to the bath and the table, to mutual consolation and instruction. Thus, whatever language must be borrowed, whatever dominant metaphor must be appropriated and exposed in the light of Christ, apostolic preachers must pick up such life-giving words and submit them to the word of Christ for the inspection of the assembly. The earliest preachers were orally oriented; we have reports of their preaching, not printed manuscripts saved on diskette. Thinking *with* their listeners, the preachers used language to meet their ears. Improvising, substituting, creating what was needed to communicate, these preachers in the field were immensely imaginative. We must be no less imaginative, no less steeped in the things of Christ, for the harvest is no less urgent in our season than in theirs.

∾

LAND MINES IN THE FIELDS WHERE WE SOW THE GOSPEL
Three forces appear as land mines in the fields to be sown with the word in and around missional assemblies: (1) our failure to take seriously our need of God; (2) our failure to appropriate a new understanding of human communication; and (3) our lack of faith in an incarnate God.

We will not find God simply by heeding the dominant voices in our society. We think we know that, yet we still cling to our household gods. North American democratic ideals about respect for the individual have been distorted to the point that we idolize individual feelings and private dreams for prosperity. Freedom of speech and the inherent invitation into difficult deliberation and debate has often deteriorated into private, home viewings of what is happening "out there." The chief instrument of communication, the television, is shaped by entertainment and marketing strategies to retain viewers. Many of the programs include little or no reflection about the historical or global context or the ethical implications of an issue or event.[5] The benefit of television, its demonstration of the power of images to communicate, albeit with little critical analysis, is largely ignored by preachers who extract "the message" from the gospel story like a slip of paper from a folded fortune cookie.

Meanwhile, North Americans' ability to manage reality is being dismantled and rearranged by technological developments that allow speech and signs to flow through cyberspace in seconds. The electronic shift, like the printing-press shift, is drastically changing the ways societies transact business and imagine being in the world. The electronic shift can bring blessings, but it is also stretching and breaking old language and theories, and demands fresh speech to describe the shape of our daily existence. Preaching must cohere in this time of shifting languages and concepts of reality. Preaching must coin images and rhetoric that serve Christ in the emerging ethos of a new century, a new millennium. Preaching must name the alternatives to the way we conceive life now.

Related to this concern is the urgent matter of our failure to take seriously emerging understandings of the constructive and con-textual dimensions of human communication. How people learn, communicate, and are equipped to grasp ideas are significant areas of investigation. Preaching needs to adjust to what we are learning about how the mind constructs narrative contexts for understand-ing. Preaching must also take account of how particular cultural contexts shape hearers. We do not all hear the same thing even when the same words are used. How will preachers acknowledge the active, constructive, narrating mind in the way they shape sermons?[6]

Perhaps the hardest problem to notice is our lack of faith. Ad-vertising, films, books, talk shows, and school locker rooms are full of self-consciousness, self-realization, self-examination, and a spirituality focused on the self. We are preoccupied with angels. At the end of a millennium, we are haunted by prophecies about "Y2K." There are signs that we seek some explanation for the challenges of these times. Think about how often we are shocked: when we discover that our antibiotics are being outwitted by bac-teria's natural adaptation; when healthy, lovable Canadian and American "boys" serving needy Somalians beat and shoot them instead; when a new disease erupts in a plague of worldwide di-mensions and lurches swiftly out of control; when a princess dies

in a car crash while speeding through Paris; when the blood
supply is tainted. We place faith in technology and "progress,"
though we know the past limits of human ingenuity. We place
faith in science, though we know how hypotheses have changed
through history. Even so, we are shocked when the "now," "beautiful," or "scientific" fail.

Do we really expect to see God? Because we are versed in scientific and psychological explanations for many of life's questions,
many North Americans do not think God is acting in the world, let
alone in the words of a person preaching. Moreover, we have been
numbed by a century of shocks, stunning discoveries, atrocities, and
tumults among races and peoples. Most of these horrors have been
photographed or even beamed to us live, downloaded directly via
satellite to our radios and televisions. The mess is too big. Who is
the God who can deliver us?

The God who delivers us creates out of nothing without
apology. The God who delivers embraces death as a means to birth.
This God is an all-or-nothing, saving creator who brings a new
world into being out of an awe-inspiring imagination of what will
be. This God speaks a genuine alternative to what we are making up
for ourselves. This God is an incarnate God—God in Christ—a
scandal to our hearing.

This God is not preached as a tool, a means to self-care, self-
development, or self-improvement. This God is preached for faith
that God is at work in us and all the world to save a creation in
travail. This God is not preached in order to fill us with religious
sentiment or vague spirituality. This God is preached to reveal to us
our utter dependence on a God whom Jesus reveals to be totally for
us, totally with us, totally trustworthy despite all the things we
think we see and know. This God is not preached so that there will
be large gatherings of active participants but so that the substance
of the faith is known, passed on, and living in people's lives. This
God is not preached so that we can prove God to ourselves or to
anyone else but so that we may be filled with the fruits of faith, signs
of God's gracious love in the world. This God is not preached so we
can reduce the sovereign claims of God on creation to a simple list
of behaviors we can perform. This God is preached so we can run
headlong into the arms of a steadfast commitment we have from
God to make us little Christs for the healing of creation. This God
is not preached to make modest claims about what God is up to in
history and the cosmos. This God is preached so the God who
suffers in history, making time holy and hallowing our cry, will be
seen laboring at the crux of any chaos.

Preaching such a God calls for a curious hope and a delight in difference, for wild imagination and an inexplicable love for creation. Preaching such a God calls for a complete commitment to search, listening to the scriptures, the bath, the table, the cry of the people here and now for God—listening in the silence for the clear, small, cruciform voice, the voice we hear when the blessed bread is broken in our midst.

Preaching such a God calls for freedom from fear, freedom to act with God in the grand play of God's mercy in the world which—to our astonishment—includes the mystery that God uses us, even in spite of ourselves, whether we like it or not. God takes us into partnership, choosing what is weak, in order to come to all nations and speak peace, beginning with our assemblies in scripture reading and proclamation and echoing the good news into all the world.

NOTES

1. Justin Martyr, *I Apology,* 67. For this understanding I am indebted to Gordon W. Lathrop's presentation of early reading practices in *Holy Things: A Liturgical Theology* (Minneapolis: Fortress Press, 1993).

2. For an excellent brief overview of the development of the lectionary see Frank C. Senn's *Christian Liturgy: Catholic and Evangelical* (Minneapolis: Fortress Press, 1997), 657–60.

3. Apology of the Augsburg Confession 14.32, in *The Book of Concord: The Confessions of the Evangelical Lutheran Church,* trans. and ed. Theodore G. Tappert et al. (Philadelphia: Fortress Press, 1959), 255.

4. This term, and the entire helpful discussion of which it is a synecdoche, is taken from Herman G. Stuempfle's *Preaching Law and Gospel* (Philadelphia: Fortress Press, 1978).

5. For a good examination of this issue, see Marva Dawn's *Reaching Out without Dumbing Down: A Theology of Worship for the Turn-of-the-Century Culture.* (Grand Rapids, Mich.: Wm. B. Eerdmans, 1995), 19–24.

6. For two constructive attempts to address this concern, see David Buttrick's *Homiletic* (Philadelphia: Fortress Press, 1987) and Richard Eslinger's *Narrative Imagination* (Minneapolis: Fortress Press, 1994).

Holy Baptism: Promise Big Enough for the World

Mons A. Teig

My wife and I had stopped for dinner at a restaurant, and four women at a nearby table were engaged in animated conversation. When I sensed they were talking about religious things, I tuned in. Evidently parents were resisting baptizing their child but were feeling pressure from grandparents, who thought the baby should be baptized. One of the women apparently agreed with the grandparents and reported that she told the parents, "I think you should have the child baptized. It won't do any harm if you do!" Compare that comment to Aidan Kavanagh's description of baptism:

> When we are dealing with baptism we are discoursing about Christian initiation; when we are into initiation we are face to face with conversion in Jesus Christ dead and rising; and when we are into conversion in Jesus Christ dead and rising we are at the storm center of the universe.[1]

According to the one view, we apparently do not expect much to happen at baptism. The other description, however, suggests that we should run for shelter or look for an ark when a baptism takes place. The way we practice baptism in our congregations communicates as clearly as dinner-table conversation or books how we understand and interpret baptism in our own modern missional situation.[2] Our liturgies are embodied theology and events of the gospel.[3] At the end of his study of the doctrine of baptism, Edmund Schlink stresses that the event of baptism in which God acts

HOLY
BAPTISM:
PROMISE
BIG ENOUGH
FOR THE
WORLD

can be obscured if this act is developed neither in word nor in accompanying actions. There is a flatly mechanical way of baptizing which is satisfied with the barest essentials even when there is no emergency.... While the validity of such Baptisms cannot be questioned, the perfunctory manner of their administration permits neither the baptized nor the congregation to recognize the riches of what God is here doing for them.[4]

This chapter focuses on several baptismal motifs that express the mission of God and then concludes with three issues that invite both further thinking and action in our mission work.

∼

Baptism: GOD'S SACRAMENT OF EVANGELICAL OUTREACH
God's saving mission in the world points us to baptism. Baptism is the sacrament of mission, of conversion, of evangelism. Many commentators speak today about the passing of Christendom or their perception that we have entered a post-Christian era. Many church leaders are concerned by reports of declining membership or active involvement in the life and mission of the church. The issues of outreach, evangelism, and church growth, therefore, get leaders' attention. The sacrament of baptism must be at the center of the conversation for any church that seeks to be obedient to God's mission, command, and promise.[5] Gordon Lathrop underscores this connection between evangelism and baptism: "Baptism needs to be available as the deepest possible response to the newcomer's inquiry about God and grace. *Our evangelism, if it is to tell the truth about Christ and not just be a program for "our" new members, must be entirely baptismal.*"[6]

Theologian Robert Jenson writes:

> For any missionary community, initiation must be the chief rite, and Christianity has always retained enough missionary self-consciousness to regard baptism as the chief sacrament, or at least as the gateway to other sacraments.... In all strands and strata of the New Testament witness, no distinction is conceived or conceivable between the church's doing its mission and people being baptized. Paul assumes that all believers come into the fellowship by baptism.... In Acts the very syntax is controlled by the supposition that to be converted, to enter the church, and to be baptized are all the same thing.[7]

The mission of making disciples has forever been linked with baptism through the command and promise of Matthew 28. Jesus made baptism a sacrament of conversion, a missionary sacrament, when he gave this commission:

> And Jesus came and said to them, "All authority in heaven and on earth has been given to me. Go therefore and make disciples of all nations, baptizing them in the name of the Father and of the Son and of the Holy Spirit, and teaching them to obey everything that I have commanded you. And remember, I am with you always, to the end of the age." (Matt. 28:18-20)

Early missionary preaching in the book of Acts again led directly to baptism. Peter's Pentecost preaching provoked both this response and the church's proclamation of the promise in God's mission to the world:

> They were cut to the heart and said to Peter and to the other apostles, "Brothers, what should we do?" Peter said to them, "Repent, and be baptized every one of you in the name of Jesus Christ so that your sins may be forgiven; and you will receive the gift of the Holy Spirit." (Acts 2:37-38)

Baptism is what God does when the Spirit provokes repentance through the preaching of the gospel promise. The inbreaking storm of the royal rule of God in Christ Jesus catches us up into God's promised future. In this baptismal washing with the gospel word, each person is made a citizen of this new community ruled by the one who is given all authority in heaven and on earth, and the old citizenship is renounced.

Martin Luther's Large Catechism and Small Catechism still speak persuasively to us about the great gifts this missionary sacrament offers and in which the baptized are to live. Luther rhapsodizes about baptism's benefits:

> In Baptism, therefore, every Christian has enough to study and to practice all his life. He always has enough to do to believe firmly what Baptism promises and brings—victory over death and the devil, forgiveness of sin, God's grace, the entire Christ, and the Holy Spirit with his gifts. In short, the blessings of Baptism are so boundless that if timid nature considers them, it may well doubt whether they could all be true.[8]

One student told how her nephew echoed Luther's praise of baptism's benefits. As the water was still dripping from his infant sister's head, four-year-old Christopher's raspy voice filled the sanctuary: "That was absolutely amazing!"[9] Elaine Ramshaw expresses similar awe: "Only the promise that is big enough for the whole world is truly big enough for an infant."[10]

HOLY
BAPTISM:
PROMISE
BIG ENOUGH
FOR THE
WORLD

If, indeed, we believe these absolutely amazing things the Bible and theology say about the promises of baptism and baptism's role in God's saving mission for the whole world, then those promises and perspectives will shape how baptisms are done and how pastors and congregations prepare for this threatening and saving flood. Such a significant gospel event deserves robust and significant celebration, so the promise of God is seen and heard, experienced and believed, once done and forever remembered.

Reflecting on the subtitle of this book, *Worship in an Age of Mission*, I start from the perspective that Jesus Christ is God's liturgy/service and God's mission for the sake of the world. The church's liturgy begins with God's work among us in Christ through the saving and sanctifying event of word and sacrament. In our worship, then, we respond to the work of God through Jesus Christ in the power of the Holy Spirit by faith.

~

Exploring baptism's breadth and depth

Too often we have been minimalist in our teaching about baptism and our practice of this missionary sacrament. Although we are cleansed through the ordinary experience of washing or bathing, the word brought to the water expands our vision and experience of God's mission.

This breadth of meaning is summarized as follows in the ecumenical discussion distilled in the document *Baptism, Eucharist and Ministry (BEM)*.

> Baptism is the sign of new life through Jesus Christ. It unites the one baptized with Christ and with his people. The New Testament scriptures and the liturgy of the Church unfold the meaning of baptism in various images that express the riches of Christ and the gifts of his salvation.... Baptism is participation in Christ's death and resurrection (Rom. 6:3-5; Col. 2:12); a washing away of sin (1 Cor. 6:11); a new birth (John 3:5); an enlightenment by Christ (Eph. 5:14); a reclothing in Christ (Gal. 3:27); a renewal by the Holy Spirit (Titus 3:5); the experience of salvation from the flood (1 Peter 3:20-21); an exodus from bondage (1 Cor. 10:1-2) and a liberation into a new humanity in which barriers of division whether of sex or race or social status are transcended (Gal. 3:27-28; 1 Cor. 12:13). The images are many but the reality is one.[11]

BEM then summarizes these biblical images under five main motifs. They all point to God's mission activity for the sake of the world.

A) ***Participation in Christ's Death and Resurrection.*** Baptism means participating in the life, death and resurrection of Jesus Christ.... By baptism, Christians are immersed in the liberating death of Christ where their sins are buried, where "old Adam" is crucified with Christ, and where the power of sin is broken....

B) ***Conversion, Pardoning and Cleansing.*** The baptism which makes Christians partakers of the mystery of Christ's death and resurrection implies confession of sin and conversion of heart.... Thus those baptized are pardoned, cleansed and sanctified by Christ, and are given as part of their baptismal experience a new ethical orientation under the guidance of the Holy Spirit....

C) ***The Gift of the Spirit.*** God bestows upon all baptized persons the anointing and the promise of the Holy Spirit, marks them with a seal and implants in their hearts the first installment of their inheritance as sons and daughters of God....

D) ***Incorporation into the Body of Christ.*** Through baptism, Christians are brought into union with Christ, with each other and with the Church of every time and place. Our common baptism, which unites us to Christ in faith, is thus a basic bond of unity....

E) ***The Sign of the Kingdom.*** Baptism initiates the reality of the new life given in the midst of the present world. It gives participation in the community of the Holy Spirit. It is a sign of the Kingdom of God and of the life of the world to come. Through the gifts of faith, hope and love, baptism has a dynamic which embraces the whole of life, extends to all nations, and anticipates the day when every tongue will confess that Jesus Christ is Lord to the glory of God the Father.[12]

James White suggests five main biblical motifs which convey the life and work of Jesus Christ in the power of the Holy Spirit.[13] Each of the motifs carries implication for the church's liturgy, life, and mission. Each one focuses on God's self-giving in baptism.

The first motif points to the preaching of Christ crucified (1 Cor. 1:23) and its embodiment in the visible word of baptism. Here we turn to Romans 6, where baptism is described as union to Jesus Christ and his work. This union is something that only God can and does give. It is a sign of being joined in Christ's death to sin and being alive to God in Christ Jesus. Life and resurrection are now our future. The paschal or Easter focus is the center of our faith and baptism. It is no wonder that the early church saw the Vigil of Easter as a prime time for baptisms. (The revival in our present day of the catechumenate and baptisms at Easter is an opportunity I will discuss later.)

The second gift of baptism is incorporation into Christ's body on earth—the church. Contrary to the idea that the church is a

HOLY

BAPTISM:

PROMISE

BIG ENOUGH

FOR THE

WORLD

voluntary association—that belonging to the church is recom-
mended but optional—baptism into Christ grafts us into Christ's
body, the church. If you are in Christ Jesus, you are in Christ's body,
the church. Being grafted into the church is God's decision. The
church is a community inducted into God's mission in Jesus Christ
in the power of the missionary Spirit. It is a servant community that
has an identity as "a chosen race, a royal priesthood, a holy nation,
God's own people, in order that you may proclaim the mighty acts
of him who called you out of darkness into his marvelous light"
(1 Peter 2:9).

Martin Luther stresses the principle that this mission is given to
every baptized person over against the idea that some people are
given higher offices. He asserts the ministry of the laity when he says
that baptism ordains into priesthood. "For whoever comes out of
the water of baptism can boast that he is already a consecrated
priest, bishop and pope."[14] Gibson Winter observes that people do
not discover the meaning of baptism unless they are drawn into the
church's missionary activity.[15] In his seminal book *Worship and
Mission,* J.G. Davies stresses the importance of the baptized being
caught up in the mission of God that is expressed and embodied in
worship and life in the world. Davies asserts that "a laity which
is...passive in the forms of worship in which they are expected to
engage will inevitably remain passive in the world. Whatever they
fail to be in worship, they will fail to be in mission because of the
unity of the two."[16]

According to White, "a third form of God's self giving experienced in baptism is the gift of the Holy Spirit itself. This is a direct
pouring out of God's being, the giver literally is the gift."[17] This
Spirit is part of the whole saving movement of the triune God and
deserves strong ritual emphasis in our liturgies of baptism. "God
our Savior...saved us...through the water of rebirth and renewal
by the Holy Spirit. This Spirit he poured out on us richly through
Jesus Christ our Savior, so that, having been justified by his grace,
we might become heirs according to the hope of eternal life" (Titus
2:4-7). Upon incorporation into Christ and the community of faith,
one experiences the continuing gift of membership in the community of God's life-giving Spirit. This Spirit is "a missionary
Spirit."[18]

The fourth image White stresses is forgiveness of sin. This
image is underscored every time we confess the ecumenical Nicene
Creed, in which "we acknowledge one Baptism for the forgiveness
of sin."[19] Indeed, baptism is a washing with God's word of
promise. God forgives and reconciles us in a once-for-all action that

incorporates us into the community that continues to be nourished
by the word in sermon and meal. Now life has a baptismal shape.
Every day we begin and end in the name of the Father, Son, and
Holy Spirit.

The baptismal shape of our lives means that daily we die to sin
and rise to the promise of newness of life. In the Sunday liturgy in
many congregations, this daily dying and rising is emphasized when
the presiding minister leads the Brief Order for Confession and Forgiveness from the baptismal font. The presider might dip her or his
hand in the water to help make the baptismal connection. Of
course, this connection means we should always uncover the font
and put water in it, even though a baptism may not be celebrated in
a given week. People passing the font may dip their hand in the
water and make the sign of the cross, retracing the sign of the cross
made over them at baptism. This action can provide a strong reminder about the source of our individual and communal life. An
international consultation has summarized the central role of
baptism for our weekly worship:

> Baptism incorporates people into the worshiping assembly by bringing
> them into Christ, by burying them together with him that they might
> also live with him. Baptism proclaims Christ in sign and word. It is a
> gift given for the whole community, celebrated in their presence and
> frequently remembered. Actually, the Christian life is nothing else than
> a daily return to Baptism and its gifts; *Baptism into Christ is the well-
> spring from which the whole of Christian worship flows.*[20]

Baptism is a foundational doctrine and practice. It is not a
private family affair inserted into our communal life that makes the
Sunday liturgy longer. Edmund Schlink stresses baptism's link to the
whole Christian message and mission:

> Hence the doctrine of baptism can be isolated neither from the
> message concerning Christ, nor from the Lord's Supper, nor from the
> church. Since the New Testament does not treat Baptism in isolation,
> the church's doctrine, even when Baptism is treated monographically,
> must constantly keep in view the relationship between Baptism and
> proclamation, Lord's Supper and church. It is precisely in the combi-
> nation of all these events that God deals with [humanity].[21]

White's fifth image, new birth, is closely related to forgiveness.
Like being joined to Christ's death and resurrection, new birth
signals the radical, once-for-all action of God that makes us part of
the new creation.

This breadth of meaning in baptism helps us to see that being in

HOLY
BAPTISM:
PROMISE
BIG ENOUGH
FOR THE
WORLD

Christ is the same as being baptized. Baptism is the way God joins us to God's mission in the world for us and for all people. In both the disciple-making commission of Matthew 28 and the missionary activity of Acts, baptism is the answer to inquirers' question, "What should we do?" (Acts 2:37). A baptizing community is always engaged in disciple making. Like St. Paul, we realize that Christian living and ministry flow from the grace that God gives us in baptism. We are a healing and reconciling community because we live out of the boundless blessings of baptism. For the baptized, life can never be the same. "Should we sin because we are not under law but under grace? By no means!" (Rom. 6:15). Living in the old way is not an option. We are dead to that. We belong to another gracious power.

In baptism we renounce one ruler and pledge allegiance to another. There is the reality that we are "aliens from the common-wealth of Israel, and strangers to the covenants of promise.... But now in Christ Jesus you who once were far off have been brought near by the blood of Christ.... So then you are no longer strangers and aliens, but you are citizens with the saints and also members of the household of God" (Eph. 2:12-13, 19). Members of God's household can no longer give allegiance to the old life.

When my great-grandfather, a Norwegian immigrant, became a U.S. citizen, the transition was marked by his taking an oath to declare his new allegiance. On that day (according to the natural-ization certificate), Ole Larsen was "permitted to take the oath to support the Constitution of the United States, and the usual oath whereby he renounces all allegiance and fidelity to every foreign Prince, Potentate, State, and Sovereignty whatever, and more par-ticularly to the King of Norway and Sweden." Baptism into Christ is no less radical a change in a person's orientation in life.

We renounce "all the forces of evil, the devil and all his empty promises" and profess our faith in our new ruler through the words of the baptismal creed.[22] Now we enjoy the gift of citizenship. We no longer live under the authority of the old country. In his letter to the Romans, Paul speaks of a decisive transfer of authority in baptism: "Should we continue in sin in order that grace may abound? By no means! How can we who died to sin go on living in it?" (Rom. 6:1b-2). Robert Jenson says, "Thus it is the heart of Paul's argument to the Romans that they *have been* baptized, that this event is irrevocably a part of their pasts and that *therefore* a kind of life is closed to them that would otherwise have been open and inevitable."[23]

Proclamation of the gospel calls for a response of faith. "If the

Gospel is received by faith, it cannot be done without a desire for Baptism. For the Gospel concerning Jesus Christ is also the call to Baptism in the name of Christ."[24]

~

Baptism and the church's life and mission today

A variety of issues invite further discussion about the implication of baptism for mission. The following discussion will focus on three issues, namely, the need for the church to be more intentionally focused on being a baptizing community, to understand that the catechumenate is a way of making Christians, and to recognize the call to lifelong baptismal living and vocation.

The Challenge of Being a Baptizing Community

Baptism is about *being* church, not simply about voluntarily choosing to *associate with* a church. Being church, a member of the body of Christ, is part of what it means to be baptized.[25] So when we talk about and do baptisms, we must also talk about what baptism means for being church and what being church means for responsible baptismal practice and mission. Although Jürgen Moltmann is discussing the European state church and implications of that context for baptismal practice, his correlation of church and baptism is instructive for North American Christians as well. He says:

> Baptism can only be practiced in accordance with its proper meaning if the church's public form and function in society is altered at the same time, and if the church becomes recognizable and active as the messianic fellowship of Christ. A convincing baptismal practice can only be acquired together with a convincing church.[26]

Although baptismal practice may vary, it speaks a great deal about our theology of baptism and our understanding of its role in the life of the church. James White, a North American liturgical scholar, underlines this principle:

> This appropriation of the riches of baptism applies to practice just as it does to theological reflection. Without the active participation of a congregation, the whole image of incorporation is dissipated. The sealing of the Holy Spirit (Eph. 1:3) needs the sign of anointing or laying on of hands. These are not peripheral matters but important pastoral matters for giving expression to what God does in baptism. What is done will inevitably shape what is believed about baptism.[27]

47

HOLY
BAPTISM:
PROMISE
BIG ENOUGH
FOR THE
WORLD

The practice of baptism and our call to be church has implications for specific liturgies in *Lutheran Book of Worship* and its companion volume *Occasional Services*.

Private baptisms, for example, are inconsistent with the biblical examples and the reality that through baptism we are incorporated into Christ's body. In light of our earlier discussion, a private baptism is a contradiction in terms. How can the reality of baptism into Christ, of belonging to one another, be communicated when we treat the congregation as if they do not have a stake in this event? Even when baptism is held immediately after the Sunday liturgy, the congregation is still in danger of losing its identity as a baptizing community. Although Protestants have rightly been very critical of the private mass, they need to evaluate their own acceptance and practice of private baptism, which suggests that baptism is a private or family affair rather than a communal, public event.

The practice of private baptisms, prevalent in the past throughout a number of denominations,[28] tended to load most if not all of the responsibility for further Christian nurture on parents. Therefore, we have sometimes asked whether we can responsibly baptize infants when we have serious doubts about the parents' resolve to teach their children and worship with them. If only family and friends are present for baptisms, then our ritual practice communicates that parents and sponsors have a responsibility that the dismissed congregation does not also share. Regardless of the responsibility we might claim for the congregation, our ritual action in this instance delegates all responsibility to the pastor and parents.

In the American *Book of Common Prayer*, the celebrant asks the gathered congregation, "Will you who witness these vows do all in your power to support *these persons* in *their* life in Christ?"[29] United Methodists have included several questions and responses for the congregation as well. The pastor asks the congregation: "Will you nurture one another in the Christian faith and life and include *these persons* now before you in your care?" The congregation responds in unison:

> With God's help we will proclaim the good news and live according to the example of Christ. We will surround *these persons* with a community of love and forgiveness, that they may grow in *their* trust of God, and be found faithful in *their* service to others. We will pray for *them*, that *they* may be *true disciples* who *walk* in the way that leads to life.[30]

Bryan Spinks has offered an important critique regarding the placement of these congregational commitments in the baptismal rite. He argues that by placing charges of duties for parents and congregation prior to the baptismal washing, we may be teaching that baptism is a bilateral covenant. In his opinion, if such a charge of duties is to be included in the rite, it should follow rather than precede the action of baptizing, thus pointing to God's unilateral action in baptism.[31] When these charges follow the washing, "such imperatives are not the demands of a law that cannot be fulfilled. On the contrary, they are based on God's gracious deed and give expression to this deed."[32]

Although *LBW* provides for congregational responses following the act of baptizing, using a response similar to those cited above would challenge the congregation to see its ongoing responsibility for the baptized. Instead of loading all the responsibility on the parents and sponsors, we should ask whether congregations are willing to shoulder their proper responsibilities for the newly baptized, who has been initiated into the local expression of the one, holy, catholic, and apostolic church. We have heard the African proverb that it takes a village to raise a child. We should explore the reality that it also takes a church to raise the baptized.

The congregation's importance in baptism and the public, communal nature of this sacrament is addressed in the Lutheran rite Baptism in an Emergency, or what we might have in the past called a private or emergency baptism. The instructions suggest that if a person survives, she or he is then brought before the congregation for a public recognition of the baptism.[33] This public rite provides a crucial link between the baptized and the local faith community that nonemergency private baptisms fail to offer.

Nearly all recent baptismal liturgies from the various denominations assume the presence of the congregation and often invite congregational involvement. For example, a lay representative might lead a welcome to the baptized, who will now share the life and mission of Christ. Baptism is clearly a time for the gathered community members to affirm the promise and continuing process of their own baptisms.

Leadership roles for the baptismal rite in *LBW* could be used more effectively to express the principle that the church itself is a baptizing community and that baptism is not an action reserved to the clergy. Many pastors still fail to notice the suggestion that a representative of the congregation gives the baptismal candle to the newly baptized.[34] Instead of using the nearest acolyte or lay assisting minister, pastors might think about asking another member to carry out this symbolic action. If the candidate is an adult, perhaps his or her sponsor in the catechumenal process or a member of the evangelism committee can be assigned this task. If

HOLY
BAPTISM:
PROMISE
BIG ENOUGH
FOR THE
WORLD

an infant is baptized, then the representative of the congregation might be chosen to represent symbolically the congregation's ongoing promise to teach the newly baptized. A Sunday school superintendent or teacher could be regularly assigned this task, memorizing the words and addressing the candidate without a book in hand.

Another place in the baptism liturgy where a clear ritual and representative role for the congregation occurs is at the welcome of the newly baptized person(s) into the community of faith. Once again a representative of the congregation is assigned a role.[35] In this regard, I have observed that larger congregations with more than one pastor tend to neglect the lay representative role even more frequently than smaller congregations. Why make the effort to do what appears to be a small thing? Simply because involving lay representatives in the rite is one way to emphasize that the mission and vocation of baptism is shared by all the baptized. It might be wise to assign the task of representing the congregation to people in the community who understand this theological point. One might expand the duties of the elected officers of the congregation or the council to include the welcome at baptisms.

Here we can connect our thinking about baptism as evangelical outreach with the notion of baptism as something that brings us out of isolation, placing us in Christ—in the eschatological community of the Spirit sent from the Father. This understanding challenges the idea that in baptism we receive Christ or accept Christ. Rather, we are baptized into Christ because God accepts us and places us in a new community opened by the Spirit. Here, none of us can be an only child, but we are always placed in a diverse and strange family.

Opportunity for Making Christians

In the future, the church in its disciple making will more frequently encounter a phenomenon we are beginning to see today: adults who were not baptized as children. This experience will place us in a context more like that of the church in its early centuries, or that of missionaries who introduce the gospel of Jesus Christ to those who have not heard it. The story of an unbaptized man who encountered a life situation that sent him seeking some insight or word of meaning is instructive for all of us.

A well-dressed man entered a church building and asked a man inside if he could talk with a pastor. "I am the pastor," he replied. The visitor said, "Do you have time to talk with me?" Then followed a rapid-fire conversation that went something like this. "I don't really know why I am here. I am an agnostic. But I had the most marvelous experience of my life today, and I felt I had to talk with somebody in a church about it. I felt like I was present at creation. Today I saw the birth of my first child. And I wondered if I should have him baptized. In fact, I don't know if I am baptized. Maybe I should be baptized, too."

The pastor discovered that this man was a local manager of a retail chain. After further conversations, preparations were made to baptize both the father and the newborn son. Catechesis continued as this young family began a life of worship. Eventually the young father became active, teaching Sunday school, attending Bible study, and even serving as president of the congregation.

This incident shows the shift that occurs when we think of baptism from the perspective of an adult inquirer, rather than from the perspective of someone baptized as an infant of Christian parents. Because infant baptism has been the normative practice in many congregations, we have inadvertently lost sight of the outward, missionary thrust of baptism. The adult, however, presents us with a situation that gives rise to conversation that eventually leads to conversion and baptism. Here we see more clearly the outward focus of baptism. Davies urged the church over thirty years ago to think of worship not only in its inward direction, but in its outward direction as well.[36]

The point of relating this story is to remind readers that in tomorrow's church in North America we will not only be baptizing infants of Christian parents, but we will increasingly be in conversation with adults who were not baptized as infants. Further, we must also realize that many adults who were baptized as infants have only experienced the initial part of the missionary command of our Lord. They were baptized but not taught "to obey everything that I have commanded you" (Matt. 28:20). It is incumbent on parents and others who present children for baptism to provide continued guidance, so that the newly baptized live and develop in the nurturing, teaching, healing, reconciling, worshiping, praying, and witnessing community of faith.

One of the most promising ways of inviting inquirers or seekers to consider the Christian faith is through the newly revived practice of the catechumenate.[37] This process was once the way the church walked with seekers in prayer, Bible study, worship, and conversation about daily Christian living. It allowed people to enter into an apprenticeship of faith through conversation with lay sponsors and catechists as well as the pastor.

Our earlier discussion about the breadth of what God is giving in the baptismal gift prods us to evaluate whether we are adequately

HOLY
BAPTISM:
PROMISE
BIG ENOUGH
FOR THE
WORLD

incorporating into our faith community adult baptismal candidates, parents of infants presented for baptism, and baptismal sponsors. Many parishes of the Roman Catholic Church have learned how to involve a number of people—the baptized together with those inquiring about or seeking baptism—in the process of learning to pray, participating in worship, reflecting on the Sunday scripture readings, and deepening their understanding of the Christian faith and life. This comprehensive liturgical and catechetical approach to the baptismal process is called the Rite of Christian Initiation of Adults (RCIA).

The name of the process might mislead some people, because the term "rite" might seem to imply a single liturgical action. The RCIA, however, is a flexible process for responding to the needs of inquirers or seekers. The process may last most of a year or longer; it may also be much shorter. Central to the experience is assigning a sponsor to walk with the candidate through the process—to share in Bible study, pray with the candidate, discuss the Christian life, and worship regularly. A lay catechist regularly brings together the sponsors and candidates for study, discussion, prayer, and faith development. The priest is part of this process at specific times but especially presides at the liturgies that involve the gathered parish in prayer, blessing, support, and welcome of these candidates. The liturgies of the catechumenal process remind the community that it is in fact a baptizing community.[38] Unlike the method of holding a pastor's class of which the congregation is unaware, the catechumenal process counts the entire congregation, sponsors, and lay catechists—along with the pastor—as important partners in the journey toward baptism and beyond. This is a model for being a missional congregation oriented to baptism as the sacrament of God's mission to us through Jesus Christ in the power of the Spirit.

Lutherans in Canada were leaders in adapting for their context a form of the catechumenate that attends to Lutheran theology and mission.[39] Methodists are also encouraging congregations to explore this process of welcoming new people into the church through baptism.[40] For a somewhat longer time, the Episcopal Church has implemented this process in parishes and has provided resources for local leaders.[41] The Evangelical Lutheran Church in America (ELCA) has also encouraged congregations to explore the catechumenate. *Welcome to Christ* materials introduce the catechumenate to Lutheran congregations and leaders.[42]

Further resources are being developed for adults who have been baptized but never incorporated into the life and mission of the church. In order to make clear that their baptism is indeed God's once-for-all action and gift, these people are treated as "affirmers" who now seek to unpack and discover the gift of their baptism. They are received into the local worshiping community through Affirmation of Baptism. Their baptism was not invalid, so rebaptism is not an option. As Luther said in his Large Catechism, "Baptism is valid, even though faith is lacking. For my faith does not constitute Baptism, but receives it. Baptism does not become invalid even if it is wrongly received or used, for it is bound not to our faith but to the Word."[43]

Many catechisms have been developed since the sixteenth century to address a pastoral need. Our context requires a modern catechumenal process that honors the full Sunday lectionary readings and the varied richness of the church's liturgical heritage. The process must provide a structure for seekers as they encounter the strange new world of the Bible and the church's worship life.[44]

This catechumenal process is similar to methods of Christian education based on the Sunday lectionary readings. Such approaches allow parents and children to share experiences in worship and Sunday school that are focused on scripture and provide a basis for conversation in their life together as a family. Integrating reflection on the lectionary (Bible) with worship, prayer, and opportunities for daily baptismal living helps Christians to deepen their life in relationship to others and the world.[45]

The Call to Lifelong Baptismal Living and Vocation

Several of the newly revised liturgies for burial begin with a reference to the baptismal promise in Romans 6, where Paul speaks of baptism as uniting us with Christ in his death and resurrection. Luther vividly portrays death in baptismal terms because all of life and death is related to baptism.

> As we can plainly see, the sacrament or sign of baptism happens quickly. But the spiritual baptism, the drowning of sin, that it signifies lasts as long as we live and is completed only in death. It is then that a person is completely sunk in baptism, and that which baptism signifies comes to pass.[46]

Like birth, baptism means life. "It is done once, yet it is for all of our life."[47] In practice, we need to discover ways to communicate this principle for baptismal living. If I say, "I *was* married," you will likely assume that my wife has died or I am divorced. But if I say, "I *am* married," you will assume I have a wife and that on a certain date I *was* married and still *am*. Although it is true and essential to say that I *was* baptized, it is also necessary to assert, "I *am* baptized."

HOLY
BAPTISM:
PROMISE
BIG ENOUGH
FOR THE
WORLD

We frequently hear people say, "I am not a pastor; I am only a layperson." I cannot imagine someone saying, however, "I am not a pastor. I am only baptized." The need to affirm this baptismal identity is one of the reasons lay people ought to serve as assisting ministers in worship,[48] and all worshipers should be reminded that baptism ordains to priesthood in the world. The point of lay people carrying out worship roles such as proclaiming the scripture readings or offering the intercessions is not to make the baptized "para-pastors" or assistants to the clergy. It is rather to symbolize in worship their vocation in and for the world.

The ELCA statement *The Use of the Means of Grace* reflects a healthy orientation to mission for the sake of the world and daily life, particularly in the last part, "The Means of Grace and Christian Mission." The title of principle 52 summarizes well what it means to live out our baptism—"Baptism Comes to Expression in Christian Vocation"—and the principle itself says:

> Christians profess baptismal faith as they engage in discipleship in the world. God calls Christians to use their various vocations and ministries to witness to the Gospel of Christ wherever they serve or work.[49]

The statement goes on to quote part of an earlier confirmation ministry report:

> As baptized people, we see our daily life as a place to carry out our vocation, our calling. All aspects of life, home and school, community and nation, daily work and leisure, citizenship and friendship, belong to God. All are places where God calls us to serve. God's Word and the church help us to discover ways to carry out our calling.[50]

This outward orientation for mission is clearly expressed in the final liturgy of *Welcome to Christ* rites for the catechumenate. After the baptism of adults at the Easter Vigil and continued reflection on baptismal living and vocation during the Easter season's fifty days of rejoicing, Affirmation of the Vocation of the Baptized in the World may be celebrated on the Day of Pentecost.[51] This service can also be adapted for adults who were baptized as infants but who are only now becoming actively involved in the church's life and mission through the affirmation of their baptism. The introductory address for this brief rite begins:

> Dear Christian friends: Baptized into the priesthood of Christ, we are all called by the Holy Spirit to offer ourselves to the Lord of all creation.... Through Holy Baptism our heavenly Father set us free from sin and made us members of the priesthood we share in Christ Jesus. Through word and sacrament we have been nurtured in faith, that we

may proclaim the praise of the Lord and bear God's creative and redeeming word to all the world.[52]

Note also that this act of affirming baptismal vocation takes place as part of the sending rite at the conclusion of the eucharistic liturgy. Holy Baptism is thus understood as induction into the mission of God toward the world. This focus on the vocation of all the baptized is also symbolically expressed when a lay assisting minister speaks the dismissal at the end of the Sunday service, providing a transition as worshipers prepare to live their worship in and for the world. Those brief sending words, "Go in peace. Serve the Lord," grow out of a baptismal calling to be always caught up in the mission of God through Jesus Christ, and in the power of the missionary Spirit to be evidence of the first fruits of the age to come.

How that vocation will be carried out will depend on our context and gifts, and our discernment of the Spirit's leading. The ministry of the baptized is captured in poetry by Herbert Brokering:

Once there was a girl
who wanted to be a minister
when she grew up.
Everyone told her to stop saying it
because it was silly,
so she did.
She became one anyway
and didn't tell the people.
She washes feet,
says the people's names,
tries to get Sundays off,
sometimes works all night,
and helps the people go to sleep.
She can make a bedroom
feel like Communion.
She is very pretty.
When she was ordained,
they gave her a white cap.[53]

Whatever cap the baptized wear in daily life (and we usually wear several), we have opportunities for baptismal living. In worship the baptized are regularly nourished by communion and holy conversation. Could we imagine that because Christ is in us and we are in communion with God and all the saints, the places we live might "feel like Communion"? Ultimately the gift of baptism is to be expressed through the lives of ordinary people

HOLY
BAPTISM:
PROMISE
BIG ENOUGH
FOR THE
WORLD

like us. This extraordinary gift of God is for our ordinary days. Thanks be to God.

NOTES

Parts of this chapter originally appeared as an article, "Baptism, Evangelism, and Being Church," in *Word & World* 16, no. 1 (Winter 1994): 28–35.

1. Aidan Kavanagh, *Made, Not Born: New Perspectives on Christian Initiation and the Catechumenate* (Notre Dame, Ind.: University of Notre Dame Press, 1976), 2.

2. What we do in liturgy matters because it is an event of the gospel on which theology reflects. See Mons A. Teig, *Liturgy as Fusion of Horizons: A Hermeneutical Approach Based on Hans-Georg Gadamer's Theory of Application* (Ann Arbor, Mich.: University Microfilms International, 1992).

3. Two books that argue this perspective cogently and carefully are Gerhard O. Forde, *Theology Is for Proclamation* (Minneapolis: Fortress Press, 1990), and Robert W. Jenson, *Visible Words: The Interpretation and Practice of Christian Sacraments* (Philadelphia: Fortress Press, 1978).

4. Edmund Schlink, *The Doctrine of Baptism,* trans. Herbert J.A. Bouman (St. Louis: Concordia Publishing House, 1972), 205.

5. *The Sacred Actions of Christian Worship,* ed. Robert Webber, vol. 6 of The Complete Library of Christian Worship, 8 vols. (Peabody, Mass.: Hendrickson Publishers, 1993). Part 3, "Baptism," provides a history of baptismal practice and a brief summary of how major denominations present a theology and practice of baptism today.

6. Gordon W. Lathrop, foreword to *What Is Changing in Baptismal Practice?* Open Questions in Worship, vol. 4 (Minneapolis: Augsburg Fortress, 1995), 4.

7. Carl E. Braaten and Robert W. Jenson, eds., *Christian Dogmatics*, vol. 2 (Philadelphia: Fortress Press, 1984), 315–16.

8. The Large Catechism 4, 41–42, in *The Book of Concord: The Confessions of the Evangelical Lutheran Church,* trans. and ed. Theodore G. Tappert et al. (Philadelphia: Fortress Press, 1959), 441–42.

9. This was related to me by the Rev. Laurie Natwick.

10. Elaine Ramshaw, "How Does the Church Baptize Infants and Small Children?" in *What Is Changing in Baptismal Practice?* 13.

11. Faith and Order Commission Paper No. 111, *Baptism, Eucharist and Ministry* (Geneva: World Council of Churches, 1982), 7–8.

12. Ibid., 8–10.

13. James F. White, *Sacraments as God's Self Giving: Sacramental Practice and Faith* (Nashville: Abingdon Press, 1983), 36–42.

14. Martin Luther, "To the Christian Nobility of the German Nations," quoted in Eric W. Gritsch and Robert W. Jenson, *Lutheranism* (Philadelphia: Fortress Press, 1976), 71–72.

15. Gibson Winter, *The Suburban Captivity of the Churches* (Garden City, N.Y.: Doubleday, 1961), 152.

16. J.G. Davies, *Worship and Mission* (London: SCM Press, 1966), 148.

17. White, *Sacraments as God's Self Giving*, 38.

18. Davies, *Worship and Mission*, 29.

19. Nicene Creed, *Lutheran Book of Worship* (Minneapolis: Augsburg Publishing House; Philadelphia: Board of Publication, Lutheran Church in America, 1978), 64.

20. Eugene Brand, ed., *Worship Among Lutherans* (Geneva: Lutheran World Federation, 1983), 6, emphasis mine.

21. Schlink, *The Doctrine of Baptism*, 40.

22. *LBW,* 123.
23. Robert W. Jenson, *Christian Dogmatics,* vol. 2, eds. Carl E. Braaten and Robert W. Jenson (Philadelphia: Fortress Press, 1984), 321. Two sections by Jenson, "Sacraments of the Word" and "Baptism," are foundational theological statements for a discussion of Christian baptism.
24. Schlink, *The Doctrine of Baptism,* 123.
25. 1 Cor. 12:12-13 and Gal. 3:27-28. Both baptism and communion are seen in terms of reconciled unity and cooperative common ministry. In fact, failure to discern and live this gift of unity in Christ leads to sickness and even death, the opposite of what these communal sacraments offer.
26. Jürgen Moltmann, *The Church in the Power of the Spirit* (New York: Harper & Row, 1977), 232.
27. White, *Sacraments as God's Self Giving,* 42.
28. Maxwell Johnson, *The Rites of Christian Initiation: Their Evolution and Interpretation* (Collegeville, Minn.: Pueblo Books, 1999), 233. Maxwell Johnson, a Lutheran pastor who teaches at Notre Dame, has provided a thorough, insightful book about baptismal practice and theology from Christian origins, through the Reformation up to the present. He provides historical context for thinking about renewal of baptismal practice today.
29. *The Book of Common Prayer* (1979), 303.
30. *The United Methodist Book of Worship* (Nashville: United Methodist Publishing House, 1992), 89. Two additional forms for congregational pledges of responsibility to newly baptized people are provided in this book for celebrations of the baptismal covenant.
31. Bryan D. Spinks, "Luther's Timely Theology of Unilateral Baptism," *Lutheran Quarterly* 9 (spring 1995): 26 and 42. See also Johnson's use of Spink's article in his discussion of "creeping Pelagianism" in *The Rites of Christian Initiation,* 380–81.
32. Schlink, *The Doctrine of Baptism,* 79.
33. *Occasional Services* (Minneapolis: Augsburg Publishing House; Philadelphia: Board of Publication, Lutheran Church in America, 1982), 17.
34. *LBW,* 124, rubric 16.
35. Ibid., rubric 18.
36. Davies, *Worship and Mission.* Frank C. Senn, *The Witness of the Worshiping Community: Liturgy and the Practice of Evangelism* (New York: Paulist Press, 1993), expands on Davies' work.
37. Edward Yarnold, S.J., *The Awe-Inspiring Rites of Initiation: The Origins of the RCIA,* 2nd ed. (Collegeville, Minn.: Liturgical Press, 1994). Most of this book consists of the fourth-century baptismal sermons of Cyril of Jerusalem, Ambrose, John Chrysostom, and Theodore of Mopsuestia. These sermons on the rites of initiation were addressed to the newly baptized or those preparing for baptism. A modern discussion of the ancient rites, their dissolution, and present-day developments can be found in Johnson, *The Rites of Christian Initiation.*
38. *This Is the Night* (Chicago: Liturgy Training Publications, 1992). This thirty-minute video, shot on location at a Texas Roman Catholic parish, communicates the local flavor and excitement of inquirers preparing for baptism and the experience of baptism at the Easter Vigil. The viewer senses that the parish is a catechumenal and baptizing community of faith.
39. *Living Witnesses: The Adult Catechumenate,* (Winnipeg, Man.: Evangelical Lutheran Church in Canada, 1992). This church has developed a set of liturgical rites, a process guide, and a network of people as resources to introduce the catechumenate to its congregations.

HOLY
BAPTISM:
PROMISE
BIG ENOUGH
FOR THE
WORLD

40. Daniel T. Benedict Jr., *Come to the Waters: Baptism and Our Ministry of Welcoming Seekers and Making Disciples* (Nashville: Discipleship Resources, 1996).

41. Ann E. P. McElligott, *The Catechumenal Process* (New York: The Church Hymnal Corp., 1990).

42. Four resources in the Welcome to Christ series are now available. They are *Welcome to Christ: A Lutheran Introduction to the Catechumenate; Welcome to Christ: A Lutheran Catechetical Guide; Welcome to Christ: Lutheran Rites for the Catechumenate* (Minneapolis: Augsburg Fortress, 1997), and an eighteen-minute video resource, *Welcome to Christ: Preparing Adults for Baptism and Discipleship* (Chicago: Evangelical Lutheran Church in America, 1998).

43. The Large Catechism 4, 53, in *The Book of Concord*, 443.

44. Marva Dawn, *Reaching Out without Dumbing Down: A Theology of Worship for the Turn-of-the-Century Culture* (Grand Rapids, Mich.: Wm. B. Eerdmans, 1995). The catechumenal process is a way to deepen worship life by introducing new worshipers and seekers to the rich and varied traditions of worship without trying to appeal to the lowest common denominator.

45. A recent approach to this concept is provided by the Life Together series (Minneapolis: Augsburg Fortress).

46. "The Holy and Blessed Sacrament of Baptism, 1519," in *Luther's Works*, ed. Helmut T. Lehmann (Philadelphia: Fortress Press, 1960), 35:30–31.

47. *The Use of the Means of Grace: A Statement on the Practice of Word and Sacrament* (Evangelical Lutheran Church in America, 1997), application 14B.

48. *Occasional Services*. In the order Recognition of Ministries in the Congregation, the call of lay people to ministry within the congregation is rooted in baptism: "Baptized into the priesthood of Christ, we all are called to offer ourselves to the Lord of the Church in thanksgiving for what he has done and continues to do for us," 143.

49. *The Use of the Means of Grace*, principle 52.

50. *The Confirmation Ministry Task Force Report*, 5; *Together for Ministry: Final Report and Recommendations of the Task Force on the Study of Ministry* (Chicago: Evangelical Lutheran Church in America, 1993), as quoted in *The Use of the Means of Grace*, background 52A. See also Gustav Wingren, *Luther on Vocation* (Philadelphia: Muhlenberg Press, 1957) for an extensive discussion of baptismal vocation as service for "the other"; see especially pages 28–31.

51. *Welcome to Christ: Lutheran Rites for the Catechumenate*, 58–61.

52. Ibid., 59.

53. Herbert Brokering, *"I" Opener: 80 Parables* (St. Louis: Concordia Publishing House, 1974), 61. Copyright © 1974 Concordia Publishing House. Used by permission.

Holy Communion:
Taste and See

Mark P. Bangert

MARKET RESEARCH has become a fact of life for North Americans. We assume the products and services familiar to daily life—breakfast cereal, children's toys, life insurance, political leadership—have been developed with the guidance of surveys and focus groups. We understand that the new sandwich offered by a fast food franchise was subject to months of study in test kitchens before it was made available to the public. We pay attention when automobile ratings are published, and we want to know what the expert wine tasters say are the year's best vintners and varieties of grapes. Some people test so that others might taste.

Whatever one thinks about it, the tools of market research are being used even to discover what people think about worship. What time should the service be held? How long should it be? What elements appeal to the people the congregation wishes to attract? What kind of music should be sung? What topics should be addressed in a sermon? What do unchurched people think about the meaning and place of holy communion in worship? Here the taste test is usually not about whether to use wine or grape juice, wafers or loaves. Rather, congregation leaders ask questions about who is welcome at the table, and who is not; which elements of the celebration are necessary, and which are dispensable.

How can we go about testing these things? To begin with, we need to develop an educated palate, that is, to discover and distinguish the components of holy communion and how they affect our taste—how communion affects our relationship with God, ourselves, other people, and God's creation. In other words, does our eating make any difference in how we live and move and have our being as Spirit-led people in the world? What part does holy communion play in the church's mission?

Most of us need guidance to develop this taste. The church used to call this guidance catechesis. We tend to think of the catechetical process as a formal one involving classes and mentoring. Catechesis might begin long before we are aware of it, however. Stimulated aurally by the assembly's hymns and the repeated cadences of "the body of Christ, the blood of Christ," engaged visually by the candle light refracted from vessels of precious metal and images emanating from brightly colored stole and chasuble, and responding tactilely to the traced cross on the forehead, the very young, brought to the table in the warm arms of parents, begin their instruction in the faith. Infants so initiated to life at the table busily start to compile their own catechism on the meaning of life in Christian community, particularly, for purposes of this discussion, holy communion.

Nourishing as they are, the child's apprehensions are only the beginning of catechesis, and the community needs constantly to help that child—as well as older children and adults, whether new to the Christian faith or longtime members of the community—further explore the richness of holy communion. As each of us, child and adult alike, changes and grows, we continue to probe the holy mysteries.

Although the church has many gifts to offer the maturing Christian, we all risk impoverishing ourselves in our search for a more satisfying tasting of holy communion if we bypass Luther. There in his catechisms, small and large, we find anchorage but also a doorway to ever deeper insights into this holy meal. Luther calls us back to three basics:

1) God in Christ stands behind the sacramental event. It is Christ's feast, not ours.[1]
2) The purpose of holy communion is to give God's people, individually, the forgiveness of sins, life, and salvation.[2]
3) This meal is for the hungry of heart.[3]

Still, changing attitudes among all generations and contemporary culture's impact on personal faith and the dynamics of parish life prompt further musings about the Lord's supper. We explore with the hope that we might discover for ourselves dimensions of grace of which we were not previously aware. Such is the nature of the holy meal: it denies simplistic reduction and invites us into the wonders and riches of Christ. The taste is always more complex than our descriptions. Luther's catechesis is not passé, however. Today's younger generations, for example, are said to be searching for authentic life and community, and to them Luther might say,

"You will not be satisfied until your hearts rest where these words are heard: 'Given and shed for you for the forgiveness of sins.'" Luther's insights, we can see, continue to speak today.

In this chapter we will look first at three dimensions of eucharistic worship that will enrich our participation in holy communion. Each is biblically rooted, each connected to the central image of the body of Christ. Limiting our focus in this manner is not meant to minimize the role of the word in the assembly's gatherings for holy communion. Rather, urgent and perplexing issues about the relationship of worship and outreach (evangelism, witness, mission) become clearer when we explore the richness of the body image. The three explorations evolve from these questions:

1) What are the dynamics of Sunday parish worship? Why do Christians gather to worship?
2) How are we what we eat and drink?
3) Where can the stranger find God's witness in this world?

In the second part of this chapter, we will use our conclusions from these explorations to evaluate three increasingly popular parish sacramental practices.

1) Customizing worship for the generations;
2) Giving place to children at the table;
3) Sacramental feeding of the unbaptized.

We will see that while these practices offer resources for moving into the future and advancing the church's mission, they also invite us to return to the past, to the foundations of the Christian meal. Our task for today is to evaluate this trio of sacramental practices, so we can fully grasp the opportunities at hand.

"The body of Christ for you"—words of promise, words of hope, words of mission, words by which to live, and words of gospel. What now do they mean? Let us begin to develop our ability to discern, to test our taste.

~

SEEK THE LIVING AMONG THE LIVING

Luke's first clue to the resurrection is stark: "When they went in, they did not find the body" (Luke 24:3). A group of seekers—Mary Magdalene, Joanna, Mary the Mother of James, and others—came to the tomb early in the morning on the first day of the week, intending to embalm the body of the one they loved. They found much to their surprise that the stone was already rolled away. With this twist, the evangelist Luke begins the last chapter of his gospel, a compilation of interrelated events.[4] As one firmly rooted in the community of those who regularly broke bread together, Luke shows us that the resurrection of Jesus quickly leads to a whole series of first-day-of-the-week events, now related in Luke 24.

Seekers came to embalm Jesus but could find no body. Perplexed about this, the evangelist continues, they were reminded by the two angels that they should not seek the living among the dead but should instead remember the words of Jesus that "the Son of man must be handed over to sinners, and be crucified, and on the third day rise again" (Luke 24:7). If the women came only to mourn their dear friend's passing, to recall all that he had done and said, then their visit was fruitless, according to the dazzlers. The physical body of Christ was not available, but a new body in Christ was available for them outside the burial place of Jesus, now risen.

The evangelist is not yet done with his amazing narrative. "On that same day" (24:13), he goes on, two disciples were walking away from Jerusalem, where the crucifixion had taken place. They were despondent over their crushed hopes concerning Jesus of Nazareth. The Living One joined them, permitted them their moment of mourning (a moment fit for an empty tomb), and then, like the dazzling angels, explained that the crucifixion was a step to glory. To teach them, Jesus "interpreted to them the things about himself in all the scriptures" (24:27) and patiently lead them to recognize that the events of the past days were not good plans gone awry but were, in fact, the great design of God fulfilled in Jesus' own death and resurrection.

Still, the two kept walking away from Jerusalem, because they thought the body was nowhere to be found. Only when Jesus, now the host, was at table and took bread, blessed it, broke it, and gave it to them were their eyes opened, as the evangelist says, so that they might see the Living among the living. The body had now been found, on this first day of the week, the first day of the new creation.[5]

We make one final observation about this resurrection account. The two disciples, still on that first day of the week, left Emmaus and returned to Jerusalem. There they gathered with the other disciples, as if compelled by their own experience of the resurrection to come together immediately as sign and seal that they had found the body.

Over the years, the church has easily found the breath to trumpet God's action in the resurrection of Christ and the reality that the first day of the week upsets all we know about life and death. Christians have not always been clear about what comes between death and resurrection. Yet they have always gathered expectantly on Easter morn to hear the gospel accounts of empty tombs, loud noises, rolled-away stones, and dazzling angels. What seems to be even less clear among today's faithful are the links among the tomb, the resurrection, the defecting disciples, and the epiphany of Christ in the breaking of bread. But those links are important to Luke.

Like Paul, who wrote a few decades earlier to the Corinthians, Luke found that he could explain the gospel more effectively by telling what Jesus did at meal time.[6] Through the story of the Emmaus disciples, he talked about what Christians of his age experienced every first day of the week: the appearance of Christ in the breaking of bread. We break bread on the first day of the week precisely because the empty tomb made possible the apprehension of Christ's body by those who now eat and drink from his hand. To break bread is to meet, hear, touch, feel, and taste the living Jesus, crucified and risen. Several observations illustrate how radical this reorientation came to be.

To begin with, first-century Christians, experiencing Christ as the new lamb of God's *pasch,* naturally looked to the yearly Passover observance as a way to structure their weekly communal gatherings. Contemporary practice makes us a little immune to the significance of such a shift.

> Unlike the Israelite Passover, the Christian Passover is celebrated once a week on the first day of the week, and even daily, besides its solemn celebration in the Paschal Triduum.... The Christian Passover enables its participants to situate themselves in their history, one which reaches back to the climax of Jesus' life in the passion-resurrection.[7]

For most Jewish Christians, God's decisive deliverance through the new Passover lamb meant the cessation of the strict, annual Jewish ritual, though important aspects of Passover were reflected in the Christians' weekly practice and annual observance of Jesus' death and resurrection. Clearly, however, it was the resurrection of Christ together with his appearances in the breaking of bread that propelled these early believers to weekly gatherings where they experienced God's new presence in Christ outside the empty tomb.

Second, these first-day-of-the-week gatherings, reminiscent of family Passover observances, were distinctive precisely because they were *communal* experiences of the Risen One. In Luke 24 people encountered and met the Living One in groups: the two Marys and Joanna, the two Emmaus disciples, even two angels announced (and amplified) the news from the tomb. Even more significant was the return of the Emmaus disciples to Jerusalem so that they might be with the others. It is as if the Living One attracts as many people as possible so that the body might be experienced as truly living. This yearning for fullness continues in Luke's second book, where in Acts 2 we sense the excitement of Pentecost notably through the addition of thousands more who continued in the apostles' teaching, the breaking of bread, the prayers, and in the *koinonia* (fellowship).

Third, just when people of the Sunday gathering were tempted to think that they were the significant feature that attracted others to a bursting community—that they themselves were inviting Jesus into their irresistible (expanding) midst—Jesus suddenly appeared as the host and made it clear that resurrection meals occurred precisely because the Lord Christ was at the center of such meal epiphanies.[8]

To find the body, then, was to seek the Living among the living (as many as possible) on the first day of the week, when the Resurrected One imprinted the living through the breaking of bread—shorthand in some Lukan and Pauline materials for the holy communion and its predecessor meals.[9]

$\sim$

O TASTE AND SEE

Nowadays, thankfully, most of those preparing for first communion in our congregations have been spared the dreadful fear that used to descend on confirmands who imagined themselves to be among the damned who ate and drank unworthily. But there are enough of us around who remember how sternly these words of Paul—"For all who eat and drink without discerning the body…" (1 Cor. 11:29)—pierced our well-intentioned, if not hungry, souls. Discerning the body, we were instructed, meant to be clear about what that bread and wine really were. So summoning our best efforts, we worked to get the definitions right.

Some fussing over the meaning of *soma Christou* (Paul's "body of Christ") is worthwhile. Sacramental presence and the reason we still dance around that mystery is central to grasping the promise of holy communion and keeps several other insights sharp, too. O taste and see that morsel of bread, shaped from the fruits of creation by human hands and skill, so that in such tasting you might know the Resurrected One full of life, salvation, and the forgiveness of sins—as Luther would have it. Real presence is how we describe the eating and drinking linked to these gifts of grace and explain how the eating and drinking and gifts are Christ himself. Real presence is a way to apprehend what and how great the gift of the holy communion is.

Some people would have us believe that God's gracious giving is clearest only when scriptural words alone are spoken over bread and wine. Ponder, however, the richness of a greater thanksgiving, one that proclaims the grace revealed in the new covenant life of Jesus, now available in the eating of bread and wine. Personal benefits of such feasting are inherent in the very notion of the great thanksgiving, as if to say that there is no greater thanksgiving possible for those who have left the tomb to seek the Living One. The great thanksgiving not only begins to fill the body with the wondrous meaning it mysteriously bears, but it invites, even assumes, the powerful reception of the gift given. To receive from the hand of God forgiveness of sins, life, and salvation through blessed bread constitutes the highest thanksgiving, the highest worship we can give.[10] Graciously receiving God's bounty, moreover, gives great honor to the host of this meal.

Paul would surely urge us rightly to discern these gifts of bread and wine, and so taste the body of the Living One. Rightly discerning the body of Christ in the bread prevents the Christian assembly from imagining itself as the center of the meal, thinking that it must project itself as an agreeable bunch of personalities whose purpose for meeting is to attract new and fitting recruits. Christians gathered around holy food take no delight in themselves apart from the one who gives himself as the loaf and cup of salvation. For those in the baptized assembly, the attraction in the meal is the gifts, not the assembly itself.[11]

Yet, in 1 Corinthians 11, the apostle invites us, possibly with a knowing grin on his face, to think of the body of Christ in still another way. The entire letter deals with problems leading to parish disunity (1:10; 6:7ff; 8:10ff, and so forth). Saving his best arguments for last, Paul argues that the church's internal divisions manifest themselves in the way communion is celebrated in their midst (11:18-19). Some go ahead and eat by themselves, others go hungry, and still others are drunk. Liturgical practice belies that which they eat (11:20). The bread and wine are meant to shape an assembly that clearly reflects the unity all have in the Living One. What is not discerned, Paul warns, is the body of Christ as church. That failure to discern can only bring judgment, which in the Corinthian case comes in the form of debilitating dissension.

Like Luke, the apostle makes his clearest proclamation of the gospel by pointing to the meal. Hence, "as often as you eat this bread and drink the cup, you proclaim the Lord's death until he comes" (11:26). In other words, the Living One is recognized in the icon of the community—real presence can be perceived both in the community's eating and in the community itself. The meal is about people. The Lord's supper is the liturgical epiphany of the church, and if authentic, cannot help but show forth the brokenness of humanity[12] and at the same time enact "signs of how life is to be lived."[13]

Paul's own take on that radical vision of community shows up in subsequent chapters. He hammers away at varieties of gifts given by one Spirit (12:4ff). Diversity is meant to be savored (12:27ff) and to be fueled always by love (13:1ff). Honoring one another's varied gifts shows forth the body of Christ, and such honor must extend also to worship (14:20ff.). Paul simply is not willing for the sake of ease to reconfigure the body by separating those who speak in tongues from those who do not. A way must be found to accommodate all.

The composition of the assembly and the behavior of the assembly is at the heart of being the body of Christ—that which we eat. By permitting diversity to fracture the Christian community, the body of Christ dilutes its witness, siphons off power for its mission, and soils the gospel. The body of Christ is seen even as it is tasted. Blessed bread and wine and the community are not two things but one. So Joseph Cardinal Bernardin wrote: "Without liturgy [holy communion] we forget who we are and whose we are; we have neither the strength nor the joy to be Christ's body present in the world."[14]

≈

YOU ARE WITNESSES OF THESE THINGS

To eat worthily, in the apostle Paul's view, is to see more clearly. To see what? The body of Christ as both food and community. But that is not the end of Paul's vision. Behind food and community lies God's love affair with this creation. Luke the evangelist can be of help here. Consider how he wants the faithful to see that God's presence in this world is an embodied presence, coming as it does into this world in an eating trough, heralded by angels and witnessed by shepherds (Luke 2). God's commitment to embodiment is not lost in subsequent chapters. One way to look at the gospel of Luke, according to Eugene LaVerdiere, is to note how Jesus' ministry becomes manifest—or is to be seen—in a series of ten meals.[15] The Christ undertakes his mission by going to the lost and the lonely and having meals with them. Eating, particularly eating with others, is one of the clearest traits of incarnation. After the resurrection the Living One still shows up at meals. True to his purposes, Luke portrays the resurrected Lord as the embodied Christ who eats with the gathered ones in Jerusalem, delivers one last teaching about his identity, and commissions them to be the transformed embodiment of God's continuing presence in the world: "Repentance and forgiveness of sins is to be proclaimed in his name to all nations.... You are witnesses of these things" (Luke 24:47-48).

From then on, no Christian assembly can gather without being dispersed, and no Christian assembly can disperse without gathering. It took some time for the disciples to grasp fully what this new embodied presence in the world really meant. But already in the first chapter of Luke's second book, Acts, the disciples began to take on apostleship by finding a way to replace Judas, to bring to twelve the number of the disciples-turned-apostles. A new Israel is inconceivable without the twelve tribes. Only then could the story tracing God's embodied presence beginning in Jerusalem and going to the ends of the earth continue.

Clarity about church as embodied presence of God in the world is essential for the contemporary mission of the church. North American immigrant churches, due in large part to their own perceived need for physical survival and national identity, most often kept to themselves. To be sure, strangers were occasionally invited in. In fact, the admonition to bring others to church fueled evangelism efforts well into the twentieth century. Elsewhere the notion of church as embodied sanctuary took on a slightly different shape. As Frank Senn and Gordon Lathrop have noted, evangelical churches were drawn to the camp meeting and urban revival patterns to deliver news *about* the mission with the intent to receive the wayward through conversionlike altar calls.[16]

Acts records another model for mission. Embodiment is also, if not chiefly, out there. Healings took place in the public places and evangelism in the marketplace. The community adopted a lifestyle that astonished even the uncommitted, such as Pliny the younger, who is supposed to have noted how the Christians loved one another. In short, the mission of the postresurrection embodiment of God takes place apart from the assembly as frequently as it does within the assembly. The business of the gathering is the same as the business of the dispersal. This unity of liturgy and mission is unveiled in the meal.

In a particularly poignant way, the author of 1 Peter provides lively images for energizing mission in dispersal. In chapter 2 the writer invites the church, the body of Christ, to think of itself as a chosen race, a royal residence, a holy nation, and urges these people then to shed any notion that they are "not a people," but rather to live as "God's people" (1 Peter 2:9-10). If, as some surmise, this

epistle was addressed to newly baptized adults, these recently catechized believers—now named the "elect" in the epistle—would
grasp the impact of these words, for they would remember that
God spoke to Israel of old and said, "Now therefore, if you obey
my voice and keep my covenant, you shall be my treasured possession out of all the peoples.... You shall be for me a priestly kingdom
and a holy nation" (Exod. 19:5-6). Just as the first Israel was to be
God's presence to the nations, so the new Israel—even this besieged,
suffering, yet washed remnant—is now to be the presence of God to
the nations.[17]

How can this chosen race live up to its name? By doing all those
things that caught the attention of Pliny. Maintain good conduct
among the Gentiles (1 Peter 2:11), live as free people without letting
freedom be a pretext for evil (2:16), honor the emperor (2:17),
employ gifts for one another (4:10), and do service to glorify God
(4:11). In short, live as the body of Christ in the world.

The body of Christ in the world, as the new Israel, depends for
its life on the sustenance freely given by its head and on the intricate
workings of its members. Learning the ways of trust in worship,
being nurtured by the presence of Christ, becoming bold in the
Christ-life, and practicing oneness in the Spirit, for example,
provide the patterns for going in peace and serving the Lord. Evangelism is the public acting out of the compact, focused gestures and
communications of the church at worship. But once worship has
gone evangelistically public, another tendency begins to emerge.
The enactment of the church's mission in the daily lives of its
members is drawn back into the patterns and processes of its
common meal.[18]

Christians are always tempted to keep liturgy and evangelism
far apart from each other. Our task is easier that way. Evangelism
can be ignored altogether, or it can be reconfigured as if it were a
matter for specialization, a function for the interested few. Without
a close bond between liturgy and mission, worship is too easily
transformed, as if it were merely an aesthetically pleasing ingredient
in one's personal quest for things spiritual—liturgy reduced to a
ritual hot water bottle for those with spiritual chills. Turned in on
itself in such a way, liturgy evolves into a spiritual concert for the
lonely.

Liturgy and mission, however, are one and the same. How can
this be? Among other things, ritual is a kind of shorthand for extraliturgical behavior.[19] The family sings "Happy Birthday"
because members wish to mark the importance of this singular life
in their midst. By themselves, song, candle, and cake are insignifi-

cant unless they are accompanied by the thousands of other ways
the celebrators manifest their love and care for this individual
throughout the year.

Rituals establish patterns for the way things really are, patterns
that continue well beyond the holy time and space. They unveil the
deep, hence real, dynamics of personal relationships; they carefully
mark the doorways to extraliturgical life, so that participants might
perceive meaning and purpose in ordinary life. Through repeated
conventions, rituals show us how to act, reveal what is valuable,
and provide patterns of behavior toward the creation and all those
who have not yet tasted the goodness of God.

A characteristic of worship as ritual is that the significance of
what is done far exceeds what is apparent. Ritual concentrates
meaning. Some people think of worship as a kind of "symbolic
transformation."[20] Whatever image is helpful here,[21] it is clear that
in Christian liturgy worshipers are enabled to apprehend the overwhelming mysteries behind creation and redemption. The incarnation and resurrection of Christ—yes, his real presence—are mani-
fested through simple eating of bread and drinking of wine. Precisely
because of this simple eating and drinking, these worshipers learn
how to recognize the mysteries of Christ's presence among the lowly,
poor, and meek but also among the rich of means and poor of spirit,
all hungry to know the name and goodness of the one in whom they
live and move and have their being. Ritual reduces in order that it
might expand. Worship and mission are the same.

This fact is what frightened the detractors of Jesus. If he had
eaten only an occasional meal with tax collectors and prostitutes,
his detractors might have turned away from the obvious indiscre-
tions Jesus displayed rather publicly in his eating habits. But these
meals, too, were foretastes of the reign of God. It was clear that
Jesus meant to display in concentrated form what the mission of
God was about: all people are called, including children and others
from the highways and byways (Luke 14:23). Jesus' meal behavior
struck at the crumbling premises of the religious establishment. As
early Christians merged this kind of meal practice with the Passover-
based Lord's supper, they turned into targets for social ire.

The severity of this rift becomes clear in first-century meal practice among people of means. Biblical scholar LaVerdiere describes
the Hellenistic symposium as a social event built around a lavish
meal to be followed with learned discussions. According to
LaVerdiere, this pattern found its way into the Lukan account of the
Lord's supper: the writer places Jesus' farewell discourse immediately after the meal (22:14-38). LaVerdiere continues:

As a reclining banquet, the symposium was for free people only, that is, adult males. At times women, boys and slaves were brought in during the second part of the symposium for the drinking feast but their purpose was to serve as prostitutes or the like. A reclining banquet could become quite depraved.

By welcoming everyone to the eucharistic symposium—including women, children and slaves—the early Christians opened themselves to accusations of gross immorality and of subverting the social order.[22]

But subvert they must, both in mission and in meal. Although we have moved in our discussion from worship to mission, the movement from mission to worship reveals the whereabouts of this body of Christ. Christian worship always takes its cue from its mission, wrote Joseph Cardinal Bernardin. "Only those who live out... proclamation daily discover finally why it is not a dirge that we sing when we gather but praise."[23] Worship and mission are one in such a way that "the actions of the assembly offering Eucharist are signs of how life is to be lived; caring equally for all those whom we see and helping to provide for those we cannot see, ensuring that the resources of the earth are distributed to all."[24] Simply put, "our mission is to be the body of Christ in the world—to be the new creation."[25]

In these days people need and can be drawn to the liturgical mode of the eucharistic mission of God, but the church dare not pretend with them that liturgy is the end of the invitation and call. In fact, the liturgical mode should make clear through its own unfolding that God's mission flows into all of life: "Go in peace, serve the Lord." What is inside is out, and what is outside is in. In many parishes this unity awaits serious epiphanies.

~

Promise, hope, and mission

Awakened to mission in the twenty-first century, congregations from all denominations are beginning to hear the Spirit's call from those who cannot yet bless the God of Jesus the Messiah. Members of these communities know that the gospel needs to be heard more clearly than ever before. It is usually easier to sense a vocation in these matters than to put such a calling into practice. Nevertheless, goading and advice are offered by many people. Unless enthusiasm and commitment are tempered by a sure grasp of the gospel's mission, however, communities of faith can be diverted from God's mission in their midst and through them to the world. A growing number of voices decry popular paths to apparent parish growth.

Some worshiping assemblies captivated by the idols of size need the cleansing, freedom, and clarity that the resurrected Christ can again bring to them through rededication to word and sacrament. At the same time, other assemblies need to open the doors, to let in the mission of the gospel, to scrutinize their esoteric liturgical practices for signs that the connection between worship and mission has been broken.[26]

What overrides all concerns is the pressing need for congregations everywhere to regain a sense of the unity of worship and mission. To do that is to sense the local epiphany of God's presence in the world, a presence that cannot be reduced to an instruction manual for making your church grow. On the other hand, a handful of current sacramental practices deserve attention for what they might mean for parish life in these times.

We will consider three practices with the hope that any proposal for worship and mission will be welcomed with thoughtful scrutiny. Parishes moved to take on these practices, for whatever reason, will do well to expand on the process below by setting the practices and any others alongside observations made above.

∼

Customizing worship for the generations

Much of the excitement about worship at the turn of the millennium derives from the sense that public worship is an ideal meeting place for the various generations to become acquainted with the Christian gospel. Hence every effort must be made to bring people to the meeting. Such passion is not new. Christians throughout the twentieth century admonished one another to bring a neighbor or a friend to church, though little attention was given to making the stranger feel at home. What is new about this contemporary missionary zeal is its insistence that the church attend to *how* it clothes itself for the unchurched. The "church growth movement," as it is popularly known, is so well known, so frequently reviewed,[27] and in some quarters so taken for granted that to raise questions about any part of the movement is sometimes misunderstood as a blanket dismissal of the church's responsibility to follow the Spirit to the ends of the world. Indeed, commitment to connect the gospel to every generation continues to yield blessing, as we will point out.

But who are these people commonly lumped together into generations? Fast-paced changes in experience, education, technology, and operative values help to create what Strauss and Howe have called "cohort groups,"[28] which more broadly constitute somewhat distinct "generations." According to the discreet groupings pro-posed by these authors, many of the people others might call "the unchurched" come from one of three generations: baby boomers (those born between 1943 and 1960), the "thirteenths" (those born between 1961 and 1981—also known as "generation X"), and the millennials (those born after 1982).[29]

The way to engage these generations, so the theory goes, is to shape the public meeting in such a way that the gospel gets through to those targeted. Although such an aim gives birth to a host of complicated questions about worship and culture,[30] the liturgical solutions originally proposed and now widely used do often result in immediate numerical growth spurts. Most dramatic seems to be the increased number of worshiping groups (or "starts," as they are called bureaucratically) gathered from residents of homogeneous, fast-growing suburban developments. Struggling urban parishes looked on with interest, hope, and a hunger for assistance. It was not long before leaders of these new congregations began to talk about different kinds or styles of public worship: traditional, con-temporary, alternative, and blended. A short look at each of these may be useful.

Linguistic usage suggests that "traditional" has to do with something that is handed over, inherited, something that provides cultural continuity via established or customary patterns. To remain healthy, Christian assemblies of worship adopt a yes/no posture over against the "traditional." On the one hand, because the gifts of grace handed over in proclaimed word and sacramental eating and sacramental washing bring life to people of every culture and gen-eration, worshipers are hesitant to give up received ways of making these gifts available. Such hesitancy probably arises from a shared sense that some aspects of what is handed over (for example, washing with water rather than with milk) transcend every time and place. Tradition of that sort calls forth a yes from the gathered faithful and understandably prompts a concern to guard what is more precious than gold or silver. Many worshiping communities find that text and music from *Lutheran Book of Worship* and *With One Voice* present a still clear, if not the clearest, pattern for expe-riencing the gifts of grace. Members from these groups value the bonds such liturgies provide with worshipers of other times and places. They treasure the safety and security of what is known, even though intense commitment to what is comfortable can lead dan-gerously to liturgical idolatry.

Distinguishing what is nonnegotiable about the gifts of grace from what lends them apparent cultural currency is no easy task, for whenever Christians set out to protect generational or national values, patterns, or expressions in their worship assemblies, whenever they hold more dearly the way the gifts of grace come into their midst rather than the gifts themselves, they have lost the ability to say no to all that impedes the ever-recreating energies of the Holy Spirit through the gospel.

"Contemporary" means what exists, lives, comes into being at the same time, is marked by signs of the present time. If worship among Christians is not contemporary—deliberately concerned in preaching, prayer, and offering with issues of this life and the world as it is now—then it is dead. But "contemporary worship" has come to mean something different in the language of worship stylists. For them contemporary designates particular worship "formats," use of "praise music" or Christian contemporary music, informal dress and behavior, and messages geared toward the needs of the people. Without prejudice, such a style of worship would be more accurately described as a loosely organized program with an edifying message, built around a single style of performed music in a deliberately informal manner.

"Alternative" usually refers to the style just described, especially as it is proposed as an equally effective (or better) choice over against the traditional pattern of assembly worship.

Finally, "blended" means that elements from the traditional are used together with elements of the contemporary so as to offer something for everybody. Often blended liturgies are a laudable attempt to deal with the spectrum of generations in a typical parish.

It remains to be said that the history of Christian assembly around word and sacrament shows that Christian worship has always been "blended," especially in terms of music (which seems always to be the Rosetta stone for determining the pedigree). Luther's forays into church music included simultaneously Gregorian chant, Christian pilgrimage songs, metrical settings of the psalms according to models from Calvinist France and Switzerland, the latest in Latin and German polyphony, newly composed pieces according to the guild music of the Meistersinger tradition, and a few songs baptized into service from nonreligious sources.[31] The varied pedigree of Luther's music needs to be known lest we misrepresent Luther as the first prophet of contemporary Christian music.

Emergent terminology such as this gets pressed into service for noble reasons. The generations are different enough, the reasoning goes, that it makes sense to customize worship styles to fit the targeted cohort groups. Yet customizing inadvertently encourages divisiveness, because it invites people to choose or reject an assembly on the basis of style. Actually, the choice/rejection possibility calls into question the related practice of time-slot liturgies. For too long accepted without consideration of consequences, such scheduling likewise creates divisiveness, if not virtual coexisting congregations, in parishes. But the problem, it seems, runs deeper. Planning separate services according to time, style, or generation tempts us to think of Christian assembly as a gathering of the like and liked (and convenient separation from the different and unliked).

Such was not the inclination of those first disciples described in Luke/Acts, however. Hungering for the body of Christ, they set out for Jerusalem, desiring to eat together with the whole company, learning to recognize the presence of the Risen One always in the full gathering. Reading chapter 24 of Luke together with the first few chapters of Acts reveals a kind of spiritual giddiness among the primary followers, a giddiness that drove them together, equipped by the power of the Spirit to overcome the barriers of language and culture.

What would happen if we were to leave behind notions of the meal liturgy as the place where we might find a personal dose of spiritual caffeine?[32] What would happen if we were to let ourselves be drawn into the Spirit-led foolishness of gathering the full body of Christ in a local place, to come together because it is there that the Risen One desires to make epiphany? Do we hear such sanctified giddiness as a challenge to find the way for all to gather and meet the Christ? What would we give up so that others might be included? How would each of us revamp our personal wishes to restructure the worship of our own community? How might we benefit from a Spirit-led insistence on the unity of the body of Christ, a unity that creates longing less for a eucharistic club of the like-minded and more for an experience of the multitude that comes from the four corners of the earth?

The desire to customize worship tends to create segmented parishes and to mirror the kind of partitioning that under political and military manipulation evolves into the myriad war-torn lands of the world. Interestingly, the apostle Paul, ever on the watch for liturgical disunity, as we see in 1 Corinthians 10–12, continues his discussion of unity and worship in chapter 14. There he cautions against the disunity that results from imposing individual agendas on the assembly's worship (14:26ff.). Individual gifts serve only when they are introduced for the edification of all. In the larger measure of these matters, unity evolves not from cultural or generational preference but from the Risen One in the midst of diversity. Customized worship retards the spiritual growth and benefits that derive from committing ourselves to the stranger; the church's witness to the world gains strength from its demonstration of and faith in Christ's work of reconciliation.[33]

Thankfully, those who are zealous for continuing the mission of God to the people, nations, and generations of this world have awakened in the whole church a commitment to the gospel's own ministry of preaching to the poor, recovering the sight of those who are blind, and setting at liberty those who are oppressed (Luke 4:18). Moreover, they have taught all Christian assemblies to attend to hospitality, to foster new ways to contextualize worship for the generations of this age, and to let go of those nonessentials so that the gospel might be ever clearer in word and sacrament.

Desiring then to recognize the Risen One in the fullness of the body of Christ, let Christ set the agenda for Christian assemblies. Let the assemblies give attention to the fullness of the appointed readings so that all might apprehend and experience the mystery of his incarnation, death, and resurrection. Let those readings be proclaimed with every oral art that serves the miracle of sounded gospel, as Luther has it.[34] Let us evaluate, learn, and build on the church's own traditions of drama and music. Let it be known that liturgy is timeless by its very anchor in the Timeless One, that Christ was not invented for boomers, Xers, or millennials but is the Messiah for every age.

Let the chief service of a parish be on the first day of the week and designed to seek out the Risen One in the breaking of bread. Let parishes explore new ways to use the sacred concert as a place to hear praise bands, praise choirs, praise handbells, praise organs, and praise congregations. Let the sacred concert be a means to offer the riches of all Christian musical traditions, and thereby to meet those who seek the Christian community through what is familiar. Let the vesture of worship leaders be not an occasion for parading singular greatness, but rather the tool to transcend idiosyncrasy for the sake of mission. Let honor and respect for all the people determine behavior and style, so that none is excluded. And let liturgy employ intimately and simultaneously the tongues and cultures of all, so that we might taste the city of God in its splendor (Rev. 21:22-27).

~

Giving place to children at the table

If evangelism is the invitation to people "to enter more deeply into Jesus and the community that bears his name,"[35] then children by definition are among those invited into that community that receives the stranger. How children are invited is less the subject here than how they are a part of the community's witness. Their place in the eucharistic assembly is ultimately more important than whether or not a parish offers latchkey services, for instance, especially when outreach is understood to be more than marketing human services.

Our thinking on these matters is guided by Jesus' own meal practices and by the apostle Paul's efforts to describe the singularity of meal and church. Earlier we discovered that Jesus saw children as coworkers in the reign of God and insisted that they not be kept at a distance but be welcomed, as into his own presence, because "it is to such as these that the kingdom of God belongs" (Mark 10:14). In fact, a child provides the model for entering into God's presence (Mark 10:15). In the Hellenistic symposium, children were used and abused. In the reign of God, they are embraced and blessed.

Divisiveness, we learn from 1 Corinthians, cripples the church and makes it a sham. In his letter to that church, the apostle clearly reprimanded the eucharistic practices in Corinth because their ritual meal belied what they claimed it to be. Paul was not even tempted to parse politely; instead he made it clear that

> [w]henever the community is insensitive to the requirement of transcending human barriers, particularly by favoring the rich, by excluding racial groups, disadvantaged or disabled persons, children or elderly people in its way of life, then that community contradicts the will of God and violates the Eucharist because it does not discern the body.[36]

Full inclusion of children in holy communion, therefore, enacts what the body of Christ is. Even as the apostle Paul pleaded for manifest congruence between its meal practice and what the church in Corinth confessed itself to be, so Christian assemblies today stand to benefit from Paul's critique by asking hard and honest questions about the role of children in worship and how that role essentially shapes the congregation's witness to those being invited ever more deeply.

Consider two scenarios. The cherub choir, that group of ebullient singers from the first grades of school, garbed in little red gowns with white tops, is preparing to sing during Sunday worship. There they are, lined up in front of the church, prepared to sing the song they carefully rehearsed. They do a fine job, offering a gift to the assembly. But then there are the parents, video cameras in hand, doting uncontrollably, and finally, with their applause, succumbing to the temptation to relegate the children to objects for their own gratification.

Or this: Saturday evening concludes a twenty-four-hour senior choir retreat. One of the basses brings his eight-year-old son for closing worship, which in this case is the setting of evening prayer from *LBW*. In the midst of a darkened prayer chapel, the young boy joins the rest in singing all the parts, most from memory. He neither expects nor asks for recognition. Rather, he knows his gifts are welcomed and he is welcome, just as in those times when he helps to carry bread and wine in the Sunday offertory procession in preparation for his own participation.

Which scenario begins to implement the vision from 1 Corinthians? Of course, this is not an easy choice, because there are mitigating circumstances and issues left unnoted here. Can it be said, however, that parishes often seek to incorporate children in worship in order to please the parents, because we expect to be entertained? Children as diversion? as entertainment?

Far better for them, for the adults, and for the witness of the church for the children to be offered the roles and tasks in worship that their baptismal vocations afford. Here we look first at what that rightful place might be and then, second, at what kind of image that might provide both for the faithful and for the seekers.

Children have a right to be nurtured in the assembly in languages they understand. Let the readings, then, be offered in ways that address children (and, perhaps, the child in each adult?). Let children do the reading. Let there be proclamation designed and fit for children, yet offered as proclamation for the whole assembly. And let preachers take care that this proclamation not take the form of predictable moralisms derived from objects or stories. Let the simple gesture of blessing be weighted over against many words. Let biblical images flood sermon and prayer.

Children have a right to offer their own gifts to the assembly. Let them make monetary offerings from their allowances. Let young servers assist the ministers and not merely light candles. Let children serve the sacrament to all. Let children join the offertory procession even with their own gifts. Let the children lead the psalm and sing in order to elicit the voices of parents and the eschatological vision of the crowds who shout hosanna!

Children have a right to the meal. Although this is not the place to rehearse the many twists and turns of liturgical history leading to the exclusion of children from holy communion, it is clear that withholding holy communion from the newly baptized is indefensible historically and theologically. In its 1997 sacramental practices statement, *The Use of the Means of Grace*, the Evangelical Lutheran Church in America added its voice to the growing ecumenical consensus by affirming, "Admission to the Sacrament [of the Altar] is by invitation of the Lord, presented through the Church to those who are baptized."[37] Pastoral considerations in these matters always guide practice, but the document goes on to explain that "infants and children may be communed for the first time during the service in which they are baptized."[38] With this advice, the document begins to reclaim the rightful place of infants and children in the eucharistic meal, acknowledging that in the postapostolic church it was always understood that "baptism was initiation into the eschatological body of Christ, which is realized in the eucharistic fellowship."[39]

Children have a right to the meal. Let parishes welcome them to the table, then, and resist the temptation to present them with substitute snacks. Let infants come when they are baptized.[40] Let instruction and reflection[41] accompany children at every step of the way. Let confession and forgiveness in the parish be for children, too, and let it be freed from generalized acknowledgments of incapacities and momentary slips in behavior.

Jesus observed that children receive the reign of God in a way adults should imitate (Mark 10:15). Full participation in the eucharistic meal by the young demonstrates simply and mightily that everyone relies on the nurturing God who provides food for all suckling children of faith. In communing children we observe the reign of God in which the baptized of any age, no matter how well instructed, always *receive* the gifts of forgiveness of sins, life, and salvation.[42] Attending to the right of children is far more than a new program to keep them interested in Sunday assembly. Rather, the presence of children at the meal enables all to know themselves not as those who decide for God but as those called, gathered, enlightened, and sanctified by the power of the Spirit. Children at the table are signs of God's grace.[43]

Christian communities that give children their rightful place at the meal make a compelling witness to those being drawn to Jesus and the gospel. Instead of offering a religion that grants approval on the basis of instruction and the acceptance of specified conventions, such communities live out that eschatological vision that proclaims God's tireless gathering of all humans, young and old, no matter what their emotional, physical, or intellectual capabilities. Indeed, the full participation of children in worship is essential to the witness of the church.

Finally, Christian assemblies whose table is open to all the baptized also enact what God means by family. Here, children are not to be treated as if they were underdeveloped adults, treated as if

they were living dolls or toys for adults, or even considered the full
measure of the community at worship. Rather, they are to be honored for their own gifts, challenged in the faith, instructed by experience, and above all to be held dear for their trusting hearts, which point adults back to their own dependence on God's grace.

LaVerdiere keeps reminding us that the meal is not so much about food as it is about people.[44] The presence of infants and children at the table declares the meaning of the food there eaten. Infants and children at the table proclaim the reign of God through sign and action. By the power of the Spirit, the nations and generations will see the vision of the city of God and come to it.

∾

SACRAMENTAL FEEDING OF THE UNBAPTIZED

Just how the Holy Spirit "calls, gathers, enlightens, and sanctifies" the whole church is not ours to know fully nor ours to fashion programmatically. To be sure, the Spirit's calling comes through the gospel, Luther insisted, and thereby he brought focus to a typically Lutheran insight about the relationship between the Spirit and the means of grace.

Can and does the Spirit call through holy communion? To ask the question makes many anxious, especially if an affirmative answer leads to using the meal liturgy as an evangelistic opportunity. For those anxious ones, there is some comfort in knowing that the World Council of Churches, obviously acknowledging growing sympathy for the sacramental feeding of the unbaptized, affirmed instead that "Roman Catholic and Reformation Churches agree that baptism is necessary for participation in the Eucharist."[45]

Still, current parish practice suggests that because people are increasingly mobile and the number of the unbaptized is growing, the likelihood that the unbaptized will commune is greater than ever before. Surely the practice of hospitality will help us to deal with these occasional visitations without much fuss. But having done that, we need to ask whether communing the unbaptized comprises an opportunity for mission.

First, matters of hospitality. There are all sorts of reasons why on an individual basis we do not turn away the unbaptized from the table. In former times—out of love, it must be said—those who sought to honor the tradition made sure that none would incur the wrath sure to come upon any who unworthily reclined at this table. In 1 Corinthians, however, we have learned that the apostle Paul was not prescribing gatekeeping procedures in order to protect the unworthy from receiving the sacrament to their own "damnation," as the word *krisis* (judgment) was formerly translated. Judgment was for those who failed to be what they ate.

The Lord's supper is not our own. It is Christ's supper. Christ hosts the meal and through the church invites the most unlikely to participate (Luke 5:27-39). What is required at this table is that a person has a "genuine and living faith in Christ."[46] After hearing that the disciples wanted to turn the five thousand away, Jesus instructed them instead to provide hospitality for the Bethsaidan crowds (Luke 9:12-13) by feeding them with bread broken and blessed by Jesus in a way that is strongly reminiscent of the Lord's supper.[47]

Although Christ's invitation through the church is to all the baptized,[48] we are also advised that

> when an unbaptized person comes to the table seeking Christ's presence and is inadvertently communed, neither that person nor the minister of Communion need be ashamed. Rather Christ's gift of love and mercy to all is praised. That person is invited to learn the faith of the Church, be baptized, and thereafter faithfully receive Holy Communion.[49]

In this way, those who follow from afar are brought into Christ's presence in a manner and with a dispatch perhaps surprising even to themselves. Once there, they are nurtured by the faithful, so they might join fully in the mission of the church.

But can this somewhat irregular pattern become the basis for reaching out to the many more hungry ones out there, those who would not even count themselves among the followers from afar? In other words, are there any reasons to use holy communion as an opportunity for evangelism? In some respects, the church cannot help such evangelism from occurring. The fact that they were "witnesses of these things" (Luke 24:48) presented the disciples with the opportunity to take the apostolic witness to the nations. There among the nations, they preached, healed, and baptized. Presumably through such powerful witness, the Spirit led still others to join the apostles as they took the good news to all nations. Gradually the thousands baptized at Pentecost were joined by thousands more, so that the new royal residence of God, described in 1 Peter, might be manifest to the far corners of the earth.

With Jerusalem as the epicenter, the church quaked its way into all nations. We read in Acts that there were often meetings at the margins that brought together the bearers of good news and those who had not seen or heard.[50] Seldom do we get a glimpse of how it felt for those first apostles to come home at night or to regroup around testimony and meal. Yet that may be the very point. For those first witnesses, giving testimony through word and daily life was the theological and practical outcome of hearing the word, praying, and eating at the table of the Lord.[51] Worship and witness were thought to be a unitary activity given integrity by being in two modes.

When worship and mission are seen and enacted as one, and when circumstances permit open assembly, individuals can and will be drawn to the Spirit's activity through the gospel in both modes. All of life is the place for evangelism; therefore, the meal can be a place of evangelism. But the meal must never be reconfigured as prelude to mission or as a recruiting station for witness.

In the gospel of Luke, the feeding of the five thousand occurs in a portion of the gospel that deals with mission (Luke 9:1-50). The disciples had just returned from going out and preaching the reign of God. Jesus invited them to withdraw with him to Bethsaida, but the crowds followed. As evening came the disciples wanted to send the crowds away, but Jesus helped them to understand that meal hospitality could not be denied the crowds (9:10-13). The feeding, although hosted by Jesus, required the assistance of the twelve (the new Israel), indicating that the disciples were deliberately being called and drawn into the mission of their Lord. There was to be no mistake: the disciples were being called not only to the five thousand in Bethsaida but to the thousands beyond that gathering (twelve basketfuls of bread were left over). In fact, the Bread of life is for the whole human race, and he and his saving ministry are to be most clearly experienced in the meal.[52]

In this miraculous feeding, we are to perceive not only an image of holy communion but the nature of the mission of Christ through his twelve apostles and through the church, his body. Meal hospitality demands that none be turned away. Rather, they are welcomed even when provisions (energy, time, and nourishment) seem inadequate.

The evangelizing mode at the margins and the liturgical mode are one and the same. Those who come to be healed and to discover the Christ are welcomed and not turned away. Just where they discover the Christ is not ours to predict.

So, then, can the holy meal be an opportunity for evangelism? The answer must be yes for these reasons: (1) It is Christ's meal and surely a means by which the Holy Spirit can awaken or confirm faith in an individual;[53] (2) Jesus, the one denied hospitality at his birth, makes meal hospitality a central sign of the gospel as embodied in his presence among humans;[54] and (3) for some the meal mode of Christ's mission may be, at least at first, more compelling than the evangelizing mode of the single unitary mission.

Still, there are serious responsibilities connected to the communing of the unbaptized. In a typically winsome style, the framers of *The Use of the Means of Grace* remind us that unbaptized people who come to the table are "invited to learn the faith of the Church, be baptized, and thereafter faithfully receive Holy Communion."[55] Behind that gentle rhetoric resides a strong reminder that the meal is not an end in itself but is always an icon through which one is drawn into the pervasive mission of the church, that is, to faithful living as part of the body of Christ in the world.

Even though, for instance, Jesus directed the disciples to extend meal hospitality to all five thousand people in Bethsaida, this open invitation followed a day in which he "welcomed them, and spoke to them about the kingdom of God, and healed those who needed to be cured" (Luke 9:11). The meal followed catechesis and physical epiphanies of the mission of God. It served as a summary of the mission already proclaimed and then offered to those who would hear the call.

That mission is about much more than enjoying the goodness of God in bread and fish, in bread and wine. Early interpretations of the meal in both 1 Peter and 1 Corinthians make it clear that the meal explicitly calls forth commitment to the mission mode of the community. The disciples learned just that as they prepared to feed five thousand with paltry resources. "The call to conversion is part of the call to table-sharing."[56] In the meal, Luther suggests, Christ sacrifices us by turning us into what we eat,[57] and with that we have taken on a task and identity that is clearly countercultural.[58]

Now a Christian community gathered around word and sacrament must make the nature of the mission task clear to those who are attracted to its table. Without both baptism and Lord's supper, there can be no Christian.[59] Regular participation in holy communion assumes the participant desires to be graced with the holy bath and the mission it comprehends. Otherwise, the meal itself becomes a sham, a lie—not unlike the rituals emanating from Corinth. The meal always serves as an epiphany of God's mission and thereby strengthens and enlightens the faithful. It becomes the royal residence for the faithful in the world. Such purpose dare never be displaced in favor of reconstructing the feast to solicit new allegiances, for it is "at the table of our Lord Jesus Christ that God nourishes faith, forgives sin, and calls us to be witnesses to the gospel."[60]

Inside out; outside in. The challenge is to perceive and live this singular field of rebounding energy that we call mission in a way that clearly offers the promises of God in Jesus Christ. And then, by God's grace, we will taste and see.

Draw us in the Spirit's tether,
for when humbly in your name
two or three are met together,
you are in the midst of them.
Alleluia! Alleluia!
Touch we now your garment's hem.

As disciples used to gather
in the name of Christ to sup,
then with thanks to God the giver
break the bread and bless the cup,
Alleluia! Alleluia!
so now bind our friendship up.

All our meals and all our living
make as sacraments of you,
that by caring, helping, giving,
we may be disciples true.
Alleluia! Alleluia!
We will serve with faith anew.[61]

NOTES

1. "No matter whether you are unworthy or worthy, you here have Christ's body and blood by virtue of these words which are coupled with the bread and wine." The Large Catechism 5, 18, in *The Book of Concord: The Confessions of the Evangelical Lutheran Church*, trans. and ed. Theodore G. Tappert et al. (Philadelphia: Fortress Press, 1959), 448.

2. "By these words the forgiveness of sins, life, and salvation are given to us in the sacrament." The Small Catechism 6, 6, in *The Book of Concord*, 352.

3. "But what is given in and with the sacrament cannot be grasped and appropriated by the body. This is done by the faith of the heart which discerns and desires this treasure." The Large Catechism 5, 37, in *The Book of Concord*, 451.

4. Eugene LaVerdiere, *Dining in the Kingdom of God: The Origins of the Eucharist according to Luke* (Chicago: Liturgy Training Publications, 1994), 153ff.

5. Ibid., 154.

6. Ibid., 2.

7. Ibid., 124. See also Apology of the Augsburg Confession 24.1, in *The Book of Concord*, 249: "In our churches Mass is celebrated every Sunday and on other festivals." This statement from the Apology is the basis for principle 35 of "Holy Communion" in *The Use of the Means of Grace: A Statement on the Practice of Word and Sacrament* (Evangelical Lutheran Church in America, 1997). Principle 33 from that document reads: "In this sacrament the crucified

and risen Christ is present, giving his true body and blood as food and drink. This real presence is a mystery."

8. Ibid., principle 37: "Admission to the Sacrament is by invitation of the Lord, presented through the Church to those who are baptized."

9. Johannes Behm, κλάω, *Theological Dictionary of the New Testament*, ed. Gerhard Kittel and trans. Geoffrey Bromiley (Grand Rapids, Mich.: Wm. B. Eerdmans, 1964), 3:736–43.

10. So "the highest worship in the Gospel is the desire to receive forgiveness of sins, grace, and righteousness." Apology of the Augsburg Confession 4.310, in *The Book of Concord,* 155.

11. Mark Olson writes: "Consequently, evangelical activity, if it is to have credibility, must be addressed to all. *When evangelism applies only to those outside the community of faith, the gracious gift of transformation in Christ becomes trivialized into a campaign for new member recruitment and institutional growth"* [Olson's emphasis]. "What Is Evangelism?" in *How Does Worship Evangelize? Open Questions in Worship,* vol. 3, ed. Gordon W. Lathrop (Minneapolis: Augsburg Fortress, 1995), 8.

12. Jim Wallis, "Set Apart—On Behalf of Everyone," *Sharing One Bread, Sharing One Mission*, Med. Jean Stromberg (Geneva: World Council of Churches, 1983), 56.

13. Barbara Liotscos, "The Future of Liturgy: Some Thoughts and Dreams," *Worship* 71, no. 1 (January 1997): 50.

14. Joseph Cardinal Bernardin, *Guide for the Assembly* (Chicago: Liturgy Training Publications, 1997), 5.

15. LaVerdiere, *Dining in the Kingdom of God,* 9.

16. Lathrop, "New Pentecost or Joseph's Britches? Reflections on the History and Meaning of the Worship Ordo in the Megachurches," *Worship* 72, no. 6 (November 1998): 482–500. Frank C. Senn, *Christian Liturgy: Catholic and Evangelical* (Minneapolis: Fortress Press, 1997), 687–706.

17. Because of their interest in this text as support for the "priesthood of all believers," Lutherans have often missed its implications for the unity of liturgy and mission. See John Hall Eilliott, *The Elect and the Holy* (Leiden: E. J. Brill, 1966).

18. Commenting on Karl Rahner's theology of worship, Michael Skelley writes: "The Church's liturgy is the ritual celebration of this universal process of God's self-communication to the world and our free acceptance of God's self-gift. Worship, therefore, is to be seen 'not as divine liturgy *in* the world, but as the divine liturgy *of* the world, as manifestation of the divine liturgy which is identical with salvation history.' For Rahner, the liturgy of the Church is the symbolic expression of the liturgy of the world." *The Liturgy of the World: Karl Rahner's Theology of Worship* (Collegeville, Minn.: Liturgical Press, 1991), 19.

19. "Ritual mastery is the ability...to take and remake schemes from the shared culture...[and] deploy them in the formulation of privileged ritual experience, which in turn impresses them in a new form upon agents able to deploy them in a variety of *circumstances beyond the circumference of the rite itself"* (emphasis mine), in Catherine Bell, *Ritual Theory, Ritual Practice* (New York: Oxford University Press, 1992), 116.

20. Susanne Langer, *Philosophy in a New Key* (New York: New American Library, 1951), 52. See also Mark Searle, "Liturgy as Metaphor," *Worship* 55, no. 2 (March 1981): 98–120.

21. For some people, it might be useful to think of ritual's purpose as iconic. The icon is an art that "uses images and forms drawn from the material world to

transmit the revelation of the Divine world, making this world accessible to understanding and contemplation," in Leonid Ouspensky and Vladimir Lossky, *The Meaning of Icons,* trans. G. Palmer and E. Kadlousovsky (Crestwood, N.Y.: St. Vladimir's Seminary Press, 1983), 30.

22. LaVerdiere, *Dining in the Kingdom of God,* 18.

23. Bernardin, *Guide for the Assembly,* 23.

24. Liotscos, "The Future of Liturgy," 50.

25. Senn, *The Witness of the Worshiping Community: Liturgy and the Practice of Evangelism* (New York: Paulist Press, 1993), 87.

26. Senn, taking his cue from Paul Hoon, describes how culture can corrupt worship through utilitarianism and aestheticism. See *The Witness of the Worshiping Community,* 24–29.

27. See the literature presented in the citations at n. 16.

28. William Strauss and Neil Howe, *Generations: The History of America's Future, 1584 to 2069.* (New York: William Morrow, 1991), 44.

29. Ibid., 32.

30. Many of these questions are addressed in the publications and statements resulting from a six-year study on worship and culture sponsored by the Lutheran World Federation: *Worship and Culture in Dialogue,* ed. S. Anita Stauffer (Geneva: Lutheran World Federation, 1994); *Christian Worship: Unity in Cultural Diversity,* ed. Stauffer (Geneva: Lutheran World Federation, 1966), and *Baptism, Rites of Passage, and Culture,* ed. Stauffer (Geneva: Lutheran World Federation, 1999).

31. Johannes Riedel, *The Lutheran Chorale* (Minneapolis: Augsburg Publishing House, 1967).

32. See Richard R. Gaillardetz, "Doing Liturgy in a Technological Age," *Worship* 71, no. 5 (September 1997): 429–51. The author fears that worshipers no longer distinguish between "thing" and "device," looking to communion as a private dispensing of grace rather than as opportunity for engagement with the whole people of God.

33. *The Use of the Means of Grace,* principle 45: "Practices of distributing and receiving Holy Communion reflect the unity of the Body of Christ and the dignity and new life of the baptized."

34. Luther continued to be amazed by sound and asserted that because the gospel came to life as sounded word, it immediately shared an alliance with music. "For 'gospel' *[Euangelium]* is a Greek word and means in Greek a good message, good tidings, good news, a good report, which one sings and tells with gladness." "Preface to the New Testament, 1522," in *Luther's Works,* ed. Helmut T. Lehmann (Philadelphia: Fortress Press, 1960), 35:358.

35. Olson, "What Is Evangelism?" 9.

36. *And Do Not Hinder Them: An Ecumenical Plea for the Admission of Children to the Eucharist,* Faith and Order Paper No. 109, ed. Geiko Müller-Fahrenholz (Geneva: World Council of Churches, 1982), as quoted by Senn, *A Stewardship of the Mysteries* (New York: Paulist Press, 1999), 163.

37. *The Use of the Means of Grace,* principle 37.

38. Ibid., application 37D.

39. Senn, *Stewardship of the Mysteries,* 168.

40. Senn makes a distinction between "infant communion" (normally understood to be the culmination of a process of initiation) and "children's communion" (access to the table because children have more understanding than they are usually given credit for by adults). Ibid., 155.

41. "Experience is the child's primary source. Experience and intellectual instruction do not always have to happen at the same time. Sometimes children can

experience something with explanation or instruction being offered later." *And Do Not Hinder Them*, 164.

42. "At the table of our Lord Jesus Christ, God nourishes faith, forgives sin, and calls us to be witnesses to the Gospel," *The Use of the Means of Grace*, principle 31.

43. The Small Catechism 2, 6, in *The Book of Concord*, 345.

44. LaVerdiere, *Dining in the Kingdom of God*, vii.

45. Senn, *Stewardship of the Mysteries*, 162.

46. "Epitome," Formula of Concord 1, 7.18, in *The Book of Concord*, 486.

47. LaVerdiere, *Dining in the Kingdom of God*, 68–69.

48. "Admission to the Sacrament is by invitation of the Lord, presented through the Church to those who are baptized." *The Use of the Means of Grace*, principle 37.

49. Ibid., application 37G.

50. Acts 3:2-6; 8:4; 8:26; 8:40; 9:32ff; 11:18; 11:20-21; 13:4-6; 14:6; 16:11-12; 17:1; 17:22; 19:21-22; 20:2; 28:1, 8; 28:14.

51. Acts 4:23-31; 5:42; 13:42; 14:27; 15:12; 15:41; 18:23; 20:7; 20:17-24; 21:17-19; 28:30.

52. LaVerdiere, *Dining in the Kingdom of God*, 60ff.

53. The sacraments "are signs and testimonies of God's will toward us for the purpose of awakening and strengthening our faith." The Augsburg Confession 8.1, in *The Book of Concord*, 35.

54. LaVerdiere, *Dining in the Kingdom of God*, 66.

55. *The Use of the Means of Grace*, application 37G.

56. Robert Hurd, "A More Organic Opening: Ritual Music and the New Gathering Rite," *Worship* 72, no. 4 (July 1998): 302.

57. "A Treatise on the New Testament, That Is, the Holy Mass, 1520," in *Luther's Works*, ed. Helmut T. Lehmann (Philadelphia: Fortress Press, 1960), 35:99. "From these words we learn that we do not offer Christ as a sacrifice, but that Christ offers us. And in this way it is permissible, yes, profitable, to call the mass a sacrifice; not on its own account, but because we offer ourselves as a sacrifice along with Christ."

58. See "Nairobi Statement," *Christian Worship: Unity in Cultural Diversity*, 27.

59. The Large Catechism 4, 1, in *The Book of Concord*, 436.

60. *The Use of the Means of Grace*, principle 31.

61. Percy Dearmer, 1867–1936, alt. *With One Voice: A Lutheran Resource for Worship* (Minneapolis: Augsburg Fortress, 1995), no. 703. Copyright © Oxford University Press. Used by permission.

Liturgical Year: Within the World, Within Its Time

Mark W. Oldenburg

I T MAY SEEM rather surprising to talk about mission and the liturgical year in the same breath. For some folks, "the liturgical year" conjures up such questions as, What color paraments should we use for a wedding on St. Swithin's Day? or, Can you sing "alleluia" on the festival of the Annunciation, even if it's in Lent? Many people associate the liturgical year with a list of the most picayune rules in creation, which are enforced by the rubrics police—a mean-spirited squad of folks who delight in finding and squashing minor infractions. The liturgical year fits as well with outreach and service as brown shoes with a tuxedo.

The practice of the liturgical year, however, can be one of the most engaging, attractive, transformative tools in the church's storehouse. On Christmas Eve, church buildings overflow with people, many of whom may have come not to celebrate the incarnation but to indulge their nostalgia for the sight of candlelight, the smell of pine, and the sound of "Silent Night." Yet the candlelight, pine, and carols of Christmas Eve—and the proclamation they surround—can awaken a hunger deeper than nostalgia and hint at a way to satisfy that hunger. In fact, Christmas Eve is a time for the church to remind itself that part of the message of the incarnation is God's constant willingness to use creation—including candlelight, pine, and carols—to bear the divine Word.

The liturgical year is a tool that not only gathers strangers but has the potential to impel the baptized into service. Hymns on All Saints Day may help us to carry out a ministry of caring for those

LITURGICAL

YEAR:

WITHIN

THE WORLD,

WITHIN

ITS TIME

who grieve. Prayers on the Sunday prior to Labor Day might encourage us to view our occupations as our response to God's calling and the way we participate in God's work of creation. A sermon on the festival of the Holy Innocents might call on us to use the political power we have been given in order to protect today's victims. In general, every Sunday's readings, with their dynamics of indicative followed by imperative, call and response, forgiveness and new life, provide example after example of how we, having been gifted by peace, go into the world to serve the Lord.

Despite its reputation, the liturgical year is indeed a powerful and popular tool for the church's mission, and anyone who doubts the significance of the role the liturgical year has long played in our culture has missed large portions of folklore. Many cultures commemorate the dead on or around All Saints Day, often displaying greater faith in the communion of saints than many theologians find acceptable. Santa Lucia Day celebrates the presence of light during the darkest portion of the year. Las Posadas, on which crowds follow those portraying the holy family in their search for an inn, not only hallows hospitality in general but links today's homeless, aliens, and refugees to Mary and Joseph. Even Ground Hog Day, coinciding with the festival of the Presentation, takes its cue from Simeon's hymn about the infant Jesus being "a light to lighten the Gentiles." In one sense, the liturgical year is more popular than the church, for many of those who celebrate Mardi Gras, Thanksgiving, or Martin Luther King Jr. Day do so in ignorance of the holidays' churchly roots.

It is not enough, however, for the liturgical year to be powerful and popular. Like many powerful tools, it is often not used to its full potential. How often has a Christmas Eve sermon simply become one more fulmination against commercialism that ignores the promise that "the hopes and fears of all the years are met" here tonight? The liturgical year, rightly understood and kept, is a gift of incredible proportions to the church. If it were not already in the church's treasure chest, those passionate about mission would no doubt invent it because of its power and popularity. In fact, that is just what has happened.

Each of the major building blocks of the liturgical year is inherently connected with the church's mission. Let us take a look at four building blocks to see how they originated in concern for mission, how faithful practice can make that concern clear and powerful in the present, and what dangers we need to avoid as we celebrate them. We will consider these facets of the church's sanctification of time: Sunday, the Pasch (Easter), the liturgical calendar

(including saints' days), and the lectionary. There are other facets, of
course, most notably the times for daily prayer, but these four are
more than enough to keep us busy.

~

Sunday

One of the enduring characteristics of the church is our ability to
fight with one another. Anyone who has sat through more than a
few congregation council meetings will be able to testify to that
trait. And anyone who believes the apostolic church was entirely at
peace has not read Paul's correspondence with the Corinthians.
Almost no topic is too small to divide Christians. It is surprising,
therefore, that there is no evidence of controversy for the better
part of two millennia over Christians' gathering as the church on
Sunday, the first day of the week. We will fight about service *time*
(that is part of what was going on in Corinth in Paul's absence) but
not about service *day*. Certain passages in the New Testament point
to the emerging practice of gathering each Sunday. From those early
days of the church until the appearance in the sixteenth century of
some Sabbath-keeping Christian communities, there was widespread unanimity in the church that Sunday is the day of meeting.

But why? Christian authors have long lifted up Sunday as the
day of creation, of the resurrection, and of the descent of the Spirit.
As Christopher Wordsworth wrote, summarizing the reflections of
writers from the second century to his own day:

> On you, at earth's creation,
> The light first had its birth;
> On you, for our salvation,
> Christ rose from depths of earth;
> On you, our Lord victorious
> The Spirit sent from heav'n;
> And thus on you, most glorious,
> A threefold light was giv'n.[1]

As satisfying as that explanation is in its trinitarian shape, it
does not explain what some regard as the earliest practice of
meeting on Sunday *evenings*. The creation began (according to
Genesis 1) at evening on the first day of the week, which according
to Jewish reckoning would be Saturday evening. If the Christian
gathering were to commemorate the creation, then it would have
made sense to meet at the close of the Sabbath—a natural time especially for Jewish Christians. Both the resurrection and the descent

LITURGICAL
YEAR:
WITHIN
THE WORLD,
WITHIN
ITS TIME

of the Spirit happened in the morning of the first day of the week (Sunday), the former before sunrise and the latter, apparently, before the middle of the morning (Acts 2:15). If the Christian gathering were to commemorate the resurrection, then it would have made sense to meet before dawn on Sunday; and if it were to commemorate the descent of the Spirit, then a mid-morning gathering would have made sense—a difficult time to meet given that Sunday was an ordinary work day throughout much of the pre-Constantinian Roman Empire. So what explains the apparent practice of meeting for a weekly celebration on Sunday evening?

Although Sunday evening was not the time of the resurrection, it was the time of the resurrection *appearances*. It was on Sunday evening that Jesus appeared in the midst of his followers. Except for the ascension as recorded in Acts (but including the ascension as recounted by Luke!), every public appearance of the risen Christ that was associated with a specific day happened in late afternoon or evening on a Sunday (Mark 16:12f.; Mark 16:14ff.; Luke 24:13-35, 36-53; John 20:19-23,26-29). It seems clear that the Sunday evening worship of the early church was connected with the appearances of the resurrected Christ. Whether the church met at the time Jesus appeared or the stories were shaped so that Jesus was said to have appeared at the time the church met is unclear. What is important is that the regular assemblies of Christians took place in continuity with the appearances of the resurrected Christ.

The descriptions of those public appearances make this continuity even clearer. On the first Easter and the days following, the disciples did not gather in order to commemorate the resurrection or to elect a new rabbi. Instead, they huddled together in fear and wonder, going over the words and deeds of Jesus and the witness of the scriptures. As they huddled, talked, and prayed, Jesus appeared. Often this appearance was in the context of a meal he shared with the disciples. That pattern reveals as much about how the first believers understood worship as it does about how they understood the resurrection.

For us, as for the first disciples, Sunday remains a time to meet in the presence of the resurrected Lord. Sunday is not a time for remembering Jesus' absence, for calling to mind his past teachings, example, and promises. Rather, Jesus' promise is that when we call to mind his life and his teaching, he will be *present*. He will be present in evangelism and initiation (Matt. 28:20) and in the reconciliation of Christians to one another (Matt. 18:20). Because he has bound himself so intimately with the church, he is as present in that assembly as we are in our own bodies (1 Cor. 12).

Therefore, the very day on which the church assembles gives a peculiar slant to that assembly itself. Meeting on a Sunday—in continuity with the resurrection appearances and in the presence of the Resurrected One—means that our gathering is an encounter with the living Christ. We do not assemble primarily to teach or to learn about Jesus but to meet him. And meeting someone always involves learning about that one. We do not assemble primarily to praise God but to hear, see, touch, taste, and be formed by the Word. And being formed by the Word means that we will respond, among others ways, with praise to God. We do not assemble primarily to declare our friendship with others like us, or our solidarity with those unlike us, but to be joined as the body of the one who meets us here. And Jesus brings us into relationship with all those like and unlike ourselves whom he also loves. Education, doxology, and fellowship, however, are by-products, not preconditions, of the presence of the crucified and resurrected one.

That presence turns out to be essential to the task Jesus sets for the church. The great commission (Matt. 28:18-20) charges the church to make disciples by baptizing and teaching. For a number of reasons the kind of discipleship outlined in the gospels is rather unusual. First, it is permanent, not a state from which one graduates; this task demands total commitment and service. What most clearly differentiates this discipleship from almost any other, however, is the relationship at its center. Although Jesus does teach, what makes a disciple is not learning the wisdom Jesus imparts. What makes a disciple is the personal relationship between the disciple and Jesus. Jesus calls the disciple into the relationship and claims that disciple's ultimate loyalty not to his teaching or to his discipline but to himself. Therefore, if disciples are going to be made, they must meet Jesus. The community's meeting on Sunday, in continuity with the promised resurrection appearances of Jesus, proclaims that this encounter is possible. The Sunday assembly is not the only gathering in which Jesus carries out the promise that ends the great commission ("I am with you always"), but it is an occasion when the fulfillment of that promise is assured. Because the community meets at a time that marks its continuity with those to whom the resurrected Lord appeared, the Sunday assembly proclaims the presence of the Crucified and Resurrected One in the here and now, which makes disciple making possible.

The dynamics of the resurrection appearances, as well as their timing, have connected Sunday with the mission of the church from the church's very beginning. Every one of the resurrection appearances began with the disciples huddled together and paralyzed with

LITURGICAL
YEAR:
WITHIN
THE WORLD,
WITHIN
ITS TIME

fear, grief, and perhaps even guilt. When Jesus appeared with news of victory over death, he brought more than a reframing of the biblical message (Luke 24:27) and a peace beyond the imagination of the world (John 29:19, 26). Having comforted his disciples, Jesus sent them into all the world to make disciples, teach, and baptize (Matt. 28:18-20). Jesus sent them as charismatically gifted witnesses of his own sacrifice and forgiveness (Luke 24:45-49), charged to carry on his ministry and speak with his authority (John 20:22-23). If the Sunday assembly is a continuation of the resurrection appearances, then it must share the fundamental dynamic of thrusting disciples into mission.

Over the course of time, the Christian observance of Sunday took on many of the trappings of the Sabbath. At the beginning, however, early Jewish Christians continued to observe the Sabbath as a day of rest and religious activity, alongside the new Christian gathering on Sunday. Saturday's significance as the Sabbath day has been preserved among the Eastern Orthodox, who generally forbid fasting on that day. For most of the rest of the church, however, Sunday observance has been seen as the continuation of those aspects of the Sabbath—time set aside to attend to the Word—that have carried over into the community of the new covenant. Thus, particularly in the United States, Sunday itself took the title of the Sabbath. A system of blue laws was enacted to restrict work and various forms of recreation on Sundays. Although many of these restrictions have been repealed in recent decades, North Americans still seem to spend Sundays differently from other days. Surveys report that Sundays are more likely to be spent pursuing cultural and charitable activities, and cultivating relationships with family and friends.

The caricature of traditional Sunday observance portrays a day of enforced joyless sobriety when certain forms of recreation are avoided as diligently as work. That practice seems far removed from the intention of scripture. First, based on Genesis 1 and Exodus 20, the Sabbath was something to be shared with God, a sign that worship, rest, and relaxation were parts of the intended order of creation without which life was incomplete. Second, based on Deuteronomy 5, the Sabbath was a matter of justice; no one—even those powerless to protest—was denied the right to rest at least one day a week. Remembering their own days as slaves, the Israelites were exhorted to treat their own servants with the fairness they would have appreciated.

In today's culture, work claims an increasing percentage of people's time and energy, and in our comparatively few hours away from work we operate constantly on the edge of stimulation over-load. The vision of a Sabbath rest away from frenetic activity—in which contemplation and relaxation are affirmed—is something the church could still offer our culture.

Sunday is not without certain dangers. The church has often presented Sunday rest and worship as an obligation rather than a gift, as a duty we owe God rather than as a time for God to meet and shape us. Because the reason for Sunday observance has often not been explained but simply enforced, the relationship between Sunday and the resurrection appearances has not been understood, and the delight of encountering the risen Lord in the community has been hidden. To borrow phrases from the rite of marriage in *Lutheran Book of Worship*, the gladness of worship can be overcast and the gift of the Sabbath can become a burden. But because God, who established Sunday, continues to bless it with abundant and ever-present support, we can be sustained in our weariness and have our joy restored.[2]

⌇

THE PASCH

If the Sunday assembly is as old as the church, then Easter is almost as old. If Sunday is intimately linked not just to the story of the church but to its mission, then Easter shares at least as much in this linkage. It might be clearer for us to call this annual celebration by its original name, *Pasch* (from the Greek word for "Passover"), because it has included not only the celebration of the resurrection that we think of when we say Easter, but all the events that swirled around that last Passover of Jesus' earthly ministry: his farewell and arrest, his crucifixion and death, his resurrection and ascension, and the sending of the Holy Spirit.

It is not clear from the New Testament whether the earliest Christians kept and "christianized" the Jewish festivals. Certainly the festivals were familiar even to Gentile Christians (Paul does not need to explain Passover imagery and the reference to Pentecost to his non-Jewish readers). But by the early second century, Christians were observing their own Passover, one that extended beyond the Jewish remembrance of the Red Sea. This celebration lasted through the night, during which Christians told the stories and sang the songs of God's creative and liberating activity, centering on the paschal mystery—the betrayal, crucifixion, death, and resurrection of Jesus. The celebration ended at dawn with holy communion. This celebration seems to have begun at first on the afternoon prior

LITURGICAL
YEAR:
WITHIN
THE WORLD,
WITHIN
ITS TIME

to the beginning of the Jewish Passover (the date of the crucifixion, according to John). But as the Jewish calendar became less familiar to Gentile Christians and Sunday became the regular day for eucharistic celebration, Easter came to be observed on Sunday morning during the week of Passover. Eventually, the Nicene Council (A.D. 325) established the Sunday following the first full moon after the spring equinox as the day when Easter would be observed.

Early on, at least in some parts of the church, the annual celebration of Easter became the chief time during the year for baptisms to be performed. The time of celebration highlighted Paul's understanding of baptism as a dying with Christ—being joined in his death with the promise of being joined in his rising. (Other parts of the church, particularly in Egypt linked Christian initiation to the story of Jesus' own baptism by John rather than to the story of the passion.)

This connection between Jesus' passion and resurrection, and the entry of Christians into the church, led to an understanding of Easter and initiation that has been reclaimed in the present day. If baptism is tied to Jesus' passing through death to life, then it is not simply a rite of purification; it is death and life, the end of an old way of being and the birth of a new one. Those preparing to become a part of the church do not simply improve their moral standards, learn some new religious formulas, and receive a membership card. To be freed from the bonds of sin, death, and the devil, they must die as slaves and be reborn in freedom. The Israelites passed through the death-dealing Red Sea—from slavery into freedom—and from generation to generation Jews have identified that story as the story of their own contemporary and future liberation. In a similar way, Christians have been so closely linked in baptism to Christ that he pulls us with him in his own passage through death to life.

The paschal mystery—the story of Christ's passage from death to life—is more than an important story about someone in the past that we hear and tell as the central story of the universe. The paschal mystery is the central story of our own lives. The Easter proclamation *(exsultet),* that great song that begins the Easter Vigil, has at its heart a series of sentences that identify this night as the true Passover—the night Christ arose from death, the night all believers are rescued, and the night heaven and earth are joined. The message is not simply that time is annihilated and we are placed in the land of Goshen and the Red Sea, or at Golgotha and the empty tomb. Rather, this night is the true night of the Passover, of the resurrection, and of our liberation, because on this night we ourselves are carried through death to life. That rescue occurs in the present. We are not carried back to the first century. Christ triumphs *now!*

The exodus and the passion were both times when God proved faithful and powerful, rescuing the chosen people beyond their wildest expectations. This night is such a time, as well, when God proves faithful and powerful, rescuing us when we had given up hope. Of course, this night will be described in echoes of earlier times, and of course it is a realization of Jesus' own Pasch. Yet that realization is happening here and now, not in a misty, half-mythological dream world. The enemies from which we are rescued—death and sin, pride and self-loathing, illusion and despair—are our own enemies and would-be captors. In the Easter proclamation we have the almost unbelievable experience of hearing our own experience described in mythic terms, not because we are entering into the world of myth but because our experience is the stuff of myth. Our liberation is worthy of divine attention and has cosmic implications. We do not have to pretend to be in a time and place other than our own, because what is happening to us here and now ranks with God's chief acts of liberation. That affirmation is central to the celebration of Easter from its beginning, and it is central to the in-gathering of new Christians today as well as to the rebirth of those already baptized.

The celebration of baptism strictly defined is the culmination of the process of Christian initiation. At one time and in certain places during the church's history, those seeking to be baptized first committed themselves to a life that echoed the gospel, perhaps giving up careers too closely connected with violence (such as being soldiers) or idolatry (such as being actors) and spending time in service to the poor. They underwent a lengthy time of learning, serving, praying, and being prayed for before they were plunged beneath the waters of baptism and welcomed to the eucharistic table. This preparation, overseen by the bishop and featuring sponsors and others as mentors, was intimate and time-consuming. It was hard enough to manage in the days of persecution, when converts appeared sporadically. But when under Constantine the church came to be tolerated and then established as the religion of the Roman Empire, preparing converts for baptism became an overwhelming task. How could the church handle the flood of seekers, people who had not grown up in the faith and who had little knowledge of the scriptures or the story of salvation?

This dilemma probably sounds all too familiar. In many ways our situation is not much different from the early fourth century.

LITURGICAL
YEAR:
WITHIN
THE WORLD,
WITHIN
ITS TIME

We are eager to proclaim the gospel to the multitudes around us who have never heard it, yet we are also struggling to figure out what to do once they express an interest. One of the things the early Christians did was to establish the adult catechumenate—an organized process centered on baptism for incorporating people into the faith and life of the church.[3] They did something else, however, something closely linked with the catechumenate: they invented Holy Week.

Cyril of Jerusalem was bishop of that city in the generation after Constantine. He, more than most bishops, was inundated by pilgrims who had traveled to Jerusalem. In an attempt to engage the crowds of visitors and to celebrate and teach them the stories of the faith—especially the central story of the paschal mystery—Cyril enlisted an advantage unique to Jerusalem. He was sitting on top of the places where the stories happened! These places had recently been reidentified (with varying degrees of accuracy) by no less than the emperor's own mother. How about retracing the route of the triumphal entry? Or what about telling the story of the last supper at the site of the upper room? What about celebrating the resurrection outside the open tomb and treating the other events of Jesus' passion in like manner? The Pasch itself had long been preceded by a two-day fast beginning on Thursday night. It did not take much to connect the beginning of this fast to the events of the last supper, and the first full day of it to Jesus' passion (by this time an event marked at prayer every Friday anyway). Cyril began to give liturgical shape to these connections and held the services in the locations where the respective events were believed to have taken place.

This invention was overwhelmingly powerful. People learned what happened on those great days by walking through the events, participating in carefully crafted ritual, and listening to sermons about the various occasions. When pilgrims to Jerusalem returned home, they introduced the practices there. Holy Week swept across Christendom with amazing speed, leaving its shape—Palm Sunday, Maundy Thursday, Good Friday, Easter Vigil, and Easter Sunday— much as we have it today. That shape is still a powerful teaching tool. The pageantry of Holy Week remains powerful, compelling, and extremely useful, particularly in a culture like ours, where listeners lack biblical knowledge but expect that stories will involve many of their senses at once.

The paschal mystery is the central and most powerful Christian story. But telling it, no matter how dramatically, has never in itself been enough to prepare people for their participation in the faith and life of the Christian community. There are other stories to learn as well, so that the core story makes more sense, and all these stories have implications for understanding the faith and for faithful living. We want to see new habits developed and old behaviors transformed. This work takes time. In Cyril's time, catechumens might have spent years in preparation, as would those public penitents who were interested in returning to the fellowship of the church. Each of these situations required intense preparation during the days immediately before Holy Week. This time of practicing the disciplines of prayer, fasting, and study was what we have come to know as Lent.

Early on, the church as a whole started accompanying catechumens and penitents on their journey through Lent. The members not only wanted to keep company with the people on the church's margin (not unlike some teenagers who, when a friend is undergoing chemotherapy, shave their own heads so she does not have to be bald alone), but they also recognized in Lent a marvelous opportunity for continuing education and rededication. The church as a whole kept making use of this opportunity, even when the season's original customers disappeared. Within a few generations the culture as a whole came to be permeated with Christianity. Nearly everyone was born to Christian parents and baptized as an infant; there were no adults to catechize. At the same time the practice of private confession took the place of public penitence, so that there were no more groups of penitents to welcome back at the Pasch. But Lent continued to serve as a time of particular discipline.

Lent continues, not only as a time of preparation for those to be baptized at Easter (as in the renewed practice of the adult catechumenate), but as a time of rededication for all members and prospective members. The disciplines of Lent—repentance, fasting, prayer, and works of love—are useful tools for transforming the church. Unfortunately, fasting has become almost the sole discipline of the season. But fasting was never supposed to be merely about giving up something, but rather about our identification with Jesus and his life given for others. Fasting is about freeing time and resources for better uses. Money that might have been spent on a nonessential item and the time spent in consuming it are instead invested in service or advocacy on behalf of the poor. Lent can be a time for the rededication of resources to the active mission of the church.

The celebration of Holy Week—exactly because it is powerful—can be dangerous. The danger of telling a story dramatically is that it remains only a drama, a reenactment of something that happened long ago and far away to someone else. Making the great Three Days—Maundy Thursday, Good Friday, and Easter—into

LITURGICAL
YEAR:
WITHIN
THE WORLD,
WITHIN
ITS TIME

commemorations of past events can lead participants to believe that Jesus was really only present in first-century Palestine and is not present in the here and now. Dramatic representations, especially if they overshadow or replace proclamation, can lead contemporary worshipers to believe that in order to encounter Jesus, they must take on the role of one of the characters in the drama. The church runs the risk of proclaiming that Jesus is not present here and now, within the assembly, but only long ago and far away. Powerful dramatization of the past must be balanced with equally powerful proclamation for the present if these dramatic presentations are to have their full import (something that is true of Christmas pageants as well as reenactments of the last supper).

Dramatizing Holy Week can be dangerous but need not paralyze us. Anything that is powerful will have its own dangers. Adapted to the needs of the Christian assembly today, Holy Week can be as great a tool for forming new Christians, reforming the baptized, and sending us forth in mission as it was at its birth in the fourth century.

~

THE LITURGICAL CALENDAR

One way of thinking about the liturgical calendar is to divide celebrations into two groups: those with movable dates and those with fixed dates. The movable celebrations are all associated with Easter, and the dates of these celebrations have to be determined every year. They always fall on the same day of the week (Ash Wednesday, Easter Sunday, Ascension Thursday) but never on the same date from one year to the next. This movement takes place because these festivals depend on the historic connection between Easter Sunday and Passover, which is marked by the first full moon of the spring. Using a lunar calculation to determine the date on which Easter is celebrated in our solar calendar results in a movable rather than a fixed date.

The fixed celebrations of the liturgical calendar can occur on any day of the week but always on the same date. We have no trouble remembering from year to year when to celebrate Christmas (December 25) and the Epiphany (January 6), because the dates of those festivals never change. A number of lesser festivals of the Lord are also a part of the calendar of fixed celebrations, including the Presentation (February 2) and the Annunciation (March 25). Most fixed celebrations, however, are festivals and commemorations of saints, people who have exemplified the life of faith in a particular way, perhaps to the point of martyrdom. In origin and practice, the fixed celebrations of the liturgical calendar share with the Pasch strong connections to the church's mission.

The earliest annual observance we know of held to celebrate the life of a saint was the second-century eucharistic gathering of the Christians of Smyrna on the anniversary of the martyrdom of their bishop, Polycarp. Polycarp was the first of thousands of saints known to have been remembered by the church in an organized way on a particular date. With the development of the calendar of the saints came St. Patrick's parades, Valentine cards, Santa Lucia candles, and other practices associated with the remembrance of our forebears in the faith.

Although these remembrances can take on a life of their own, quite apart from their gospel origin, they can also be strong reminders of the cloud of witnesses that surrounds us. Lucy is remembered for her courage, Valentine for his steadfast love, Patrick for his evangelical fervor—all virtues and gifts needed in the present age as well. The festivals and commemorations can be occasions for stirring up these gifts, for freeing ourselves from lethargy or self-limitation through the example of those who have gone before us. As the delightful children's hymn for All Saints Day expresses, we can be shaped and impelled by examples of saints who have lived before us:

> They lived not only in ages past,
> there are hundreds of thousands still,
> the world is bright with the joyous saints
> who love to do Jesus' will.
> You can meet them in school, or in lanes, or at sea,
> in church or in trains, or in shops, or at tea,
> for the saints of God are just folk like me,
> and I mean to be one too.[4]

At the same time as the liturgical calendar holds up for us models of faith, it also recognizes the homegrown, day-to-day aspect of sanctity. For the people who first commemorated him, Polycarp was not some far-off, half-mythological figure. He was well known to the people who had been taught and baptized by him and whose names he had known. He was part of their story. Every group, and certainly every congregation, tells stories about these sorts of figures when members get together. These stories are part of the distinct heritage and identity of each particular Christian community. Hearing, retelling, and adding to these stories is part of the process of making a stranger at home.

LITURGICAL
YEAR:
WITHIN
THE WORLD,
WITHIN
ITS TIME

The calendar also offers us a vision of who we are that is wider than we might otherwise have. That we honor and remember people who appear and speak in ways different from us is a way of proclaiming that what binds us together is not how we look or speak. I remember the impact it had on me when I sat down in a church of a different denomination, unsure whether I was welcome, only to look up directly into the stained glass image of Martin Luther in one of the church's windows. Imagine the effect on an Ethiopian worshiper, new to the United States, to hear in the announcements some June 21 that the church would be commemorating Onesimos Nesib, a translator and evangelist for the Mekane Jesus Church. The liturgical year reminds us of the catholicity of the church across race and class, time and space—and serves as a powerful argument that not all Christians have to act the same!

The most important reason for celebrating the life and death of saints, however, is that in these lives, we see Christ and are reminded of his dying and rising. In the remembrance of the saints, we hear and celebrate the same Word that we hear and celebrate at the Pasch or at Christmas. The saints might be called Christian heroes, exemplary models for our own Christian walk, but they are much more than that. With their very lives, they proclaim Christ to us and for us. These people who lived in particular times and places show us that Jesus Christ suffered, died, and rose from the dead for us, who live in this particular time and place. The paschal story is the central story of the universe, and as we are reminded by our precursors in the faith, it is also the reason we bear the name "Christian."

There is, however, another more familiar and even more powerful set of festivals in the calendar of fixed celebrations—the festivals revolving around Christmas. Each year about the second week in December, newspapers print a letter from some spoilsport attacking Christmas as simply a pagan festival. According to legend, Christians of Rome, offended by the revelry of Saturnalia, established a competing festival (or simply renamed the old one) celebrating the birth of Jesus. The trouble with this story is that it is not entirely clear that Saturnalia is older than Christmas. In fact, there is at least a possibility that the pagans in Rome, jealous that the Christians had an excuse for a party on December 25, established a feast in opposition to it!

Whichever came first, though, there is no doubt that in many cultures Christmas, as well as the festivals that occur in many cultures at the winter solstice, gets much of its impact from exactly the same source as Saturnalia. Christmas uses the cosmos itself as an audiovisual tool. The days have stopped getting shorter, the sun is starting to peak higher above the horizon, and although the worst of winter is yet to come, light and life will not be permanently frozen. The rise in our spirits, this thumbing our nose in the face of gloom, this hint of the return of brightness can be connected (with the eyes and ears of faith) to the birth of the Christ, the light of the world. The worst of winter may be yet to come, but the Son of God, like the sun, is victorious. This attempt to link the gospel with the turn of the seasons is effective.

Of course, there is more to Christmas than a christianizing of a solar festival. Christmas became widely popular in the early church because it was such a powerful witness against heresy in its testimony to Christian teaching about the incarnation of God in Jesus Christ. Theological arguments then and now pale beside the celebration of Jesus' birth as the very Word of God.

Christmas is also a great festival of social ministry, a time when we share resources not only because of the example of the magi, who brought gifts to the Christ child, but because of the example of God, who gave the gift of the Christ child himself. The songs and stories of Christmas invite us to join in. What is Charles Dickens's *A Christmas Carol* but a story based on the theme that conversion means a change in attitude toward the poor? The end of December is filled with the cries of those who recognize their bondage to consumption and hectic busyness, and who long for a community and a celebration that offers liberation. The church is able to offer exactly this liberation in simple joys and common service.

One final category of fixed observances includes the civic holidays. Some holidays in the United States such as Thanksgiving or Martin Luther King Jr. Day have purposes close enough to the church's mission that it is natural for the church to celebrate them. Other holidays, such as Presidents' Day or Columbus Day, seem to be observed less for their spiritual nature than as days off from work or school, and occasions for sales in shopping malls. Yet other days—Mother's Day and Father's Day, or the summer trio of Memorial Day, Independence Day, and Labor Day—attract cultural attention or hold some mythic power; that is, they bind us together and give meaning to our lives.

Although occasions in this final category are frequently ignored by those who prepare the assembly's worship, the church has the opportunity—indeed the obligation—to mark them in two ways. First, because the occasions are popular, they are on the hearts and minds of the assembly. Therefore, prayers of intercession on Mother's Day that do not express thanksgiving and petition for

LITURGICAL
YEAR:
WITHIN
THE WORLD,
WITHIN
ITS TIME

mothers are not genuinely prayers of the people on that day. Simple honesty demands that in our worship we attend to an occasion that garners so much popular attention. This attention need not be idolatry. In fact, the second reason why such cultural festivals ought to be marked is that they celebrate institutions that function in our culture more like icons than idols. Labor Day, for instance, gives us the opportunity to consider our occupations in the context of God's ongoing work of creation, a work in which we all share.

The gospel-centered observance of civic holidays, like the commemoration of saints and the festivals of Christ, not only provides the church with the opportunity to gather together those who wish to give thanks, but it gives Christians an opportunity to meet with those who do not even know to whom thanks are due. Such observance also gives the church an opportunity to reframe our understanding of life in the world in which we have been set and to rededicate our efforts to serve God in this world.

~

THE LECTIONARY

The final building block of the church year is the round of biblical readings appointed to be read on Sundays and festivals. Like Sunday, the Pasch, and the liturgical calendar, this ancient practice began not with a desire to straitjacket the community but to form it and to impel it into mission. In fact, the concept of a lectionary might be older than the church. The story of Jesus' first sermon (Luke 4:16ff.) implies that in the Jewish synagogue of his day, there was an order to reading the law and the prophets. In addition to the association of texts with certain festivals—Red Sea story at Passover, Esther at Purim, or Ruth at Pentecost—patterns developed in the regular reading of scripture: both the pattern of continuous reading from a single book and the pattern of thematic relationship between texts.

If scripture is to be read and interpreted at the public assembly, there are two basic ways to determine what should be read. The first is to decide on the message to be proclaimed, and then choose passages that seem to relate to it. Passages can be chosen that relate topically to the message that is to be delivered. Until recently, this was the favored practice among most American Protestants. The strength of this practice is that it intentionally relates scripture to contemporary events, desires, and needs. Its danger is precisely the same. In addition, it requires preachers to find biblical support for a predetermined message, instead of listening first to the word on its own terms. Rather than viewing the world through the lens of the Bible, it is easy to fall into the trap of viewing the Bible through the lens of our own culturally determined opinions. Combine this danger with the almost unavoidable habit of choosing only one's favorite parts of scripture, and the significant weaknesses of this practice are obvious.

The other possible way of choosing readings is to follow some sort of disciplined, predetermined table. This table might simply outline a continuous reading—every Sunday a chapter of Isaiah, a chapter of Romans, and a chapter of Mark. A more complex schema like that provided by the Revised Common Lectionary includes some continuous reading but is distinct in that it is finally structured in relation to the liturgical calendar. In either case, the choice of readings for a given liturgical gathering is not simply left up to its local leaders but is in some way prepared for them. The weakness of this practice is its tendency to irrelevance; the readings for a given Sunday might not relate well to life events of the community. Its strength is that the assembly is freed from the limited imagination of its leaders. The particular strength of a lectionary shaped to follow the liturgical calendar is that it specifically keeps in front of the assembly the rhythm of God's work in Jesus Christ, who became flesh; taught and preached and healed among us; suffered, died, and rose again.

The tradition of a lectionary might have begun in Jewish synagogues and rather early became characteristic of Christian practice. Hearing the Bible read, explained, and applied is one of the central experiences that forms the assembly and its members. Indeed, it was this use that shaped the Bible we have. The canon of scripture was established based on the writings universally approved for reading in Christian assemblies. It is this pattern of use that ensures a variety of authoritative perspectives are available to each local community for its use. A lectionary also ensures that the word has a wider scope than the parts of the scripture that current congregational leaders find congenial or even appropriate. It exposes the assembly to the formative power of many stories.

One way of approaching the appointed gospel readings is to view them not simply as a way to teach the life of Jesus but as an ordered exploration of the effects of the presence of Jesus. We might understand the gospels in general as stories about what happened to people when Jesus broke into their lives. Indeed, contemporary hearers can understand that in the reading and proclamation of scripture, Jesus, who is himself the Word of God, breaks into our lives today.

LITURGICAL
YEAR:
WITHIN
THE WORLD,
WITHIN
ITS TIME

The gospel accounts during the season of Advent do not simply recount the events leading up to the birth of Jesus. Rather, they lead us through the experience of recognizing that things are not yet what God had promised they would be, and that if God's promises are going to be carried out, it will take divine action. In the meantime, we are to hope and wait actively. After four weeks of this waiting, we are ready to hear that God breaks into the world to fulfill promises in unexpected ways. Advent does not simply prepare the way for Christmas; it prepares the way for the inbreaking of the reign of God however and wherever that happens.

Similarly, the gospel readings of Lent do not simply recount Jesus' foreshadowings of his own passion and death. Rather, they lead us into a progressively closer relationship with Christ, identifying us more and more intimately with him and his mission. After six weeks of this growing intimacy, we are ready to hear about God bringing us, with and through Christ, into new life. Lent does not simply prepare the way for Good Friday; it prepares the way for the new life of the gospel, however and wherever that happens.

Likewise the gospel readings of Easter do not simply retell stories about the appearances of the risen Jesus to his disciples. Rather, they lead us through an understanding and experience of the new life of the resurrected Christ. They progress from the stunning joy of victory over death to the anticipation of the Spirit's activity in the Christian community.

An ordered pattern of readings according to the liturgical year—what the lectionary truly presents—offers a means by which the stories we hear can build on one another. The thematic and theological relationships of the stories, rather than a purely chronological progression, forms us in the gospel and impels us to live it out in the world.

~

Conclusion

The celebration of the liturgical year is one of the most powerful, effective tools the church has for living out the mission on which it has been sent. That mission, of course, is not to teach the world the minutiae of liturgical time, as enjoyable as that task might be. The mission is to join the very body of Christ to the very mission of God. The observances and practices that can be generated from the building blocks of Sunday, the Pasch, the liturgical calendar, and the lectionary are delightful and potent allies in that cause.

It might be that the liturgical year is so powerful (and so scan-
dalous) exactly because it reflects the central motif of God's own
self-revelation. By this self-revealing, God chooses to be placed
within this world and within time. The incarnation of the Word as
Jesus of Nazareth is not an exception to God's usual ways of
working but the defining paradigm. God always works through cre-
ation—human address, bread and wine, and water. The idea that
the spiritual is at war with the material is foreign to a God who
created both heaven and earth.

MARK W.
OLDENBURG

The liturgical year is inescapably incarnational. It depends on
the way cosmic matter works—the changes of season, seedtime and
harvest, the phases of the moon, and the elevation of the sun. It
marks the quotidian events through which God delights to speak. It
sets the proclamation of the mighty acts of God within the everyday,
assuring us that God does not simply work in the long-ago or far-
away but is present here and now. Used well, it can keep the strange
and wonderful gospel from being too remote to be heard by our
neighbors or to affect our care of them.

NOTES

1. Christopher Wordsworth, "O day of rest and gladness," *Lutheran Book of Worship* (Minneapolis: Augsburg Publishing House; Philadelphia: Board of Publication, Lutheran Church in America, 1978), no. 251.

2. *LBW*, 203.

3. For a contemporary adaptation of the catechumenate, see *Welcome to Christ: A Lutheran Introduction to the Catechumenate; Welcome to Christ: A Lutheran Catechetical Guide;* and *Welcome to Christ: Lutheran Rites for the Catechumenate* (Minneapolis: Augsburg Fortress, 1997).

4. Lebia Scott, "I sing a song of the saints of God," *The Hymnal 1982* (New York: Church Hymnal Corp., 1985), no. 293.

Liturgical Space: Faith Takes Form

Walter C. Huffman

At the national Shrine of the Immaculate Conception in Washington, D.C., a huge mosaic of Christ in majesty towers over the high altar. With stern countenance and fierce eyes, he watches worshipers below. Fire emanates from his head. Muscular arms are outstretched, open hands showing wounds from his crucifixion. On the baldachin beneath this mosaic stands the figure of a girl, simply dressed, arms extended in a gesture of kindness and blessing. The prayer on the visitor's card reads:

> Mary, holy mother of God, so pure, so blessed by God, Mother who loved your child, who held your son dead in your arms, your prayers are powerful with God. *You understand us.* Pray for each of us.[1]

Even the religiously illiterate can read the message communicated by this space. The contrast between the image of *Christus Pantocrator* and the simple maid from Nazareth is striking. Jesus is God—awesomely God! Only Mary can handle this fearsome apparition. She gave birth to him; she held his lifeless body in her arms. In her humanness, she understands us. She can help us.

Visual indoctrination takes place in most Christian worship spaces. Behind the altar of a country church in southern Ohio is a large painting of Jesus in the garden of Gethsemane praying to heaven. Neighboring churches display renditions of Warner Sallman's *Head of Christ* or sculptures of Jesus as the good shepherd. Countless children have grown into adulthood believing that Jesus—or God—looks like the figure in these artistic expressions. In mosaic or stained glass, sculpture or fresco, by the shape of the room and its furnishings, messages are communicated and received. We are shaped by spatial and visual images that either encourage community or reduce us to audience, that cause us to speak or be silent, that point hierarchically to one leader or to the presence of Christ in our midst. Our spaces are outspoken when expressing a community's convictions on the significance of liturgical leadership, music, preaching, baptism, and eucharist. Whatever the style—Romanesque, Baroque, Byzantine, Gothic, prairie, or nondescript—spaces shape our perception of God and our call to the missio Dei.

Space is a primary component in the formation of the people of God. We need to develop a new appreciation of the impact of liturgical space if we are to assist the church at worship and at work in proclaiming Christ to the world. At the rededication of the House of Commons after World War II, Winston Churchill said, "We shape our buildings, and afterwards our buildings shape us." Churchill's words could serve as warrant for this chapter's call to critique the formative effect of liturgical space.

We need a theology of liturgical space. We have given significant attention to the meaning of liturgical time and its relation to salvation history, but we have forgotten that history always has a geography. For Christians, the incarnation was spatial and geographical, as well as temporal and historical. We need a theology of space, not merely as an esoteric subject for scholarly discussion, but as an essential component of liturgical orthopraxis.

~

Holy place or holy people?

David, victorious over his enemies, established Jerusalem as his stronghold. After moving into a new palace, he proposed building a house for the ark, and by inference, the Lord of the ark. Through Nathan, the prophet, the Lord responded to this suggestion by reminding him: "I have not lived in a house since the day I brought up the people of Israel from Egypt to this day, but I have been moving about in a tent and a tabernacle" (2 Sam. 7:6). That refusal is followed by the promise to build David a "house" (that is, to establish a family dynasty). Yahweh's reply to David seems to be, "You know I am not a God who dwells in temple-houses. I am the God who goes with and dwells in the midst of the people."

We cannot help but wonder whether David was really worried about Yahweh's homelessness, or this master politician needed a royal chapel to legitimize his rule. We also wonder whether there was more to Yahweh's promise than a covenantal affirmation of

David. In the rejection of a temple-house for Yahweh we detect a strain of opposition toward the construction of such holy places. This meeting between David and Nathan is intriguing, because it initiates centuries of alternation between the two complementary but often contrasting viewpoints: *domus dei* or *domus ecclesiae* (house for God or house for the people of God).

WALTER C. HUFFMAN

Israel's identity was formed in the wilderness as a pilgrim people following a nomadic Lord. Many believed Israel was at its best as a people when it was untouched by the encumbrances of cities and their pagan influences. Many people in ancient Israel decried the incursion of foreign practices and attitudes that developed within the temple's precincts. Even at the dedication of the first temple, Solomon thought it important to point out in his address that Yahweh's real home is in the highest heavens (see also Hosea 5:15; Deut. 26:15). From the beginning, there were those in Israel who had serious misgivings about the concept of *domus dei*, a house for God.

Centuries later, the Babylonian exiles saw themselves as Israel on a perilous journey in the wilderness awaiting a new exodus. The space-time coordinates were different, but the result would be the same. Their chaos would be womb for the creation of a new community. In a foreign land, separated from the temple and its worship, these exiles created synagogues as places for liturgical, educational, and community activities. Before *synagogue* came to refer to a specific space, it meant "assembly" or "congregation," a meetinghouse for the people of God.

Fast-forward to the Qumran community, which was in transition, unsettled in time and space but moving toward the fulfillment of divine promises. These priests went into self-imposed exile, believing the temple in Jerusalem was defiled and its practices corrupt. As they longed for a new and perfect temple, they viewed their community as their holy place. They awaited a heavenly temple that would descend to earth as Yahweh returned to live in the midst of the people.

Jesus' attitude toward the temple in Jerusalem was ambiguous at best. When he referred to its destruction, the evangelists spun these sayings as references to his own death and resurrection. His action at the temple shortly before his crucifixion is even more problematic. John Dominic Crossan has suggested that Jesus did not purify the temple; he attacked and symbolically destroyed it. Crossan says that we should not refer to Mark 11:15-19 as the purification of the temple. Buying, selling, and money-changing operations conducted in the outer courts of the temple were necessary components in the sacrificial enterprise of the temple. When Jesus' parents brought him to the temple for the purification sacrifice, "they offered a sacrifice according to what is stated

in the law of the Lord, 'a pair of turtle doves or two young pigeons'"
(Luke 2:24). Certainly they bought the birds in the outer court of the
temple. There was nothing necessarily wrong with such business. Even
though Mark may try to tone down this radical act, he knows that
Jesus was not just purifying but symbolically attacking the temple. He
knows, because he carefully partners this action with the cursing of the
fruitless fig tree in 11:12-14 and its withering in 11:20. The temple is
like the useless fig tree. It will be destroyed.[2]

It was inevitable that Jesus' ministry of spiritual and economic
egalitarianism would come into direct conflict with the temple and
its mentality. The temple syndrome monumentally contradicted the
ministry and mission of this wandering teacher. This seat of official
religion was prescribed, exclusive, patronal, and restrictive so that
this "symbolic destruction simply actualized what he had already
said in his teachings, effected in his healing, and realized in his
mission of open commensality."[3] In his own life, Jesus embodied
Israel's pilgrim status, trusting in a God who moved with the people
rather than waiting idol-like for obeisance in some holy place.

Like the wilderness wanderers, the exiles, the Qumranians, and
Jesus and his disciples, the first Christians saw themselves as aliens
and exiles. They had been expelled from the synagogues and subsequently had distanced themselves from the Jewish matrix. They were
poor and the object of persecution. The practical solution to their
need for Christian synagogue was similar to that of their Jewish forebears; they worshiped in homes. But *domus ecclesiae*, a house for the
people of God, was not just a practical solution. The first apologists
said it was theologically appropriate. Asked by the prefect of Rome,
"Where do you meet together?" Justin replied, "Where each wills
and can. Do you really think that we all meet in the same place? Not
so; the God of Christians is not confined by place."[4] In a classic description of Christian worship from the year A.D. 150, he states "On
the day which is called Sunday we have a common assembly of all
who live in the cities or outlying districts."[5] The absence of reference
to any particular site is noteworthy.

The leitmotif of today's liturgical movement has been the recovery of the assembly as the primordial symbol of Christian worship.
In a seminal publication, *The Roots of the Liturgy*, Eric James wrote:

> The greatest symbol that the Church possesses is perhaps that symbol
> which it unconsciously produces every time the Church gathers: the
> gathered community itself, transcending race and class, colour and
> age—the One community.... This is, of course as much vision as
> reality, but in various ways it is evident that the Church is being drawn
> towards the vision.[6]

Lutheran confessional theology affirms the importance of gathered assembly, with the significant addition that it take place around word and sacrament (Augsburg Confession, article 7). Focus on the assembly around word and sacrament has precipitated many significant changes in our liturgical life. Our people now participate in leadership roles as liturgical ministers of hospitality, word, table, prayer, and music. With these representatives, the whole people is drawn more fully into worship through language and music that are gender conscious and ethnically inclusive. Contemporary worship books and statements on sacramental practices (for example, the Evangelical Lutheran Church in America's statement, *The Use of the Means of Grace,* and the Evangelical Lutheran Church in Canada's *Statement on Sacramental Practices*) stress the communal context of baptism and eucharist, as well as occasional services.

Emphasizing the active participation of the people in worship means emphasizing the active participation of people in mission! Inevitably, worship becomes a "ritual rehearsal" for ministry. If one person does everything in worship, he or she becomes the one designated to call on the sick and prospective members, or the one primarily responsible for leading congregational programs. Affirming the gifts of others in worship is a way of commissioning them for their ministry in the world. Worship patterns people for ministry. This intersection of worship and life is the point of Paul's definition of Christian worship in Romans 12. In that passage, he refers to the offering of our whole selves in the service of Christ as true and "spiritual worship" (Rom. 12:1).

If we seriously practice a liturgical theology that sees worship as formational for Christian life and mission, then we must do more than inadvertently glance in the direction of our liturgical spaces. They will collaborate with us or contradict our good intentions. We dare not treat them casually or indifferently; they must be made to express gospel values. It is time to discuss, envision, and formulate a theology of liturgical space that will serve us in a new millennium. The remainder of this chapter points to an emerging definition of liturgical space that affects our call to Christian ministry.

∿

LIMINALITY AND PLACE

Israel in the wilderness or in exile, Qumran, the life of Jesus and his disciples, and the primitive church are examples of liminal social groups. The term *liminal* derives from the Latin *limen* (threshold) and is used by cultural anthropologists to describe a state of marginality. Separated from a given societal structure, liminal people live in a profound transitional state. To use Victor Turner's language, they are "betwixt and between" the structures of law, convention, or ceremony. In this state of marginality, individuals and communities of people tend to reorder their values. They are psychologically and spiritually malleable. Almost by nature their journey is described in religious terms. They develop a deep bond with those who share this experience with them. Turner calls this *communitas*, a relationship with others free of the distinctions of class, rank, wealth, or social status. This journey ends as liminal persons reenter society, thus renewing and transforming the status quo with new vision and energy. Such is the promise of this process: the antistructure of the liminal phase eventually gives new dynamism to a society.[7]

The author of 1 Peter speaks of Christians as aliens and exiles. If it is truly our nature to live apart from an abiding city, then we should bear the stamp of liminality in our lives, in our worship, and in our worship spaces! To speak of the liminal nature of our spaces requires a new wariness regarding their exaggerated importance to our communities. Perhaps we should call a moratorium on new church buildings. Buildings by their nature confine rather than free. Many ecclesiastical spaces are fortresslike bastions that shut out the world with stone and stained glass. Their intention is to create an alternative world. A pilgrim people, however, move unencumbered into a world of God's making rather than in an artificially controlled atmosphere. As a people in mission, the walls of our spaces must be permeable. They must open us to the world rather than symbolically confine us. A challenge facing the church today is to change our perspective on worship spaces, to make them less formidable and more formational in expressing our nature as a pilgrim people.

~

Focus on central symbols

Simplicity is one quality of liminal people and liminal spaces. When one begins a long journey, the byword is "pack light." The traveler takes along what is basic and necessary and avoids being weighed down by nonessentials. Simplicity, by this standard, affords maximum mobility. Simplicity is also valued aesthetically. In the 1894 design of a private residence, Frank Lloyd Wright wrote of his architecture as embracing a "new simplicity." In the work of this great architect we see the intersection of beauty and economy in architectural forms that successfully serve people in their living, working, and cultural interests. In recent years, there has been a new appreciation of Cistercian and Shaker buildings and furniture. In such examples, simplicity is more than a matter of aesthetic taste; these communities understand simplicity as a significant expression of their faith.

The simplicity embraced in this chapter is not so much aesthetic or utilitarian as it is a way to bring clarity and focus to our spaces. Translated into the specifics of liturgical space, simplicity means we clearly define liturgical centers and the central symbols of people, water, book, bread, and wine. It means we consciously shape spaces based on an understanding of the ritual acts and signs that make us "church." Preaching, baptism, and eucharist need their definable and appropriate places. Although we need other spaces—a presbyterium for liturgical leaders, an area for musicians, places of honor for those who wed and the dead—these ancillary places must serve the primary foci of the room. A sense of restraint should keep us from cluttering the room with secondary furnishings (such as flags, sanctuary lamps, flower stands, extraneous podiums, and musical instruments) that confuse and distract us from the importance of the central symbols. This sense of "noble simplicity," called for by the *Constitution on the Sacred Liturgy* from the Roman Catholic Church's Second Vatican Council, brings clarity to the patterns of Christian worship and facilitates the role of liturgy in faith formation.[8]

A prototype for this expression of liturgical space emerged in the work of liturgist Romano Guardini and architect Rudolf Schwarz. In 1928, at the height of the neo-Gothic, neoclassical movement, they created a small worship room in Germany that became a model for contemporary church architecture. The chapel was a large rectangular hall with unadorned white walls. The furniture was limited to one hundred black stools that could be rearranged for various functions. When the eucharist was celebrated, the worshipers surrounded the altar on three sides, and the presiding minister faced the people from behind the altar. This simple space, with its focus on central symbols of Christian worship and facilitation of congregational participation, returned to the principles of *domus ecclesiae* and served as a harbinger of the shape of liturgical space still being realized in mainline Christian communities.

The architect Edward Sovik underscored some of these same themes in his 1973 book *Architecture for Worship*. This Lutheran has been a prophetic and provocative voice on the subject of liturgical space. In lectures, articles, and the buildings he has designed, Sovik argues that "church" at its best is allergic to ecclesiastical "house of God" structures. He calls for the rejection of traditional building forms, because they fail to serve the people they shelter and encourage congregations to neglect social ministry. In ancient and contemporary church architecture, he describes such buildings as

> otherworldly by inference, detaching themselves from the architecture of the world around them. Their triumphal monumentalism magnified the authority or the prestige of the institution, or their saccharine charms insulated their habitues from the realities of the world, or their "dim religious light" provided a sentimental and esoteric escape. Where funds were not available to erect real architecture of these qualities, imitative gestures were made in the same directions.[9]

As an alternative, Sovik proposes the *centrum*. By his definition, a centrum is an ecclesiastically neutral space, a meeting room that facilitates various congregational and civic purposes. His centrum begins from the assumption that the room must be hospitable for many uses and flexible arrangements. From this starting point, he advocates flexible seating (chairs), movable platforms for a portable altar and pulpit, and some form of baptismal font that does not interfere with the openness and flexibility of the space. He speaks against axial symmetries that dictate a single architectural focus. In his book, he works out the implications of his centrum for acoustics, visual projects, musical facilities, lighting, ecclesiastical images, and art. Although the design of this space is based on the presupposition that the space will be ecclesiastically neutral and utilitarian, nevertheless, Sovik wants it to be beautiful. This master architect has been willing to think theologically about the spaces he has been commissioned to design. He does so with a sense of history and missionary purpose that should be deeply appreciated and carefully critiqued.

Sovik's call for a simple meeting room unencumbered by the liturgical debris of past centuries is a welcome one. He is right to insist that our meeting rooms be hospitable to many activities, but he is wrong to base this rationale primarily on the need for multi-purpose use. Rather, the simplification of liturgical space is desirable primarily because it clarifies our purpose and focuses our attention on the central symbols of Christian worship. Rather than minimize the furniture of the liturgical centers (baptismal font or pool, altar-table, ambo) as has often been done in the centrum approach, we must give increased attention to these significant components of a worship space. Furthermore, it is not true that a space must be neutral or cleared of all ecclesiastical symbols to be hospitable. The presence of living water in a baptismal pool evokes common human evocations that can have a positive effect on nearly any gathering.

WALTER C.
HUFFMAN

RITUALLY DEFINED SACRED SPACE

Those who advocate a return to *domus ecclesiae*, a meeting house approach to the community's worship center, fear that designating one place as sacred or holy may drain all other places of their holiness. They are wary of providing any permanent religious symbol or liturgical device in such a place for fear of separating it from other places of human concourse. Christian worship is distorted, they claim, when it is "associated with certain places instead of something which involves certain attitudes, acts, and certain kinds of people."[10]

The yearning for sacred space, however, is written into the fabric of our humanness. We cannot escape the fact that even modern people need the experience of sacred space. In today's world, that experience may indeed be fragmentary, found only in "space/time pods,"[11] but the yearning is palpable! It is inarticulately expressed every time a wedding party asks to borrow or rent a congregation's worship room for their wedding. It is demonstrated in the reverence of people who visit the Capitol rotunda, the Vietnam Memorial, or the Holocaust Museum.

In Opryland's superb auditorium, the guide often points out a circle of wood on the stage, an heirloom from the old Rymer auditorium, the birthplace of the Grand Old Opry. It is, she says, the "holy place of country music." These zones of stability and orientation provide a counterpoint to the chaos of our everyday living. They are more than special places; they are sacred spaces.

Often the sense of sacredness has been artificially induced. As church, we have often used the image of light streaming through stained glass. Lighted candles in front of icons or religious images fascinate us. We have used verticality, distance, and gradations of access between nave and chancel. We have been impressed by the unusual and bizarre, from glass cathedrals to the superfluity of Rococo architecture. These spatial devices witness not only to our need for holy place but an inability to decide what that really means.

Consider a mission congregation's farewell to a pastor and his family after the pastor had served them for a dozen years. After the Sunday morning eucharist and a community potluck with the congregation, he stepped into the worship space for one last solitary visit. It was a "boundless moment," for the empty room was suddenly full of faces and sounds from those years of worship. A thousand memories crowded his consciousness. For him the inadequate cinder block structure had become a holy place. This experience had little to do with the physical nature of the place; it had everything to do with what had transpired in it.

A member of the Society of Friends, a community that has steadfastly opposed the concept of holy places, writes of their plain meeting halls:

> Places and things do not hallow people, but the enduring faith of the people may hallow places. Where you are sitting in that calm cool place there has been unbroken prayer and worship generation after generation. In the outward and inner silences there...you may realize that... "we are surrounded by a great cloud of witnesses."[12]

Sacred space admits to many definitions.[13] The premise of this chapter is that sacred space exists where sustained and significant domestic, civic, or religious ritualization has occurred. Ritual transforms a space from ordinary to extraordinary. Before the fourth century, there is no evidence of dedication rites for new churches. Following the legitimization of the church after Constantine, the dedication or consecration of a building for liturgical purposes simply involved the celebration of the first eucharist in that building. Only later were dedications attended by extraordinary ritual exercises.[14] The parallel between the consecration of sacramental elements and liturgical spaces has been pointed out by J.G. Davies, who reminds us that consecration in both cases consists of "thankful acknowledgement of the relation of the object concerned to God the giver and blessing him for it."[15] Sacred ritual is functional, not ontological. It is, therefore, extraneous to use a rite such as Secularizing of a Consecrated Building[16] when all one needs to "secularize" a building is to stop using it!

~

ORGANIC LITURGICAL ARCHITECTURE

When planning new liturgical spaces, it is all too common for architects and building committees to give attention to the furnishings of the room as afterthought. The architectural blueprints of the building may include generalities regarding placement of people, musicians, and leaders. The shape, size, design, and location of the places for baptism, eucharist, and people are not strategically addressed. In fact, the building is often under construction before anyone becomes serious about such liturgical centers, and then the search begins for artisans and catalog possibilities.

This indifference to the internal components would have been repugnant to Frank Lloyd Wright. He spoke against the idea of architecture as one discipline, landscape another, and interior decoration a third. "In organic architecture all three are one."[17] Wright often designed everything for a house, the furniture, cabinets, window treatment, and decorations such as vases and pictures. Although he has been criticized for creating a dictated environment, Wright drew attention to the necessity of addressing all facets of a design. A building has an interior as well as an exterior, and the shape of the room is more than dimensions and forms. The furniture, artwork, cabinets—all are organic to the design. Those who design churches and liturgical spaces should heed this master's example. Consideration of liturgical centers and their furniture should be part of the initial dreaming and designing by all planners and not merely an afterthought.

In a sermon-treatise on baptism, Luther stressed that the best way to express the true meaning of baptism was through immersion. He said this form of baptism best expressed the terminological and theological meaning of the sacrament. "We should…do justice to its meaning and make Baptism a true and complete sign of the thing it signifies."[18] Just as the rite should faithfully express the meaning of baptism, so the place of baptism in our worship rooms should express the thing that is being signified. It should say that we are a people who have crossed the sea to God's promises. It should say that this is a place of being washed and purified. With Paul it should provide an image of the dying and rising inherent in the baptismal way of life. The place itself should evoke the understanding that Christians are called to bring life-giving water to a dying world. The place of baptism must be consequential, as baptism is consequential; it should have impact on the worship room as significant as the table or pulpit. This liturgical center should speak of informed baptismal themes and practice to those visitors drawn into our worship places, as well as to missionary-minded members spun out into the world. The message must be clear. This is the place where we make new Christians—children and adults! This is a place of great consequence; you should enter these waters only after great deliberation. No one should have to strain the imagination to sense some of these themes. As Christians in mission, we are those who lead across waters to new life and hope.

The place of the eucharistic meal should likewise serve eucharistic practice that is a "true and complete sign of the thing it signifies." It should be obvious to all that this is the holy meal of the people of God. That definition suggests a noble table set in the midst of the people. The chairs or pews in the space are chairs set for that dining table. When the eucharist is celebrated, only vessels with eucharistic food should be placed on this simply covered table. The presiding minister should graciously face the people for the thanksgiving prayer. The people should commune in a natural fashion around the table.

As Christians in mission, we are those who make room at table. John Dominic Crossan argues convincingly that the heart of the original Jesus movement was a shared egalitarianism of spiritual and material resources centered in table fellowship.[19] It was at table with sinners, prostitutes, tax collectors, and lepers that Jesus blasted the social and religious taboos of his day and offered an image of the kingdom of God. Nowhere is the nature of the gospel more radically proposed than at table where Jesus welcomed all—those of status as well as those excommunicated by existing social structures. By cultural standards of that day, his behavior was scandalous. Even as an invited guest, Jesus became host, welcoming people of every social rank and arranging the seats so that all were treated equally. Jesus created a "welcome table" no longer based on social status but on the liberating God for all people. John Taylor writes in *Enough Is Enough*:

> The great breakthrough of the New Testament is that the generosities of the old covenant are extended to all [people]. They are no longer an expression of family or tribal or religious solidarity; so they are no longer restricted to a limited circle only. They are for all [people] in all circumstances and in every place. Such is the unbounded liberality and fellowship of what might be called "the eucharistic life," the life that is built on gratitude, or rather on an intense awareness of who is to be thanked.[20]

Making room at the table is the preeminent act of Christian hospitality. The eucharist sets forth a welcome table where we have access to all the themes of Jesus' ministry. This is the place of revolution, truth, promise, hope, and love. This table fellowship is at the heart of the Jesus movement then and now. Our mission to the hungry and starving world is to bring guests to that table. To complete the sign, our liturgical space must match this interpretation.

In addition to our identity as those who lead across waters and those who make room at table, we are those who bear the word. Historically, the place of preaching has taken many forms. Early Christians worshiped in homes around eucharistic tables, and we therefore assume that sermons were more like shared conversation than formal oratory. When the church adopted synagogue patterns, the presiding elder's chair became the place of proclamation. After the Peace of Constantine, the church moved into basilican spaces, eventually adding an elevated ambo or podium so reader and preacher could be seen and heard. Shortly after the Middle Ages, the reading of the gospel and preaching from a pulpit were accompanied by secondary readings from a lectern.

For today's liturgical consultants and architects, the placement and size of a pulpit is a persistent problem. Reflecting a Protestant past, many congregations worship in rooms where the pulpit is the most dominant feature. Embarrassed by the ostentatious nature of such pulpits and resisting their hierarchical implications, ministers wander out into congregations to preach. On the one hand, there is health in breaking such a barrier and moving closer to the people. Often, the effectiveness of the message is proportionate to the proximity of the speaker, actor, or musician. Preaching from the center aisle or chancel steps appeals to many as a novel and engaging form of communication. For too long our ministers have been swallowed up in pulpits that resemble the bows of great ships. They have used the pulpit as a shield against a dialogical style of preaching. Mobile sermons, however, can be distracting because they draw undue attention to the preacher. Pointless meandering and the unpredictability of movement can be so distracting that the content of the sermon is lost. As this style of preaching has caught on, the pulpit or reading desk has simply been eliminated in some new spaces. Does this style not virtually eliminate the need for a place of the word and instead call attention to the word-giver? Does it not promote the actor/audience syndrome that we are trying to dismantle in our day? These are questions of practice that must be addressed as they affect the arrangement of liturgical space.

Symbolic of our ministry as word-bearers, a large, ceremonial Bible should be an important object in a worship room. The practice of placing the book on the altar is inadequate, because it turns the altar into a reading desk. Similarly, carrying the book around like Billy Graham as a device for emphasizing the connection between sermon and scripture is unfortunate. The best option is a dignified, human-sized place of the word—a reading desk with a handsomely bound Bible or lectionary. We could learn from our Jewish friends, who take scrolls from the ark, honor them with a ceremonial procession, and carefully open them for reading. In this day of bulletin inserts and untrained readers, we need to retrieve a sense of dignity concerning the book and the place of the word.

Our treatment of the place of the word and the symbol of the Bible have missional implications. The Bible or lectionary is not just text for the preacher but the congregation's big book. Lay readers as well as presider read from the same book, signifying a common ministry for all the people of God. All are called to honor the word, to found our lives on the word, and to proclaim the word. The place of the word also expresses a relationship with the places of baptism and eucharist. We should avoid the familiar practice of locating all three spaces on a raised chancel platform facing the congregation. The chancel-as-stage reinforces the liturgical actor/congregational audience syndrome. A solution is to treat the entire room as chancel in order to speak more clearly of the common ministry of the whole assembly.

∼

Establishing an ordo of liturgical space

A development in contemporary liturgiology has been the rediscovery of a basic ordo of Christian liturgy. This ordo is the historical and confessional pattern of ritual words and actions that makes us church. The ordo provides not only the foundational basis of our liturgical agenda in the Sunday assembly, however. Gordon Lathrop in *Holy Things* speaks of an ordo of praying and beseeching (including daily prayer), an ordo of holy baptism, and an ordo of the liturgical year and paschal time.[21] We need to extend that concept to encompass an ordo of liturgical space, a spatial definition for liturgical rooms crucial to the formation of Christians at worship and in mission. As one of the languages of worship, our spaces must facilitate our work as people who lead across waters, make room at table, and bear the word to the world.

The ordo of liturgical space is ritually described in the dedication of a church building in *Occasional Services*.[22] A procession of liturgical ministers moves from the threshold or entrance to the places of baptism, reading or preaching, meal, and finally into the place of the people. In this stational liturgy, leaders pause at each liturgical center for prayers of blessing to God for gifts of grace received at these locations. Water is touched, the Bible placed on the reading desk, the altar given its clothes and vessels, and the people affirmed as a center of Christ's presence. This procession is a ritual expression of the spatial ordo of Christian worship.

Establishing an appreciation of the ordo of liturgical space will not be easy. Christians bring preconceptions and misconceptions about their spaces for worship. Many would point to a decorative

cross as the primary symbol in their worship space. Some faith tra- WALTER C.
ditions emphasize the prominence of the altar; others give special HUFFMAN
place to pulpits or baptismal pools. As church, we need to be
schooled in our recognition of the shape and importance of the ordo
of liturgical space.

Over ten years ago, this writer helped to produce a study book
dealing with the history, meaning, and planning possibilities for
liturgical space. It was an interdenominational attempt to help congregations bring spaces "up to liturgical code." These booklets were
sent to every Lutheran congregation in North America seeking

> to assist congregations and institutions in developing appropriate cri-
> teria for the environment and art in their own worship spaces. It is ex-
> pected that those who enter such a study will become the catalyst for
> drawing their congregations into appropriate action in this area of
> Christian life. For some communities this study will serve as a con-
> sciousness-raising effort. For congregations that have begun a process
> to deal with their liturgical space, this study may become aid and re-
> source in that journey.[23]

Books and other publications, however, are not enough to move
people toward a theologically responsible definition of liturgical
space. We need trained people to serve as resources for congregations that wish to renew or shape new worship spaces. A practical
result of our attention to this matter is the ministry of liturgical
design consultants. A consultant can teach congregations and their
leaders in various forums, including committee meetings, adult
series, and special events. This person would be equipped to help
planners and congregations wrestle with emerging liturgical themes
as the basis for shaping the worship center. The consultant might
also help guide the design and building schedule and participate actively in the final selection of furnishings and art.

> Needless to say, his or her sophistication in the liturgical field should
> be...broad and deep, a knowledge that goes beyond acquaintance
> with patterns, to the perception of principles and possibilities. And it
> is critical that the consultant be a person of impeccable taste, whose
> judgment and sensibilities are not limited by what he knows or has ex-
> perienced. He must have the visual imagination to make judgments on
> the basis of drawings, be sensitive to color, texture, scale, and to con-
> ceive of total relationships.[24]

An ecumenical institute might be established to train these consultants. The curriculum would provide a strong dose of liturgical
catechesis, particularly addressing theological and historic patterns.

This liturgical training would reflect the present pastoral stage of the contemporary liturgical movement. Participants would gain valuable field experience from working with architects, artists, and other design consultants. Those who finish this course of study could be designated to represent their synods or regions. Congregations would be encouraged to use their services when embarking on a building project. Churchwide worship leaders would coordinate the institute and its program. To implement such a program would save millions of dollars presently spent and misspent on new and renovated buildings. All too often new liturgical spaces are outdated on the day of their dedication. Good stewardship demands that our churches begin to exercise a responsible approach in this expensive and influential area of our lives by taking seriously the vocation of these ministers of our worship spaces.

Christian faith must be incarnate. It is powerfully expressed when the faithful worship as well as serve. Something of the height and depth and breadth of the faith is also revealed through our liturgical spaces. These places of worship not only reveal the shape of a community's faith; they help to form it. If, then, we are truly concerned about mission and ministry, we will pay careful attention to the powerful influence of these spaces. We must shape and reshape our centers for worship to embody faith in Jesus Christ and his call to mission.

NOTES

1. Informational booklet and prayer card, *The National Shrine of the Immaculate Conception* (Washington, D.C.: Merkle Press, 1964), 40, emphasis mine.

2. John Dominic Crossan, *The Historical Jesus: Life of a Mediterranean Jewish Peasant* (San Francisco: HarperSanFrancisco, 1991).

3. Ibid., 360.

4. E. C. E. Owen, trans., *Some Authentic Acts of the Early Martyrs* (Oxford: Oxford Press, 1929), 49.

5. Thomas B. Falls, trans., *St. Justin, Apology I, 67*, in *Writings of Saint Justin Martyr* (New York: Christian Heritage Publishers, 1958), 106.

6. Eric James, *The Roots of the Liturgy* (London: Prism, 1962), 8.

7. See Victor Turner, "Passages, Margins, and Poverty: Religious Symbols of Communitas," *Worship* 46, no. 7 (August–September 1972): 390–412.

8. *Constitution on the Sacred Liturgy* (Second Vatican Council: 4 December 1963), par. 34.

9. Ed Sovik, *Architecture for Worship* (Minneapolis: Augsburg Publishing House, 1973), 38.

10. Ibid., 37.

11. For an interesting discussion of the nature and dynamics of sacred space in the thought of Mircea Eliade and Victor Turner, see Robert Moore and Frank E. Reynolds, eds., "Space and Transformation in Human Experience," chap. 6, in *Anthropology and the Study of Religion* (Chicago: Center for the Scientific Study of Religion, 1984).

12. F. J. Nicholson, "A Hallowed Place," *The Friend* 132, no. 12 (1975): 288.

13. See, for example, Lawrence A. Hoffman, *Sacred Places and the Pilgrimage of Life in Meeting House Essays No. 1* (Chicago: Liturgy Training Publications, 1991).

14. See, for instance, Marion J. Hatchett, *Commentary on the American Prayer Book* (New York: The Seabury Press, 1981) or J.D. Crichton, *The Dedication of a Church* (Dublin: Veritas, 1980).

15. See chap. 8 in J.G. Davies, *The Secular Use of Church Buildings* (New York: Seabury, 1968).

16. See *The Book of Occasional Services—1994* (New York: Church Hymnal Corp., 1995), 223–25.

17. "Building a Democracy," Taliesin Square Paper No. 10 (Chicago: The Frank Lloyd Wright Foundation, 1994).

18. "The Holy and Blessed Sacrament of Baptism, 1519," in *Luther's Works*, ed. Helmut T. Lehmann (Philadelphia: Fortress Press, 1960), 35:29.

19. Crossan, *The Historical Jesus,* chap. 13.

20. John V. Taylor, *Enough Is Enough* (Minneapolis: Augsburg Publishing House, 1977), 61–62.

21. Gordon W. Lathrop, *Holy Things: A Liturgical Theology* (Minneapolis: Fortress Press, 1993).

22. *Occasional Services* (Minneapolis: Augsburg Publishing House; Board of Publication, Lutheran Church in America, 1982), 166–72.

23. Walter Huffman, Ralph R. Van Loon, *Where We Worship* Process and Leader Guide, ed. S. Anita Stauffer (Philadelphia: Board of Publication, Lutheran Church in America, 1987), 4.

24. Sovik, "An Orderly Journey," in *The Environment For Worship*, ed. Secretariat, The National Conference of Catholic Bishops (Washington, D.C.: United States Catholic Conference, 1980), 66.

Music: Poured Out for the World

Paul Westermeyer

I hate, I despise your festivals,
    and I take no delight in your solemn assemblies.
Even though you offer me your burnt offerings and grain offerings,
    I will not accept them;
and the offerings of well-being of your fatted animals
    I will not look upon.
Take away from me the noise of your songs;
    I will not listen to the melody of your harps.
But let justice roll down like waters,
    and righteousness like an everflowing stream.

Amos 5:21-24

WHEN I FIRST HEARD about this book, I suggested that music be omitted from it. To omit music from a book about worship would normally be unthinkable for me, as it would be for most of the Christian church and especially for Lutherans. We live in a time, however, when the church has been engaged in power plays called "worship wars" and "music wars." This game is named death. It is played by forcing people to choose between two sides, one labeled stuffiness and the other froth, as if those were the only possible choices.

In such a time we might turn to Amos for help and ask if his cry is the only one that has any power or integrity. I hate your silly battles about worship, he would say. I hate your phony, ingrown feasts, whatever their style. I hate your musical madness and pretense. Put away from me the noise of your musical monkey business, and let justice roll down. Stop looking at your navels, and care about the world you are called to serve.

The question in such a time is whether the song has to cease. The dilemma is whether the church has to fall silent in order to be true to its being, whether in order to be true to their vocations church musicians have to abandon them because they cannot escape the prevailing malady anymore. In such a time, do musicians keep pace with Christ and the obedient confessing church by worshiping with some small community of the baptized that quietly manages, maybe underground and with only the most minimal musical resources, to keep the paschal feast each week and to welcome the newly baptized? Thereafter throughout the week, apart from daily prayer, are church musicians called to avoid all gatherings of the church as much as possible, so they can simply be the church in the world with the rest of Christ's broken and scattered body? Are they to seek a vocation in the world that provides a way to challenge systemic injustice; care for widows, orphans, victims of abuse, and the environment; teach children; speak the gospel; sing or play in some constructive "secular" musical context; or do anything Christ calls us to do for the other? Is that what Bonhoeffer's dictum might mean, that when Christ calls us, he bids us come and die?[1] Are those of us called to musical vocations in the church, including vocations that reflect on the music of the church, required to die to the very vocations to which Christ calls us?

Or is that approach a cop-out? Does dying with Christ mean staying the course right in the midst of the church's culturally driven, mean-spirited, and ingrown hatred? In the midst of the bureaucratic madness of power plays and intrigue, should we expect whatever abuse and death might come, knowing that God is faithful in spite of our disobedience? Are we to sing with our communities of faith and to reflect on them as well as we are able, whatever their state? Is that what Bonhoeffer's dictum means? When Amos voiced his prophetic cry in poetic and musical language, is that what he too meant?[2]

I have opted for the second choice and for the inclusion of music in this book. But it should be clear that everything I write here stands in the context of and under the judgment of God in Christ who cares about the world and regards our stench of corruption, musical and otherwise, for what it is.

~

Rhythms of the church's worship

To get at the background of the church's music, one has to begin with the worship the music has served. Across time one can see a gravitational pull to five rhythms in the church's worship life. They can be described briefly as follows.[3]

Baptism. The church has baptized "infants as if they were adults"
and "adults as if they were infants"[4] with water and word in the
name of the triune God. Baptism is not about how cute the baby is.
It is powerful. It grafts us into Christ's body and nerves us for the
Christian life. It requires vital, instructional, wholistic, serious, and
joyful preparation;[5] and it leads to freedom, prayer, fasting, feasting, singing, being formed liturgically, and being Christ's body in the
world.[6]

Baptism is unique. It happens once for each of us, then forms
and shapes our whole Christian life. The other four rhythms happen
across the days, weeks, and years that make up our lives.

The Year. Christians first celebrated Easter, the one festival of the
early church, and then filled out the whole year around it—a period
of preparation before it, a period of celebration after it, a Christmas
cycle (itself perhaps derived from Easter), and a cycle for remembering the saints. Our sisters and brothers who have gone before us
learned to live the Christian story in the rhythms of the year and
have taught us how to remember its fullness.

Sunday. Sunday has characteristically been a little Easter for Christians, just as Easter has been regarded as a great Sunday.[7] We have
most often celebrated word and supper, though Protestants have
tended to maximize the word and minimize the supper, while
Catholics have tended to maximize the supper and minimize the
word. For almost all of us, however, and certainly for Lutherans,
both word and supper have been the focus of our Sunday gatherings.

The variations on the central core of word and supper are enormous, but essentially we are dealing here with what "has been used
by generations of Christians"[8] and is described tersely and well in
the Lutheran statement, *The Use of the Means of Grace:*

> We gather in song and prayer, confessing our need of God. We read
> Scriptures and hear them preached. We profess our faith and pray for
> the world, sealing our prayers with a sign of peace. We gather an of-
> fering for the poor and for the mission of the Church. We set our table
> with bread and wine, we give thanks and praise to God, proclaiming
> Jesus Christ, and eat and drink. We hear the blessing of God and are
> sent out in mission to the world.[9]

The Day. The days of the week have spun around the central
Sunday celebration and have been shaped in three ways by Christians: (1) brief "cathedral" morning and evening prayer services in
which groups of Christians gather before and after work or perhaps

at a noontime break; (2) the normal prayer of the Christian at home—on arising, at meals, on going to bed, sometimes with devotional guides; and (3) the monastic style of eight offices at about three-hour intervals throughout the day and night.

Occasional Services. We live not only according to the set rhythms of days, weeks, and years. Our lives are also punctuated by their own significant points of passage. The church has therefore worshiped with weddings, funerals, healing services, services of reconciliation, ordination for some, commissioning for others, cornerstone layings, dedications, preaching missions, and similar "occasional" services.

~

PSALMODY AND THE CHURCH'S SONG

The music of the church has permeated these rhythms of its worship through psalmody and the very nature of the church's song. Psalmody is the womb of the church's music and has been central to the church's worship.[10] The psalms are not only the hymnal of the Old Testament and the songs of Israel; they are the voice of the church, as Ambrose said[11] and as one book's title aptly puts it.[12] From the first Christians up to the present, the church has continually gravitated to the psalms for the ground of its song. The psalms are not only used by different groups of Christians, Eastern and Western churches and their various subgroups, but have been employed almost everywhere in the five rhythms of worship mentioned above. The psalms stretch across the church year from the central service of the Lord's supper to the baptismal service, congregational forms of morning and evening prayer, monastic offices, free church worship, private devotions of the people, and occasional services.

From the beginning of the church's history, the psalms have characteristically been sung, not spoken.[13] That is why there is so much music associated with them across a spectrum from the simplest to the most complex.[14] At the simplest end of the spectrum are strophic tunes for metrical psalms and psalm tones designed for everyone to sing, such as those in *Lutheran Book of Worship*.[15] At the complex end there are numerous musical settings that require the most sophisticated forces, such as Igor Stravinsky's *Symphony of Psalms*[16] and some types of psalm tones, such as Anglican chant, which require considerable rehearsal to be done well. Between those two extremes are numerous other settings of psalms or texts that rely on the psalms, such as those found in anthems and motets.

~

THE NATURE OF THE CHURCH'S SONG

If you ask about the nature of the church's song and how the church has used music in the rhythms of its worship, five categories are helpful to our discussion. The remarkable gift of music has carried the church's praise, prayer, proclamation, and story.[17]

A Song of Praise. The church's song is a song of praise. Many psalms—such as 98, 100, or 150—give expression to what is implicit throughout the Bible: God is to be praised, and music is one of the chief vehicles for expressing that praise. Many of the church's leaders and writers across the history of the church, Martin Luther one of the chief among them, repeat this theme forcefully.

A Song of Prayer. The song of the church is also a song of prayer. Many psalms and hymns are prayers. Some Christians would regard all their liturgies and even the music that clothes them as prayer. This view is no surprise, any more than using music as praise is cause for surprise. Human beings both laugh and weep. Laughter is the incipient form of sung praise, as weeping is the incipient form of sung prayer.[18] The two very often run into one another and coalesce.[19]

A Song of Proclamation. The church's song is also a song of proclamation. The author of Ephesians expressed this by saying, "But be filled with the Spirit, addressing one another in psalms and hymns and spiritual songs" (Eph. 5:18b-19a). Here it is clear that music is a means by which the gospel is proclaimed. Luther referred to the parallel verse in Colossians (3:16) and wrote:

> St. Paul...exhorted the Colossians to sing spiritual songs and Psalms heartily unto the Lord so that God's word and Christian teaching might be instilled and implanted in many ways.[20]

Much of the musical heritage of the church is exegetical or proclamatory: when we sing to the Lord music helps to proclaim, to interpret, to break open the word of God to people. That is in part what happens when the congregation sings. That is why, from ancient times, biblical readings have been sung or chanted. Motets by Schütz and chorale preludes, cantatas, and passions by Bach are more complex examples of the same intent. Without a proclamatory understanding of these pieces, they are incomprehensible.[21]

The Song as Story. A less obvious aspect of the church's song is upon reflection both the most obvious and the most profound: the church's music carries the church's story. When the people of God recount the history of God's mighty acts, they invariably sing. The morning stars "sang together" at creation on behalf of the people (Job 38:7). After their deliverance from Egypt, Moses and the people sang a song (Exod. 25:1-8). The reason for the psalmists' songs of praise is that God "has done marvelous things" (Ps. 98:10). New Testament canticles such as the Magnificat (Luke 1:47-55) and the Benedictus (Luke 1:68-79) are songs that recount God's mighty deeds. The songs of Revelation tell the story of God's mighty acts in an eschatological frame of reference. From the beginning of the biblical saga to its end, from one end of history to the other, the story is a song to be sung.

The biblical story is essentially the focus of the church's hymnody. The hymns in most hymnals could be laid out in a sequential fashion to relate the entire story of God's mighty acts—from creation through Old Testament history, Christ's incarnation, the church in the world between the times, to the last things. Individual hymns often tell the story by themselves. "Oh, love, how deep"[22] is a good example. Music is the vehicle by which the community remembers and celebrates what God has done—which leads to two further points about the church's song as story.

First, music has a peculiar communal and mnemonic character. A group that sings together becomes one and remembers its story over years and generations, discovering who it is in a particularly potent way. Christmas and Easter, birth and death have different sounds and communal memories when the story is sung. Hitler knew and exploited the demonic potential of this reality. Whenever the church loses its song, a vacuum is created that the Hitlers among us will invariably fill.

Second, music spins itself out through time, as does the story the song recounts, and as does worship where the song is sung. Music, therefore, is peculiarly suited not only to tell the story but to accompany worship as well. Music and worship both exist in time, and music serves as the means by which the time of worship is articulated. The gathering rite has its musical shape, as does the service of the word or any other component of the church's worship.

The Song as Gift. Finally, the church's song, like music itself, is a gift of God. Music is a joy and delight with which God graces creation. We do not bargain for it. We do not deserve it. It is simply freely given, there for the hearing and doing, a joyous overflow of creation's goodness. This gift is affirmed in one way or another by virtually all the traditions in the church.

~

IN, BUT NOT OF, THE WORLD

The church lives *in* but not *of* the world. The music that permeates the rhythms of the church's worship is simultaneously a part of the rhythms and music of the world in which the church finds itself. As an incarnational organism, the church has to make choices about what music it will and will not use. For more than the first thousand years of its history, the church chose unison chant with no musical instruments. This choice of the early church, which found instruments too closely allied with immorality and idolatry, determined its practice for centuries and still largely determines the practice of the Eastern Orthodox.[23]

Generally those of us in the Western church simply assume that instruments will be used in our worship. That is not an issue for most of us. We have other difficulties. The last several centuries have bequeathed to us three big ones.

The first concerns emotions or feelings. For most of the church's history, emotions have not been allied with music. Emotions surely were not absent when human beings sang or heard Gregorian chant or the music of composers such as Palestrina, Josquin, Schütz, and Bach, but emotions were not central nor to be sought, from the early church throughout the Middle Ages and past the Reformation.[24] Music's powerful emotional capacities were to be stewarded carefully lest they became idolatrous.

In the eighteenth century a change that had been brewing became evident. Erik Routley points to this change in John Wesley.

> There is in him [Wesley] a creative conflict...between the residue of Puritanism and a proleptic romanticism.... No seventeenth-century Puritan would have dreamed of saying that it was music's purpose, in or out of church, to arouse emotions; if it did, they did not approve it. But to John, music's primary purpose was just this.[25]

Wesley's "creative conflict" involves contradictions that are not easy to grasp. Some people may question whether Wesley thought arousing emotions was music's *primary* purpose, but Routley isolated a pivotal issue. The seventeenth- and eighteenth-century context certainly supported music's relationship to emotions and an emphasis on the heart.[26] Friedrich Schleiermacher systematized the whole mind-set when he defined piety as "essentially a state of feeling" and made this the linchpin of his systematic theology.[27] As I have written elsewhere:

> If everything is reduced to feelings and music is to arouse them, the implication is clear. Why are the church and its worship needed at all? Why are words or even faith needed? Why not let music do its thing outside the church at wordless symphony concerts, or at rock concerts where words become unimportant vocables to carry many decibels of liminal sound?[28]

The nineteenth century and its high art music generally enhanced such a mind-set and rode it into the twentieth century. Music and feelings were linked with the tacit assumption that one can get to the bottom of reality by means of music. Members of symphony orchestras and their conductors have often expressed such sentiments. For example, Georg Solti, the fine Hungarian conductor who led the Chicago Symphony Orchestra so well for many years, said the concert hall was his church. Rock musicians and their partisans have said similar things about their venues. Our culture simply assumes music is related to emotions and that truth lives somewhere in that mix. The church often makes the same cultural assumption.

A second inheritance has to do with using music as a technique. If music could be used to manipulate feelings and everything has to do with the heart and feelings anyway, some Christians asked why they could not use music to convert people. Sometimes high art musicians or their partisans in the church have explicitly or implicitly assumed music can be used to convert, though such a perspective became more obvious at the end of the nineteenth century, when Dwight Moody and Ira Sankey used the music of gospel hymnody this way.[29] A comparable point of view today calls music a tool. Charles Grandison Finney in the middle of the nineteenth century provided broad support for such a position by embracing various techniques for purposes of conversion. He believed there were techniques, such as the anxious bench, that could be used to convert people. Confessional Reformed and Lutheran writers such as John Nevin (*Anxious Bench*, 1843[30]) and Charles P. Krauth (*The Conservative Reformation and Its Theology*, 1871[31]) challenged this posture. They pointed to creeds, confessions, the liturgy, catechetical concerns, and conversion as a daily necessity. Their underlying if unwritten presupposition was that to presume to convert people by techniques is to assume we can take the place of God and render God needless or nonexistent.

A third inheritance for we who live after the industrial revolution and after the fall of the Berlin Wall and communism has to do with our commercial culture. The ideas that music is essentially allied to feelings, where truth resides, and that it can be used with other techniques or tools to get people to do something have now been folded into a commercial culture. Some people believe, therefore, that market analysis should control worship. If baby boomers do not like to confess their sins, they say, omit confessions. If people are offended by the cross or the name of Jesus Christ, do not have crosses in your worship space and leave out Jesus' name. If people do not want to hear lessons read, do not read from the Bible.

When Christians embrace such notions, they unwittingly support Ludwig Feuerbach's assertion that the essence of Christianity is that God is a projection of humanity.[32] Karl Barth might be right that such a position is "extraordinarily, almost nauseatingly trivial."[33] But a loud and visible portion of the Christian populace has trivialized the holy in its worship by assuming that if you analyze a given slice of the population properly, you will be able to choose the right music to produce the right feeling and thereby summon up God. The underlying premise is that Christianity is one more product to be sold, often by means of entertainment, and that by attracting numbers of people and citing statistics, we can fashion our salvation and guarantee the church's existence. It is not only the Ludwig Feuerbachs who will gradually realize the emperor has no clothes. Jan and John Nameless are beginning to perceive it and will see it more clearly in the next generation when they develop some historical perspective. If you can analyze the market and sell Christianity by musical or other means, they will find themselves saying with Ludwig Feuerbach that God is simply the extension of our needs and desires.

~

URGENT MATTERS FOR MISSION

The three propositions just described effectively deny God and the church, substituting for them ourselves and our human ability to sell a product called Christianity. Increasingly frenetic marketing schemes, forms of works righteousness, are necessary to keep the lie afloat. There is little question that a skilled sales force can draw many people for short periods. Radio and television talk shows demonstrate that. So might temple prostitution. Propaganda machines developed by our century's dictators have done the same thing. There is also little question that over the long haul, such a sales force or propaganda machine plays loose with truth and produces little longtime commitment. In the church that means truth is obscured by marketing, and discipleship evaporates. Or, in the words of Bonhoeffer:

> [L]ife together under the Word will remain sound and healthy only where it does not form itself into a movement, an order, a society, a *collegium pietatis*, but rather where it understands itself as being a part of the one, holy, catholic, Christian Church, where it shares actively and passively in the sufferings and struggles and promise of the whole Church.... When the way of intellectual or spiritual separation is taken the human element always insinuates itself and robs the fellowship of its spiritual power and effectiveness for the Church, drives it into sectarianism.[34]

Libby Larsen, a composer and perceptive musical analyst, suggests that we are living at the end of the romantic period with its roots in the nineteenth century. She may or may not be right about music, but her insight points beyond music. The roots of our theological dilemmas lie in the still unresolved nineteenth-century concern about the nature of the church, as the quotation from Bonhoeffer suggests. If the church is a voluntary organization such as the Rotary Club or the Boy Scouts, it is obvious that we are compelled to embrace the above three propositions that have backed us into our current corner. Then dichotomies such as maintenance and mission make sense. Mission comes to mean what it signifies in the mission statements that can be seen in virtually every business establishment today—getting more customers to prop up your own commercial enterprise, perhaps even to prop up a dying institutional shell. To adopt such a position is to allow the artificial bubble of church attendance after World War II to loom over our consciousness as an ideal. That leads us to seek to identify the church with a cultural envelope where a patina of full church buildings was characterized by Dwight D. Eisenhower's quip, "It doesn't matter what you believe as long as you're sincere about it."

If the Apostles' Creed ("I believe in...the holy catholic Church") is right, however, and if the church is an article of faith, sustained by God in Christ who promises that the gates of hell will not prevail against it and that Christ will be with us to the end of the age;[35] if Luther is right when he says in the Small Catechism that we cannot believe by our own efforts but that the Holy Spirit calls and gathers the church;[36] and if the triune God creates the church,[37] then the church as voluntary organization does not pertain. Distinctions such as maintenance and mission do not apply. Instead the church is seen as the organism it is.[38] Its New Testament character as the body of Christ poured out for the sake of the world radically alters everything. Then it is no longer necessary to attempt to subvert the institutions of the church and avoid the real issue of service to and proclamation in the world. Then it is no longer necessary to substitute feelings for word and sacrament, to substitute a presentation by a pastor or worship team for the liturgy, to substitute an entertainer for the pastoral office, or to substitute a group of spectators for the people in *their* office. Doing these things not only denies the very nature of the church, but commits us to creating yet another sectarian movement that will be out of date by the time we get it created. Those who presume to know what the twenty-first century will look like, who want current institutions and people to acquiesce to their control, have no more knowledge of the future than any other human beings.

$\sim$

Aᴄᴛ ᴏɴ ᴛʜᴇ ᴄʀᴇᴇᴅ ᴀɴᴅ ᴛʜᴇ ᴄᴀᴛᴇᴄʜɪsᴍ
If we are really serious about mission, we will train missionaries. We will not try to subvert the pastoral office by making its holders into pseudomissionaries, nor will we try to subvert the church's being by moving its furniture around or trying to replace it as if we could make the gospel relevant or attractive or anything else. The task is for us to be relevant to the gospel. We cannot make the gospel anything. It is what it is—good news, justification, forgiveness of sins, new life in Christ. Or, said in less theological language by Garrison Keillor:

> I think that the attempts of the church to modernize its message and to look and sound contemporary are almost always foolish and counterproductive. The church is a great mystery, and there is only so far that one can go in stating the mystery in terms that do not deny its mystique.[39]

The most urgent matter for mission, then, is to follow where scripture, creed, and catechism lead and to understand the church as sustained by God. To talk about music or anything else before that is a hopeless, sectarian dead end. Following scripture, creed, and catechism is in no way to suggest that the church will not change. Of course, it will change. It is the nature of an organism to change. The church lives creatively into all human cultures and their permutations, all sorts of experimentation are certainly welcome, and we have work to do to be a church that lives imaginatively into our culture. Change and our work are not at issue. It is hostile takeovers by those who use lies, deceit, and music as their tool that have no place, nor do attempts to turn worship into any of the things our century has sought to make it—high art, folk art, education, stewardship, concerts, evangelism, entertainment, political agendas, propaganda, or anything else. Attempts to go around musicians or other members of the church and attempts to destroy consensus or checks and balances that hedge in our sinful nature must likewise be eschewed. In place of the tactics of control that presume to know the future no human being can know, the organism of the church gives up its life for the life of the world, does not seek to preserve itself, and certainly does not set out to foment internal subversion, deceit, and intentional conflict by manipulating people with guilt and shame.

The ethical issue here is generated by an ecclesiological reality. The being of the church under God's sustenance frees us to treat one another with integrity. Once we get that right, we can begin to discuss music.

∼

GIVE VOICE TO THE CHURCH'S SONG

Musical matters can be divided into two categories: what relates to the gathered church and what relates to the church scattered out in the world. We begin with the gathered church, its inevitable impulse to sing, and some presuppositions.[40]

Presuppositions

The first presupposition is obvious from what has been said: the church has a song to sing and cannot keep silent.

A second is that the music we use for that song needs to be durable, well crafted, and of the finest quality—what we can grow into, not out of; what will serve us well as children, on our deathbed, and during the journey in between. This presupposition does not suggest the romantic notion that we must attempt to compose for eternity. Music composed for specific occasions has a long, faithful history and has often endured with far more stamina than pieces that set out to last forever. This principle does mean we must pursue good craft that treats people with the same respect and concern God does. Of course, there is a place for the throwaway, but that is not the central feature of our music. The song was there before we were born, it will be there long after we are dead, and the church musician's vocation is in part to sort out what is worth the church's time and effort over the long haul. The church itself over time will do the sorting whether we like it or not. It will only keep what is worth keeping.

That is exactly what happens with folk music as well as high art music. The body has different members, and the church musician's role in the body is partly to save the church some time and do the sorting for them. Yes, the church musician will make mistakes in the process, just as all human beings make mistakes. But with love for the people, innate abilities, and training in the discipline of church music, the cantor—my preferred term for the church musician because it highlights the task of leading the people's song[41]—is in the best position to figure this out with empathy.

A third presupposition is honesty. The music the cantor chooses and the way she or he uses it must have integrity and be neighborly. Music cannot be used with the intent to manipulate. Manipulation is tyranny, and, of all people, those of us who live in our century with the recent terror of the Hitlers and Stalins ought to know about that.

A fourth presupposition is that we have to deal fundamentally with the congregation's singing. From that center grow choirs, instrumental groups, and all manner of richly textured music making, with and without professionals.

Fifth, the musician must be musical. *Musical* means things such as this: phrasing that breathes; introductions and consistent spacing between stanzas of a hymn that make it clear when a congregation is to begin singing; tempos that fit the particular piece, and the time, place, people, and season; dynamics that are neither too quiet nor too loud, but that use the whole spectrum as appropriate to the occasion.

Sixth, the ideal music in any local church is not prerecorded music imported from some outside group, no matter how good or bad that group and its music may be. While we should learn from any and all sounds in the world around us, the ideal music in a local church is the sound the people themselves make around word and sacrament. That sound is what the church musician leads and why the musician is so important. To substitute external, extrinsic sounds for the sound of the people themselves is to contravene the very nature of the Christian worshiping community. Such substitution is the same as, maybe even worse than, piping in a sermon.

The Cantor

We have now come upon the need for the cantor, the church musician, the leader of the church's song. As always, the song of the people comes into being when someone composes it and leads it, the person I would call a cantor. This once unitary role is now often divided, so composers are separate from the musicians who lead us. We also have various sorts of musicians, some with full-time and some with part-time musical responsibilities, some with more and some with less ability and training.

Though composing and leading the people in their song is one of the most exciting things a human being could do, many able and committed composers and musicians have bailed out of their musical vocations among Christ's people because they have been treated so badly by the church. The church needs to engage the finest musicians it can find, encourage them, train them, and pay them adequately for their labor.

Engaging the Finest Musicians. Artists, among whom musicians are numbered, inevitably respond to their cultures by creating works of art that reflect their time and place. Their work is inauthentic when it reflects a time and place not their own. As in every age before us, we need to seek out the finest musicians. That search can be painful because our age is fractured. Our century's finest artists and musicians obviously reflect the fracture in their work. The church has a message that transcends the fracture, but it also knows the cross and ought therefore to be prepared to express pain and anguish with the utmost honesty.

The church in its post–World War II mode of embracing sincerity without the cross has avoided its own message, however, in a Gnostic bubble that floats artificially above the world we humans inhabit. It has tended, therefore, to shut out of its purview the finest music and musicians of our age. If we are honest about the gospel we have to proclaim and the context we have been given in which to proclaim it, we will reverse our course in this matter and not shrink from the reality we have to inhabit and express. As Christians we confess a faith in which Easter does not excise Good Friday, nor does Good Friday excise Easter. Rather, the cross stands on the road to resurrection. This reality needs to infuse our music. We cannot avoid it musically or in any other way.

Encouraging Them. If you treat people badly, you not only drive them away; you destroy their gifts and their abilities to express them. Perhaps you have witnessed, as I have, an able musician beaten down by a community. The result was inevitable. The musician's gifts withered and seemed to die. Perhaps you have then watched as that same musician was embraced and encouraged by another community. The result there was inevitable, too, but this time the outcome was healthy rather than diseased. The musician's gifts came to life again with new capacities not previously apparent.

The church at its core is a community of new life that affirms the music of God's good creation and those who have the gifts to craft and express it, then encourages these gifted people to exercise their craft freely. The church has often failed to acknowledge and act on its best instincts, however, choosing instead to deny its very essence and its responsibilities. Musicians have walked away and exercised their gifts elsewhere. We must repent and attend to our duty and delight by encouraging musicians.

Training Them. If we are to encourage musicians, we must train them. That means the institutions of the church must support and provide for this training. Schools of the church—especially colleges, seminaries, and other graduate schools—are the most obvious places for such training to occur.

We need degree programs, curricula, teachers, libraries, and churches where musicians can practice—as well as the financial support to pay for them. The need is for composers and practicing cantors who are trained theologically and musically, so that they know why they are doing what they are doing, and so that they have the skills to do it well. Two sorts of programs are required. One is for those who will enter full-time service, usually for people who plan to make church music their primary vocation and livelihood. The other is for part-time musicians who spend most of their time each week in other vocations, but who are very capable of using their musical gifts to serve effectively communities of Christians. Beneath the two types of programs and musicians lie two sorts of communities of faith, those with greater and those with lesser resources. Actually the spectrum is wider than the two extremes. An enormous variety exists between the two poles. None of these is better than another. We should give thanks for the entire spectrum and train musicians to lead vigorous congregational song in all its parts.

Paying Them. The laborer is worthy of his or her hire. If the church really is the incarnational organism we confess it to be, then its servants need to be able to put bread on their tables and roofs over their heads. As Luther said a long time ago, music is more worthy of support than many other things we do. The only way to support it is to pay for it, which includes paying musicians. The need to pay musicians is as obvious as the need to pay pastors and other servants of the church, but that is still hard for some congregations to comprehend. There are good reasons for this difficulty. Immigrant and poor communities had little money and few resources when they first came to this country. Honestly held pieties identified vocations in the church as necessarily voluntary or as close as possible to voluntary. The church has learned to give thanks for the positive aspects of this past while realizing our day presents different challenges. We have learned that we need to pay pastors equitably. We need to learn this lesson equally well for musicians.

Approaching the Task

The next need in giving voice to the church's song is to figure out how the cantor, the church musician, approaches the task of composing and leading it. This issue is addressed in curricula for training church musicians, but we can sketch out a few things here.

The cantor has to begin by choosing and composing music for congregations to sing. Questions immediately arise: Is the music well constructed, so it is worth the people's time and effort? Is it congregational? Can the people make sense of it? Do the words say what we mean to say? Is the text inclusive? Does it fit the flow of the service? Is there balance in a given service, balance over a season or a year, and balance in the use of the full biblical story and the psalms?

Texts need to be good poetry, friendly to the people—neither Shakespearean sonnets nor nursery rhymes, as Erik Routley might say. Ambrose, Clement Marot, Martin Luther, Isaac Watts, Charles Wesley, John Mason Neale, Catherine Winkworth, and the contemporary writers like the ones considered in *With Tongues of Fire*[42] are good examples.

For both music and texts we need to use:

1) the *old* and the *new*. The old helps us keep pace with our sisters and brothers who have sung the song before us and keeps alive for our children things they and their children will understand better than we do. The new helps us live into our time with its melodies and rhythms.

2) the *local* and the *catholic*. The local, what comes from our own community, helps us sing in the language of our people. The catholic helps us hear that the faith extends beyond us and helps the nomads of our society when they move around. The terms *ethnic* and *multicultural* could be used here, so long as they are not turned into useless shibboleths.

3) the *simplest* as well as the most *complex*. These words need to be understood in the context of a specific group. What is complex for one group of Christians may not be for another.

An enormous range of music is available to fit all our various
capacities and to reflect the richness of the faith. Another way
of stating this is to affirm both folk song and high art.

4) the *priestly* and the *prophetic*. God comforts and afflicts, consoles and judges. The words and music of the faith need to reflect that reality. If everything is saccharine, the faith is distorted, just as it is distorted if everything is angular and jagged. This point is related to the one made earlier about our music expressing the fullness of the faith from the cross to resurrection and all the themes that grow from that center.

When dealing specifically with the music of the congregation, the following should be considered:

1) Avoid long rests, or what amounts to the same thing, long tied notes. Congregations cannot count measures of silence or long held notes and then come in on fractions of beats.

2) The style has to be congregational, that is, folklike, not soloistic. Much of the music of our culture is solo music and will not work for congregational singing. What is overly emotive will not work either, partly because the more emotive it is the more soloistic it is, but also because overly emotive music can too easily belong to an in-group and become unwelcoming. The hymnody of the church is sometimes criticized because it appears to be the possession of an in-group. That is a fair criticism, similar to the perspective of C. S. Lewis, who regarded hymnody as the gang songs of the church. But you do not solve the problem by overemoting (and usually avoiding good craft in the process). Excess emotion increases the problem, because it makes hymn singing more closed to those outside the emotive circle. Congregational song is folklike, with a hardy and welcoming character.

3) Augmented and diminished intervals, major sixths, and sevenths are problems in congregational melody lines. With the exception of tunes that outline and prepare them carefully and support them with a clear harmonic structure, such intervals need to be avoided if a congregation is to sing.

4) Tunes have to gravitate to a tonal or modal center. As Béla Bartók discovered when he did his research in the Balkans, an atonal folk melody is impossible.

5) Tunes may be multimetric or syncopated, like the original form of the tune for "A mighty fortress is our God"[43] or the Jamaican tune LINSTEAD, which is used for "Let us talents and tongues employ."[44] Like these examples, patterns must be in a folklike idiom so human beings who do not practice before services can sing them.

6) Ranges and tessituras have to be where most people can sing. Climax and anticlimax notes can push the range, but you cannot transpose pieces up or down to a key that is comfortable to a given soloist. Nor can you group most notes of a melody below middle C or above treble C and expect congregations to sing.

7) Texts of strophic music should have the syllables structured the same way for every stanza. Soloists and choirs can add or subtract syllables, put more or fewer notes on the same syllable, or make all sorts of other alterations from stanza to stanza, but congregations will almost always have problems with these sorts of changes. Hymnody is a very disciplined business. Exercising its discipline is one of the ways cantors treat their congregations well and help them sing.

8) Simple psalm tones like those in *Lutheran Book of Worship*, their duplicates in *The United Methodist Hymnal*,[45] and the simplified Anglican chant in *The [Episcopal] Hymnal 1982*[46] are all friendly to a congregation and can be sung easily by people with or without musical training. Such tones work well with texts that have varying numbers of syllables from verse to verse. Unmodified Anglican chant and unmodified Gregorian tones, however, require much rehearsing. They work with choirs, not with congregations.

9) A good test for a piece of congregational music is whether it can stand alone without accompaniment. That does not mean accompaniments are bad or should not be used, though we usually are afraid to give the people their voice alone and should do it more often. It means the genre endemic to a congregation's song is what the congregation can do alone.[47] The more a piece depends on accompaniment, the less congregational it is likely to be.

We face an obvious dilemma when applying some of these measures. Our fractured age wants to break out of communal constraints and blast to pieces the musical checks and balances that make it possible for unrehearsed communities to sing together. At this point the Christian community sets a disciplined check on prophetic instincts that turn into antinomian snares and pronounces them idiosyncratic.

Obviously the music of choirs, organs, and other instruments is not subject to the same discipline as the congregation's song. Such music can and should be responsive to its own discipline, namely, the finest craft for the sake of the congregation. Because it is rehearsed, it does not have to and should not be poured only into the

mold of congregational strophic forms, psalm tones, or refrains.
The musician's first responsibility is to lead what might be called the
primary congregational "choir," but beyond that the cantor should
explore all manner of musical forms and styles that are only accessible to the congregation when it listens.

Organs

What about organs, our current favorite symbol for warring fac-
tions? Those who stare at the culture say everybody now alive
except for a few Luddites hates organs. Therefore junk them. Those
who stare at the church and like organs ask if it is that simple, then
note things like the number of organ builders, the number of
churches who keep installing new organs, and the number of people
(including many Asian Christians) who are attracted to them.

Behind the hyperbole lie different understandings of the church.
The organ has become a symbol for opposing ecclesiologies. If you
think you can start the church from scratch and disregard anything
from before the time you existed, you can junk anything you do not
like. If you think the church is a reality that precedes your being and
that each generation is called to reform what is presented to it, you
do not have the option of junking anything you please. Lutherans
have usually affirmed the latter option and denied the approach
that the first one necessitates. The organ is not the critical issue
here. It is a nonessential. It gives rise, however, to the deeper ecclesiological questions that need to be faced. Once we have some
clarity about them, we can make sense of less essential questions
such as those about the presence or absence of the organ.

You do not need an organ or any instruments at all in Christian
worship. All you need are human voices.[48] But if you are going to
have an instrument, the pipe organ still works best. It fills large
spaces with sound, makes sounds with air flowing through pipes
like the human voice, can therefore lead congregational singing
better than any other instrument, and can produce multiple lines
and various colors like an instrumental group with the advantage
that the sounds are under one person's control.

Second, questions of practicality and stewardship cannot be
avoided. For most congregations it is more efficient and better
stewardship for one person to practice than to attempt to get an instrumental group together week after week. Though organs cost a
lot, building a fine one is also better stewardship over the long haul
because it costs less than other instrumental solutions.

Third, worship has more life and vitality if instruments and instrumental groups are used from time to time in various configurations.

That does not suggest avoiding instruments or instrumental groups. I certainly want to use them often—all kinds of them, from orchestral and band instruments alone and in groups, to Orff instruments, bells, conga drums and other percussive pieces, and synthesizers. But breaking open texts with instrumental color is far more possible when those colors are used selectively rather than perpetually. Instruments can help us to focus on the texts; but they can also prevent us from hearing the text. That is apparently why the church persistently gravitates to unaccompanied unison song for its gatherings.[49]

Finally, one person can respond to the flow of a service in a way a group simply cannot. That is true even for those of us who improvise in the most elementary way. In virtually every worship service, there are moments when plans need to be modified. A sensitive organist can make the necessary adjustments. Even the most exceptional improvisatory instrumental group is hard-pressed to do the same thing as well.

The church has a long history of working out its relationship with the organ. The organ has a repertoire in all kinds of styles that is more deeply connected with the Christian faith than any other instrument. That alone suggests its teaching and evangelical value. When the literature is played well on real organs and used appropriately, almost everybody loves it—in spite of what we are being told to the contrary. The church will rediscover the pipe organ when the current hostilities have ceased. One hopes that will happen before a void is created and the church has done too much damage to music and musicians.

There are more organists and people interested in the organ than is admitted. If we lock up organs and do not let students practice on them, if we attack organs and do everything possible to discourage children who are fascinated by them, and if we pay organists slave wages or abuse them, of course we will not have them. All of this means we would be well advised to encourage, train, and pay organists well, as we should do with all church musicians and other servants of the church.

~

SING THE WORD IN THE WORLD, AND TEACH THE WORLD TO SING

The gathered church is not primarily about missionary activity. It is for the baptized who come together to be nourished by word and sacrament and then to be sent into the world as Christ's body. That is not to say the gathered congregation has no missionary relevance.

Visitors may well be compelled to seek baptism by entering a Christian service of worship. After all, the word of God is spoken there, the sacraments are received there, prayers for the world are offered there, and the congregation's song is heard there. These potent signs live under Jesus' promise and the Holy Spirit's breath. They are powerful both for believers and unbelievers. But they are not techniques under our control. Trying to harness them for what we think will be effective is to destroy them. They are more powerful than we think because God is more powerful than we think.

The song of the gathered church is for the baptized when they gather, hospitably open to the world, which is invited to listen and join. The church scattered, however, addresses its musical activity not to the baptized but to the world. It does this in two ways.

First, it simply sings its message in the world. There is a long history of the church's activity in this regard, probably symbolized best by oratorios. Whatever George Frederick Handel might have thought he was doing in *Messiah*—perhaps creating an entertainment that sold well in his English context, the content of which he may or may not have identified with the person of Christ—*Messiah* has, in fact, embodied the Christian message to countless people. So have the many oratorio-like compositions that set portions of scripture to music. In seventeenth-century Italy the intention to proclaim God's word was explicit when oratorios were constructed in two parts with a sermon between them. J. S. Bach's cantatas were meant to proclaim the word to gathered congregations, but they too have been employed outside worship in oratorio-like ways. So have all sorts of sacred concerts and their anthems and motets, again often taken out of the worshiping contexts for which they were originally intended and then used as proclamatory vehicles in the world.

There is no limit to the ingenuity of the church as it sings its message in and to the world. Radio, television, concerts, classrooms, restaurants, coffee houses, pubs, and other places where people gather are among the venues that offer these opportunities. A wide variety of styles to live into the culture's melodies and rhythms is possible. Let us be clear about this, however. Three desiderata must always be respected.

☐   Whatever is done needs to be honest. We are talking here about what is boldly proclamatory, and that is relentlessly honest. This is not an invitation to devious or manipulative attempts to sneak in a commercial for Jesus. That is tyranny, which denies the very freedom Jesus proclaims. What we are doing needs to be clear to those who engage us to do it.

☐ The quality needs to be of the highest order, not artificial slumming that treats people contemptuously. Of course, we identify with people in the various styles and linguistic envelopes their cultures bequeath to them. That is not the same, however, as playing down to them on the premise that they have no capacity to comprehend the finest of their and others' cultures. Trying to use commercial culture to sell them something is the most devious design of all. We are about liberating them from their bondage, whatever that may turn out to mean for them, not driving them farther into it as if we have all the answers and the right to control them.

☐ As in retreats, prayer groups, and study groups, the momentary energy of any gathering that hears the word in a certain musical envelope always has the potential to turn from a healthy group spirit into an unhealthy transmutation where wholeness is lost and partiality embraced. The enthusiasm of a given group can lead it to think it has to force its music on the whole church. Then comes the danger of the movements and orders Bonhoeffer described. The partiality of sectarian division, musical or otherwise, always has to be informed and corrected by the catholic whole. That is, no pious conventicle or group however large is the whole church, no matter what its music may be.[50] All of our groups have an idolatrous impetus. We are all required to keep pace with the catholic whole lest we turn into sectarian, lifeless, and ingrown streams.

The second way the church addresses its musical activity to the world is in service. This address is not proclamatory, though it is always possible that the word will explode when we least expect it, and elements of prayer, praise, and testimony can never be excluded from the explosion. At the level of human intention, however, the church's address is about serving the world by teaching it to sing, to play, and to delight in the joy of music.

At this point we make common cause with all those who constructively teach and practice music in the world—music educators, symphony orchestras, choral groups, small ensembles, good folk and popular groups, and theater and dance musicians. There is no reason for us to duplicate what is already happening well. We are best advised to support it.

There are more and more communities, however, where music is now neglected in schools and the public arena generally. There the church ought to fill the vacuum with the finest possible individual instruction, as well as with the finest instrumental and choral groups. We can teach the world to sing and to play. And we should do it with duty and delight.

We not only can teach the world to sing. We can delight in it with music that fills the whole sacred and secular creation with wonder, lament, and joy. If we believe the first article of the creed, we will know the music of the world participates in God's good created order—broken, of course, but incipiently good. Concert series can be set in motion. Trained individuals and groups can sing and play for old people or young people or anybody else. They can help us to dance. The overflow of God's gift of music in the creation is not only for a certain segment of the population. It is for everybody. The church knows this reality and can meet the need.

Just as numerous historical models show us how to proclaim the word in the world, symbolized by oratorios, so numerous historical models show us how to serve the world with music. These are symbolized by Christian music educators who have taken their musical responsibilities into the world, and by choral and instrumental groups that church-related colleges have spawned. The work these individuals and groups have done for generations is remarkable. Those who attack it today are engaged in one of the most wrongheaded and counterproductive moves imaginable.

In sum, if we are faithful, we will be the body of Christ we receive; give voice to the song around word, font, and table; and let the song spill out into the world. If we pour ourselves out for the life of the world, musically and in every other way, we will stop seeking to preserve ourselves. Then the ingrown madness Amos warned us against will cease, and justice will roll down as we sing the ancient song of the renewed creation into the future where Christ has ascended and leads us.

NOTES

1. John W. Doberstein, introduction to *Life Together* by Dietrich Bonhoeffer, trans. Doberstein (New York: Harper & Brothers, 1954), 8.

2. For a few more reflections about this, see Paul Westermeyer, *Let Justice Sing: Hymnody and Justice* (Collegeville, Minn.: Liturgical Press, 1998), 22–24.

3. These are expanded in Paul Westermeyer, "How Shall We Worship?" *Reformed Liturgy and Music* 31, no. 1 (1997): 3–10, an article originally prepared for the Faith, Reason, and World Affairs Symposium, Concordia College, Moorhead, Minnesota (September 17, 1996), with parts drawn from lectures at the Worship and Music Conference, Albuquerque, New Mexico (July 14–19, 1996).

4. *The Use of the Means of Grace: A Statement on the Practice of Word and Sacrament* (Evangelical Lutheran Church in America, 1997), application 18A.

5. As the preparation for baptism in the early church and in contemporary catechumenal materials indicates. See *Welcome to Christ: Lutheran Rites for the Catechumenate* (Minneapolis: Augsburg Fortress, 1997).

6. See Melva Wilson Costen, *African American Christian Worship* (Nashville: Abingdon Press, 1993), 27, 57–64, for discussion of the freedom African American slaves realized inhered in baptism.

7. For a description of the Sabbath and Sunday, see Therry Maertens, *A Feast in Honor of Yahweh*, trans. Kathryn Sullivan (Notre Dame, Ind.: Fides Publishers, 1965), 152–92.

8. *The Use of the Means of Grace*, application 34B.

9. Ibid.

10. For more detail, see Paul Westermeyer, *Te Deum: The Church and Music* (Minneapolis: Fortress Press, 1998), chap. 3, from which the following has been distilled. For yet more detail but still a brief overview of the shape of the psalter, the psalms, and their relationship to the church's worship, see Massey H. Shepherd Jr., *The Psalms in Christian Worship* (Collegeville, Minn.: Liturgical Press, 1976).

11. See James McKinnon, *Music in Early Christian Literature* (Cambridge: Cambridge University Press, 1987), 126.

12. Andreas Heinz, ed., *Die Psalmen als Stimme der Kirche* (Trier: PaulinusVerlag, 1982). Eric Werner, *The Sacred Bridge* (London: Dennis Dobson, 1960), 128, says "the one book of the Old Testament that came to be the backbone of most liturgies [was] the Psalter."

13. Willi Apel, *Gregorian Chant* (Bloomington, Ind.: Indiana University Press, 1958), 74, notes that all the early Christian writers who mention the psalms say they were sung.

14. In James Laster, *Catalogue of Choral Music Arranged in Biblical Order*, 2nd ed. (Metuchen: The Scarecrow Press, 1996), musical settings of texts from the entire Bible are listed. Of the 613 pages, 270 provide texts from the psalms. Apel, *Gregorian Chant*, 87, points out that the book of Psalms has been "called the most influential single source of texts in all music history."

15. *Lutheran Book of Worship* (Minneapolis: Augsburg Publishing House; Philadelphia: Board of Publication, Lutheran Church in America, 1978), 290–91.

16. Igor Stravinsky, *Symphony of Psalms (Symphonie de Psaumes) for Chorus and Orchestra* (London: Boosey & Hawkes, 1948).

17. For more detail see Paul Westermeyer, *The Church Musician*, rev. ed. (Minneapolis: Augsburg Fortress, 1998), chap. 4, from which the following is distilled.

18. Cf. Joseph Gelineau, *Voices and Instruments in Christian Worship* (Collegeville, Minn.: Liturgical Press, 1964), 15–19.

19. For a very helpful discussion of the primal nature and close relation of prayer and praise, as well as their relation to thanksgiving and proclamation, see Patrick D. Miller Jr., *Interpreting the Psalms* (Philadelphia: Fortress Press, 1986), 64–78.

20. "Preface to the Wittenberg Hymnal, 1524," in *Luther's Works,* ed. Helmut T. Lehmann (Philadelphia: Fortress Press, 1965), 53:316.

21. See Robin A. Leaver, "The Liturgical Place and Homiletic Purpose of Bach's Cantatas," *Worship* 59, no. 3 (May 1985): 194–202; Leaver, *J.S. Bach as Preacher: His Passions and Music in Worship* (St. Louis: Concordia Publishing House, 1984).

22. *LBW*, no. 88.

23. The congregation's singing in sixteenth-century Wittenberg, Strasbourg, and Geneva followed a variation on the same principle of unaccompanied unison song. In our day, though harmonies and accompaniments appear more readily, wherever the congregation's song is respected most deeply and finds its strongest voice, the underlying push is in the same direction. Such song appears in Taizé; the Iona community; Asian, African, African American, and Hispanic congregations where the people's singing has vitality; Lutheran congregations that can sing the first and second settings of the rite of Holy Com-

munion from *LBW* without accompaniment, and many of whom once sang the third setting from *LBW* unaccompanied in its former version (*Service Book and Hymnal* [Minneapolis: Augsburg Publishing House; Philadelphia: Board of Publication, Lutheran Church in America, 1958]); and under the leadership of John Bell, Alice Parker, Ken Nafziger, Mary Oyer, Michael Hawn, John Ferguson, David Cherwien, Mark Sedio, Michael Burkhardt, and Marty Haugen. As the decibel level and hype of music in worship increase, it becomes increasingly clear why the unaccompanied unison line is so central: the text remains the focal point and cannot be avoided or obscured; the congregation can sing it, is vulnerable, has to learn and assume its office from the inside out and without surrogates, and is not manipulated by external and potentially erotic controls.

24. See, for example, Quentin Faulkner, *Wiser Than Despair: The Evolution of Ideas in the Relationship of Music and Christianity* (Westport, Conn.: Greenwood Press, 1996), 104 and 124.

25. Erik Routley, *The Musical Wesleys* (London: Herbert Jenkins, 1968), 23.

26. I have tried to sketch this context in *Te Deum*, 226.

27. Friedrich Schleiermacher, *The Christian Faith*, vol. 1, English trans. of the 2nd German ed. (1830), ed. H. R. Mackintosh and J. S. Stewart (New York: Harper & Row, 1963), 11.

28. Westermeyer, *Te Deum*, 229–30.

29. See Ira D. Sankey, et al., *Gospel Hymns Nos. 1 to 6 Complete* (New York: Da Capo Press, 1972), unabridged republication of the "Excelsior Edition" published originally in 1895.

30. John W. Nevin, *The Anxious Bench*, 2nd ed. (Chambersburg, Penn.: Publication Office of the German Reformed Church, 1844), reprinted in *Catholic and Reformed: Selected Theological Writings of John Williamson Nevin*, ed. Charles Yrigoyen Jr. and George H. Bricker (Pittsburgh: The Pickwick Press, 1978). Nevin published *The Anxious Bench* in 1843, then revised and enlarged it in a second edition in 1844.

31. Charles P. Krauth, *The Conservative Reformation and Its Theology* (Philadelphia: J. B. Lippincott & Co., 1871; Minneapolis: Augsburg Publishing House, 1963).

32. This paragraph is distilled from Paul Westermeyer, "The Anxious Bench or Let God Be God," *The New Mercersburg Review* 24 (autumn 1998): 9, originally prepared for the Mercersburg Convocation, *Ecumenical Vision: A Lutheran and Reformed Conversation*, June 11, 1998, Trinity United Church of Christ, York, Pennsylvania.

33. Ludwig Feuerbach, *The Essence of Christianity*, trans. George Eliot (New York: Harper & Brothers, 1957), xix.

34. Dietrich Bonhoeffer, *Life Together*, 37.

35. Matthew 16:18; 28:20.

36. The Small Catechism 2, 6, in *The Book of Concord: The Confessions of the Evangelical Lutheran Church*, trans. and ed. Theodore G. Tappert et al. (Philadelphia: Fortress Press, 1959), 345.

37. *The Use of the Means of Grace*, heading for principle 2.

38. I take it that when the Augsburg Confession defines the church as the "assembly of saints in which the Gospel is taught purely and the sacraments are rightly administered" (The Augsburg Confession 7.1, in *The Book of Concord*, 32), the meaning is not that the church appears and disappears when preaching and the administration of the sacraments begin and end, but that a rhythm of the assembly is implied in the visible gathering and invisible scattering to be what it is: the body and blood of Christ it has received.

39. Quoted from *Books and Culture*, July/August 1998, in Martin Marty, *Context* 30, no. 19 (November 1, 1998): 3–4.

40. The following material about the gathered church is partly taken from Westermeyer, *The Church Musician*, chapter 11, reorganized and reworked with additions.

41. See Westermeyer, *The Church Musician*.

42. Paul Westermeyer, *With Tongues of Fire: Profiles in 20th-Century Hymn Writing* (St. Louis: Concordia Publishing House, 1995).

43. *LBW*, no. 228.

44. *With One Voice: A Lutheran Resource for Worship* (Minneapolis: Augsburg Fortress, 1995), no. 754.

45. *The United Methodist Hymnal* (Nashville: United Methodist Publishing House, 1989).

46. *The Hymnal 1982* (New York: Church Hymnal Corp., 1985).

47. See n. 23.

48. Aidan Kavanagh, in typically trenchant language, says it well: "The human voice is the premier instrument in liturgical worship, and its basic repertoire is the psalms. Mechanical devices are secondary at best, and their various repertoires are frequently tangential to the assembly's liturgical purpose." Aidan Kavanagh, *Elements of Rite: A Handbook of Liturgical Style* (New York: Pueblo Publishing, 1982), 32.

49. See n. 23.

50. It will be remembered that the Donatist congregation down the street from St. Augustine may have been louder and larger than his congregation.

Ritual Practice: Into the World, Into Each Human Heart

Michael B. Aune

AWARD-WINNING poet and author Kathleen Norris writes the following about worship in her recent book *Amazing Grace: A Vocabulary of Faith:*

> In worship, disparate people seek a unity far greater than the sum of themselves but don't have much control over how, or if, this happens. Recklessly, we let loose with music, and the words of hymns, the psalms, canticles, and prayers. We cast the Word of God out into the world, into each human heart, where, to paraphrase the prophet Isaiah, it needs to go to fulfill God's purpose. Isaiah uses the metaphor of rain to convey this—rain that disappears into the ground for a time, so that we can't see it working. And then, it bears abundantly.[1]

Her observations both echo the claim that worship has an intent of some kind and exemplify a concern with what happens in this activity. Contemporary studies of the phenomenon we call "ritual" or "ritual/izing"[2] are similarly concerned with showing both how and why certain things happen to and for those who take part. Ritual, once regarded as superstitious, magical, pathological, or just plain weird is now widely recognized to be powerful and empowering.[3] Ritual/izing is now seen to be a central dynamic in human affairs, capable of creating and renewing communities, transforming human identities, and remaking one's most existential sense of being in the cosmos. It is at once a "technology of power" and a "moral economy of the self."[4]

This theoretical way of speaking about an activity familiarly

RITUAL
PRACTICE:
INTO THE
WORLD,
INTO EACH
HUMAN
HEART

known to us as "worship" or "liturgy" might strike us as either unnecessarily complicated or stunningly abstract. So we might wonder, "Why bother at all? What could we possibly learn from this kind of discourse, one that seems so far removed from flesh-and-blood worshipers and their concerns?" Perhaps our very resistance indicates there might be something about this kind of discourse that is unsettling or challenging. Perhaps we become aware that we do have certain expectations for and about worship in the church because of our participation in it over time or because we have learned something of what the theology of our tradition says is going on there.

One of the benefits of ritual theory is to make us think about these expectations and the assumptions on which they rest. It is useful to recall that *theory* comes from the Greek *thea*, "a looking at" (the same root that gives us the word *theater*). This etiology reminds us that we have a stance, a point of view, one that provides us eyes with which to see. And what do we see when we look at the worship of the church? In the first part of this chapter, I want to consider some insights of ritual theory, asking what these can tell us about liturgical practice that we may not have noticed before. In addition, I want to explore how these insights about ritual/izing may deflate some myths we hold.

On the basis of these questions and challenges, in the second part I will turn attention to the claims we are fond of making about the relationship between what goes on in our liturgical assemblies and what goes on in the world—in short, the relationship between liturgy and mission. We will discover that the questions generally ignored or suppressed by liturgical scholarship turn out to be the very questions we need to address—questions about subjectivity (there are, after all, subjective worshipers worshiping), about liturgical style (are these simply choices between carpet and stone, mechanical amplification and natural sound, Gregorian chant and guitars—or something else, such as ethics and aesthetics?), and about the vexed relationship between what we call doctrine and practice. As we shall see, it is precisely when we address these sorts of questions that ritual theory offers us some much needed assistance and perspective.

WHY RITUAL THEORY?

Historical and theological approaches to worship are concerned for the most part with either clarifying how this activity is patterned or

interpreting what worship means, given particular doctrinal claims
and promises. For example, it is argued that the study of liturgical history can reveal a simplicity and directness of both the design and dynamic of what Christians do when they gather together. The current emphasis on the importance of the ordo or the core of this activity as including gathering, proclaiming the word, offering the intercessions of the people, eating the Lord's supper, and sending the people into the world for mission has emerged from this kind of historical inquiry into the roots of Christian worship. Similarly, to say that what occurs in worship is an encounter with God that equips believers for action in the world would be an example of an interpretation based on a doctrinal claim and promise.

Although such approaches toward understanding worship implicitly recognize that the patterning, doing, and interpreting of Christian worship is based on the notion that it is always something done by someone, somewhere, sometime, someplace, such historical and theological approaches are in the long run finally unable to articulate what really goes on in this activity and how it is significant or meaningful to those who are taking part. Nor are we able to discern very well what this activity effects in the lives, communities, and worlds of worshipers.

The particular concerns of ritual theory are generated by lived practice itself. Although liturgical theologians might say that they are emphasizing practice—for example, "liturgy is primarily an act as opposed to a theory or a creed,"[5] they are in fact making claims for what liturgy *is* in a world of theological ideas *about* practice, rather than carefully examining what particular practices might indeed do (or not do).[6]

Ritual theorists, however, are interested in learning the fine art of "scratching surfaces" of experience.[7] Consider the following:

> On our knees in church (even in the cathedral) we are face to face with the bare facts of our humanity. We praise Him, we bless Him, we adore Him, we glorify Him, and we wonder who is that baritone across the aisle and that pretty woman on our right who smells of apple blossoms.... The door at the back creaks open and we wonder, Who has just come in...? Who is the boy in the plaid shirt? When was he confirmed? Why is the lady in the first pew crying? And even as the service rises to the great poetry of the Bread and Wine we continue our observations. We see that the acolytes' red plush cushion is nailed to the oak floor of the chancel and that the altar cloth is embroidered with tulips. And then for a moment a man's knowledge of His magnificence and man's giftedness draws together, in at least a promise of ecstasy, all these bare and disparate facts.[8]

RITUAL
PRACTICE:
INTO THE
WORLD,
INTO EACH
HUMAN
HEART

These reflections by John Cheever direct our attention to the obvious but often ignored surface of an actual service of worship. A small church, sideways glances, distractions, questions, ongoing observations—this is liturgy. A ritual theorist might wonder, does liturgy proclaim what these worshipers believe? What would be the tacit theology in the rite (experience) Cheever recounts? What kind of theology is embodied by furtive questioning, wandering thoughts, and "the great poetry of Bread and Wine"? Whatever we think liturgy is, it is always an embodied practice, regardless of what theologians or pastors intend or claim is "the real meaning." Marjorie Procter-Smith reminds us, "Liturgical 'truth,' then, is not at all an abstract truth or a purely intellectual truth, but an engaged, embodied, and particular truth, a truth that cannot only be talked about, but must be done."[9]

To say, therefore, as does this volume, that the liturgical event has a missional intent "in the midst of the world, for the life of the world"[10] is only a claim. A ritual theorist would ask, How does this happen? As we move in this direction of inquiry, we begin to learn something about what theory is and what it can do. We will begin to realize that it makes us think. It forces us to examine our assumptions. It calls us to a more rigorous examination of what we thought we knew about worship. Ritual theory increases self-consciousness and self-criticism.

If we are to forge or discover some connection between what worshipers are doing in their worship and what they are to be doing in the world, we cannot be content merely to study texts, even liturgical texts. We need to observe the performance or strategic use of texts and other ritual paraphernalia in particular worshiping communities. The trick is to move from textual study and theological claim, the level of intended meaning, toward the living, breathing beings who stand, sit, speak, listen, look, walk, kneel, eat, and drink. Our attention must begin to focus on "the surface of things," for the overall doing of worship happens *somewhere* and looks and sounds like *something*.

A turn toward ritual theory can also remind us that all theological reflection is for the people who comprise the church and for the enhancement of their life in the world. It seeks to understand and account for both the ongoing human experience of God and community and the abiding significance of this experience in human living. The purpose of theology, therefore, is

> to inform the practice of being human in rites specifically and beyond them. In relation to Christian worship the question is one of the total relational aspect of our lives (i.e., relationship to God; to ourselves; to community; the world/past/present/future; self: soma, spirit, affect, cognition, action, ethics).[11]

There is much in our theological traditions that asserts that MICHAEL B.
AUNE worship is not really a matter of articulating the abstract meaning of what is being enacted but rather something having to do with being concretely human. We hear that this activity moves hearts, raises minds to God, and manifests sanctification in signs perceptible to the senses. This turn to the subject, or to worshipers, however, remains largely ignored or undeveloped by liturgical scholars because we fear the so-called excesses of our culture that allegedly privilege the subjective at the expense of the objective, and we do not want our worship to take the same turn.

Yet ritual theorists, who desire to direct inquiry toward lived practice, remind liturgical theologians that the focus of their reflection is indeed a particular human experience of worship.[12] This experience, however, more than some intense, high-voltage emotional experience or some perceived level of intimate community. There is concrete evidence that "ritual participation quite often moves people to tears, and sometimes to conversion, joy or cure...."[13] Ritual/izing serves as a vehicle of both deep emotion and affective change.[14]

As students of Christian worship have come to realize that the tried and true methods of historical, theological, and pastoral study of liturgical structures and texts are not going to enable us to interpret lived practice adequately, they have turned to various interdisciplinary approaches to cultural phenomena for the tools and concepts with which to explore more fully religious activity and the qualities of human action.[15] Exactly what the experience of worship is continues to be troublesome for contemporary liturgical study, as some recent uncritical uses of ritual theory illustrate.

For example, we find an appeal to a notion of ritual/izing that emphasizes its creative, expressive, and transformative capacities. Simply because these capacities may characterize ritual activity in some cultures and communities does not necessarily imply they function similarly in our contexts. There is no such thing as some basic mechanism or universalizing quality that, once we know what it is, will tell us how and why ritual works. Although some scholars have argued that our understanding of how and why people and communities engage in ritual/izing needs more pliability and nuance, nonetheless the tendency to overromanticize its effectiveness seems to continue unabated.

We observe such romanticizing in the various claims for the creativity of ritual/izing. It is claimed, for example, that initiation rites can cure juvenile delinquents or that communing with the earth will make right our relationship with the environment. Or perhaps

RITUAL
PRACTICE:
INTO THE
WORLD,
INTO EACH
HUMAN
HEART

ritual activity is even more powerfully salvific than this, healing all the ills that afflict modern life. This kind of romanticizing extends to the scholarly realm as well. There we hear about how ritual is rooted in the "eternal wisdom of ancient peoples" or that our capacity to ritualize is the result of some prelinguistic grammar or the residue of our "pre-reptilian brains."[16]

What is especially noteworthy and potentially troubling about such testimonies and scholarly efforts is their notion that ritual/izing is independent of any sociocultural or historical context, "a pure, inadequately tapped human resource for ameliorating the evils of modernity—specifically, the personal and communal wholeness fractured by ethnicity, religious ideology, and areligious passivity."[17] Surprisingly, there are liturgical scholars who operate with this essentially acultural and ahistorical approach. It is stated, for example, that activities such as worship and ritual are transformative. The intent is to refigure the self as a self-in-community in Christ. Such refiguring, it is argued, results in the sharing of the fruits of that new self-understanding in the political, social, economic, and ethical realms of this world. This transformation is inaugurated by worship, and if this does not happen, then the body of Christ is not built up. Ultimately, however, "the mark of liturgy upon human existence is measured by the refigured self of the act of appropriation."[18] This line of thinking suggests that the effect of worship is measured by the production of a refigured self who has indeed appropriated a different way to be, to be with others, to be with God, to be with the world.

Nagging and painful questions, however, are posed by such a purely consequential understanding of the relationship between ritual/izing and daily life. By extolling the capacity of this activity to transform everything or to construct a just, creative, and peaceable community, do we do justice to the struggle, agony, and conflict that often mark such an experience? Have we adequately addressed the questions of renewal, repentance, and the splits and contradictions of being human? Do communities that are just, creative, and peaceable actually exist, either inside or outside of the ritual/izing context? Faced with such questions, it seems that we emphasize community all the more, trying to enhance its tangible and authoritative presence, while forgetting that our exaggerations actually might undermine the capacity of ritual activity to do anything. As one scholar has written, "[M]any liturgies lose authority primarily from lack of modesty. They are trying too hard to be too much, to claim too much. [Worship] alone cannot do all the things [we] want it to do."[19]

As we return to the particular concern of this volume, one that seeks to make the connections between the church's worship and the church's mission in the world, is it possible that we, too, are not modest enough in what we are claiming? Are we unwittingly operating with a notion of ritual activity that theorists have termed "consequential"—meaning that it can solve problems in the sense of making them go away or overcoming those contradictions between religious and social values?[20]

Is this really what ritual/izing does? If we reflect on our own experience as a worshiper or a leader of worship, we would probably have to admit that no wholesale transformation of ourselves or of the social world has happened—not yet anyway. Only rarely might we actually witness such an occurrence. Yet

> [i]t would be nice, if Christians leaving their Christmas mass walk out on a world where the reality of the Christian promise makes them over into more hopeful charitable Christians, where even the most mean-spirited Scrooge among them sees the light, as we say....[21]

By admitting this lack of transformation, however, are we only revealing our own Lutheran "situatedness," which reminds us that in this world of contingencies and relativities, signs of grace are never unambiguous? If we admit that concepts of transformation are likely to be grandiose and abstract, how then can we identify and reframe our expectations and experiences of worship?

Here, a distinction made by ritual theorists helps us. Ritual/izing's efficacy is both doctrinal and operational.[22] The former refers to explanations a religion offers as to how and why this activity works. Doctrinal claims assert the function of ritual/izing within a religious system and imply certain effects that occur in the relationship between God or gods and adherents. An example of doctrinal efficacy would be the assertion that in Christian worship's gesture, word, and song, the mystery of salvation revealed in Christ's death and resurrection somehow becomes once more an event in the presence of believers at worship—an event with consequences for how they are to live in this world toward God and with others.

Operational efficacy refers to the actual communicative, sociopsychological effects on the participants. Such effects are notoriously difficult to determine, however, because those who study and interpret a particular instance of ritual/izing are brought face to face with the participants themselves. It is well known, for example, that participants cannot always explain what has happened or what exactly it is that they have experienced. The consequences may be

RITUAL
PRACTICE:
INTO THE
WORLD,
INTO EACH
HUMAN
HEART

largely unconscious or may have occurred in only one or a few people. Yet students of ritual doggedly persist in trying to understand how acts of ritualizing might have, or indeed, do have significant effects, successfully convince or move their participants, or succeed on the operational level of having social or communicative effects on people.

If we do pay attention to the experiences participants have, we discover that they report an imparting of feelings and a reinforcing of relationships take place.[23] Whatever they express does not seem to be the result of successful forays into the densest forest of symbols nor the hermeneutically adept cracking of metaphorical and structural codes. Rather, participants speak of the significance of ritual participation in an emotionally laden language of family, relationship, and commitment. Language such as "belonging," "feeling understood," "being able to function sensibly as a person with human values," indicates something that is largely, if not fundamentally, social and affective in nature. Thus, the effort of creating and locating togetherness seems to involve both a realization of the self and a transcendence of the self.[24] The knowing and being known, the loving and being loved that are experienced in ritual could be, on further theological reflection, concrete instances of what a tradition claims about the efficacy of its rituals. But how might this further theological reflection be pursued in a way that is both alert to the theoretical insights offered by ritual scholarship and attentive to the intellectual and methodological resources of a particular religious—in this instance, Christian—tradition?

A key insight emerges when one remembers that ritual/izing is considered as a particular quality of activity that is differentiated from other, usually more daily activities. As such, this way of acting is a strategic medium of a distinctive sort that seeks to deal practically with some specific circumstance (for example, a wedding or a funeral). This specificity means that ritual/izing, whether awesome or austere, is "inherently historical."[25] Hence, there is no such thing as a basic mechanism or universal quality that characterizes this activity independently of particular social, historical, and cultural contexts. We need to be aware of "the imperialistic and reductionistic dangers of imposing general interpretations forged from one culture onto data from alternative cultures."[26]

What is becoming clear is the necessity of close historical work for understanding how ritual/izing is variously located, constituted, and invoked by people, communities, and liturgical traditions. Any theological and pastoral study concerning ritual practice needs to remember that our own locating, constructing, and questioning are

shaped by the styles, practices, and expectations that we operate out
of today as we ritualize and attempt to understand what and how we ritualize. If we succeed in taking ritual/izing down from the shelf of abstraction and begin to historicize it as a particular way of acting and speaking, what might we begin to discover?

～

INTERLUDE—MOVING FROM THE THEORETICAL
TO THE THEOLOGICAL

As we undertake the task of historicizing and contextualizing Lutheran worship, we encounter at the outset an ambivalence, even an embarrassment, about sixteenth-century decisions to reshape both practice and piety (that is, a particular way of being a believer). We hear, for instance, that there is no such thing as "Lutheran liturgy" at all but only the Western rite as Lutherans have used it.[27] Although this point is indeed subtle, reminding us of our confessional commitments to an ecumenical, catholic pattern of word and sacrament and that corporate worship dare not be whimsically changed, it is nonetheless wrong because of the distorted image it presents. The distortion, moreover, presupposes a dismissal of specific ways and attitudes toward doing worship.[28] Yet we can say theologically as well as anthropologically that doctrine, forms of piety, and congregational worship that are called Lutheran do continue to give shape and intensity to human experience and to understandings of self, God, and world. Behind these matters looms the larger theological question of God's relationship to the world.

It is the Lutheran Reformation's response to this larger question that produced its reconceptualization and reconstruction of late-medieval Christianity's symbolic order. This response is variously described as "justification by faith," "the rediscovery of the gospel," and "an encounter with and discovery of the word of God." Although there is general agreement that this theological insight grew out of particular concerns with biblical interpretation and the sort of language that could be the gospel's "living voice," the matter of approaching and understanding the ensuing ritual expressions of such a religious experience and theological interpretation is much more controverted.

From the vantage point of ritual theory, we can better appreciate what the early Lutheran movement was up to with its liturgical redesign. The practices of late-medieval Catholicism asserted both that divine power was embodied in the church, the sacraments, and the sacerdotal office, and that this power was capable of working all

RITUAL
PRACTICE:
INTO THE
WORLD,
INTO EACH
HUMAN
HEART

sorts of wonders in the natural order.[29] The early Lutheran move-ment, however, engaged in a concerted ritual and theological effort to regard the workings of such power in a radically different manner. Instead of arrogantly claiming that God's unfettered sover-eignty could be controlled and manipulated, Lutheran reformers posited a different vision of reality and thereby a different ritual/izing strategy, one concerned with directing participants to places where God has already promised to be truly available and therefore presently embodied.

Hence, instead of asserting that the purpose of ritual activity is to actualize holy, potent objects, we are to seek its efficacy within the framework of the *bonum commune*—"the common good," where men and women can get on with day-to-day living, "confi-dent about the ultimate matters."[30] As the post-communion prayer of Luther's *Deutsche Messe* expresses it, the public, theological claim for a reconceptualized form and practice is that it strengthens and increases "faith toward thee [that is, God] and fervent love among us all."[31]

This reorientation of form and practice, as a ritual theorist would point out, involves a changed technology of power as well as a different moral economy of the self. Taking the example of the Lutheran reformers, then, we might say that the technology of power active in ritual/izing changes radically, now having to do with the expression, construction, and embodiment of a distinctive kind of influence located in a ministry of word, proclamation, and sacrament rather than in a hierarchical, priestly, and sacramental complex. Regarded as divine *influence,* power seems more posi-tive—not as malevolent, specific, and threatening as the term *force* might imply.[32] Thus, a better way to regard power emerges: power as constitutive of all social relationships and practices. Here power becomes an effective strategy in social relationships by which some-thing is done on behalf of others.

For the Lutheran reformers, then, the speech, song, and gesture of ritual activity are born of the desire to empower the participants so that the communities and worlds in which they live can be dis-covered, experienced over time, and embraced as beloved of God. Ritual power was therefore regarded as empowering—to significant action, to a different sense of reality, and to a changed understand-ing of the self and its responsibilities. So we find Luther writing that the fruit of receiving the Lord's supper is love: "As [Christ] gives himself for us with his body and blood in order to redeem us from all misery, *so we too are to give ourselves with might and main for our neighbor.*"[33] This empowerment for the sake of the neighbor changes the way of perceiving both self and world so that justice, harmony, and peace can take the place of injustice, suffering, and death. Here we see how a changed technology of power can lead to a different moral economy of the self in which one becomes engaged, moves further into life and closer to others so that they come to matter more. The goal of ritual/izing, finally, is the creation of a particular kind of person and a particular kind of community.

By employing this combination of theoretical awareness and the recognition of a theoretical imperative to historicize a ritual/izing tradition, we have been alerted to the changes in the technology of power and the moral economy of the self that the Lutheran Reformation sought to embody. These changes, as noted earlier, are no longer guaranteed by a sacramental system of grace, priestly orders, or hierarchical succession. Rather, divine power, now available in word and sacrament, creates faith that is simply trust in the promise of God. The one who now so trusts in God's promised goodness can live again in relationship, in mutuality. He or she can now encounter God, creation, neighbor, and history instead of remaining insulated against them and isolated from them. Here is a changed ethic,

> which moves the Good into the world. The totality of historical, created existence is the place where the Good is to be done. The Good is moved from a special spiritual or sacred area to be responsible for the whole realm of what might be described as the secular—i.e., all the natural communities of human existence are places where the imperative of responsibility is to be exercised. They are places where Christ is met and where Christ becomes incarnate for us....
>
> ...[J]ustification by faith, rightly understood as the Word's activity in death and resurrection, involves the most radical moral imperative. The Word moves us out of false saintliness, the introversion of private goodness. Spiritual isolation is at an end. One is moved into responsibility for one's neighbor just in the freedom and uncertainty of history and the givenness of creation. This is so wonderfully evident in the recognition of the neighbor: the absolute command that I recognize my neighbor as a "thou." If I do not love my neighbor, I hate my own humanity, as Luther expresses it; so intimate is the oneness of the race.... Luther approaches this...with wonder, urging us to be on tiptoe anticipating the needs of our neighbor.... [T]here is the most radical democratic witness to the claim of every person to be equally creature of God, a thou, a neighbor....[34]

We are now able to see more clearly, I think, how a changed technology of power can result in a radically reoriented moral economy of the self. It calls to mind fundamental theological claims

RITUAL
PRACTICE:
INTO THE
WORLD,
INTO EACH
HUMAN
HEART

about how believers are to experience themselves as particular kinds of selves—as hearers of Christianity's gospel who are familiar with and already influenced by the Christian message. God's self-communication in the life, death, and resurrection of Jesus of Nazareth is the way that divine power is at work in the world. The incarnation of God's self reveals God as irrevocably bound to this world and its history. What this means for those who believe is not merely that we are to imitate Christ (as if that were really possible), but that we move into the world as a particular kind of person who is empowered to act in that world and on behalf of the neighbor.

~

TOWARD PRACTICE: THE CHALLENGE OF EXPERIENCE
To ask how these things can happen requires that we now turn toward the actual practice and experience of worship itself. What specific challenges confront us in the endeavor to worship in such a way that we are empowered to live a certain kind of life, a distinctive way of life—one that this volume claims is participation in the missio Dei "in the midst of the world, for the life of the world"?[35] Such a question can be particularly daunting when we realize that the claims we make for the liturgical event might be so overpowering that they resonate in almost no way with the experience of those who are participating. Even more daunting is the question of how worshipers discover experientially what their theological tradition says they are experiencing.

The recent statement *The Use of the Means of Grace* claims the following:

> Assembly itself, when that assembly is an open invitation to all peoples to gather around the truth and presence of Jesus Christ, is a witness to the world. The regular proclamation of both Law and Gospel, in Scripture reading and in preaching, tells the truth about life and death in all the world, calls us to faith in the life-giving God, and equips the believers for witness and service. Intercessory prayer makes mention of the needs of all the world and of all the Church in mission. When a collection is received, it is intended for the support of mission and for the concrete needs of our neighbors who are sick, hurt, and hungry. The holy Supper both feeds us with the body and blood of Christ and awakens our care for the hungry ones of the earth. The dismissal from the service sends us in thanksgiving from what we have seen in God's holy gifts to service in God's beloved world.[36]

These claims, however, still reside on the level of doctrinal efficacy or belong to that so-called public world of meaning that liturgical theologians are so fond of talking about, an understanding that worship is the embodied articulation of belief. But is this what wor- shipers actually experience? Is their experience that experience of grace that Karl Rahner once described so movingly as "the visitation by the Holy Spirit of the triune God which has become a reality in Christ through his becoming human and through his sacrifice on the Cross?"[37] Or is their experience more a matter of having certain pious feelings, a festive religious uplift, or soft comfort?

It can be quite unsettling (to some people, at any rate) to ask parishioners to recall their experiences of worship. Ron Grimes, in his book *Ritual Criticism*, cites one such recollection:

> The priest and the readers came down the aisle, bowed and kissed the table. I don't remember the color of vestments he was wearing. Then they had two readings and the Gospel was read by the priest while pacing back and forth. I think he had it memorized. The sound system was not very good however. Because it is new, I think no one knows how to operate it well. I notice that the priest did a lot more movements and gestures than in other Masses. I like the things he says during the sermon, but I can never really remember the content. Then the wine and the bread was brought forward by a couple; the priest took it and put it on top of the table. We then all held hands while we prayed the "Our Father." Then he blessed us all and told us to go in peace.[38]

Grimes also observes, on the basis of having read some 305 pages of recollections, that the most striking feature is how little worshipers remember or can reconstruct from what has just oc- curred. What they tend to remember is at once terse, precise, and theologically unformed. It might be tempting to conclude, therefore, that we do not learn very much from the account just cited (or from recall interviews at all). Actually, however, we learn a great deal, particularly what Grimes calls "the phenomenology of liturgical consciousness."

> It is not linear, which makes havoc of interviewers' intentions insofar as they are preoccupied with order.... Although our participant clearly nar- rates the beginning, middle, and end of the Mass, and thus has a sense of chronological order, her attention takes side trips and goes in loops and coils. She apprehends spatially as well as temporally. For instance, she notices that the sound system is not so good and thinks she knows why. *In her experience* the homily does not follow the readings. Rather, awareness of the bad sound follows awareness of the readings and pre- cedes awareness of the sermon. The order of the liturgy and the order of consciousness are not totally congruent, and if we are serious about the study of ritual, we cannot afford to overlook this incongruence.[39]

RITUAL
PRACTICE:
INTO THE
WORLD,
INTO EACH
HUMAN
HEART

We also learn that there is no such thing as "the" meaning of worship. It is a fiction at best, because, as Grimes reminds us, "meaning is always meaning-to-somebody."[40] But because of the concern with the intellectual content of worship—those objects of belief that we noted earlier and that liturgical theologians claim are mediated to worshipers—are we to conclude that their theologically unformed responses indicate a need for better liturgical catechesis? Is it really worse than we thought after all? Or is it more a matter of finding different ways to explore what is experienced in worship and to consider whether meaning is more than the thoughts worshipers have while doing it?

As we reflect further on experience, however, we become aware that it always involves inner and outer aspects. On the one hand, there is some sort of psychological apprehension such as the imparting of feeling or the reinforcing of relationship(s). On the other hand, because worship is sound and light and movement (among other things), it is a physical expression. But even as we turn our attention to what ritual theorists tell us—that ritual/izing is radically embodied—we still encounter difficulties. For instance, do the closed eyes of a worshiper indicate ecstasy or boredom? Is the worshiper's rhythmic movement a response to or involvement in a hymn being sung? Or is the movement instead some psychic twitch? Although we may receive some clues from such body language in worship, it is much more likely that body language reminds that much of what we experience is really incommunicable.[41]

Although it is certainly important to remember that experience—including what is experienced in worship—is difficult to analyze and talk about, for several reasons we still need to try to take it seriously. Even though it is elusive and ambiguous, we are challenged by the gap that yawns between our theological models for the interpretation of what occurs in worship and what actually does happen. We also need to recall that our theological interpretations might be so overpowering that they resonate little with those who are worshiping. Unless worshipers are able to discover experientially what their tradition says is available in the liturgical event, the theological claim is only a projection that exists nowhere in a living community. It also denies and neglects a crucial form of human discourse and behavior.

Yet as we proceed, albeit tentatively at first, toward a definition or a description of experience, it is helpful, if not necessary, to be aware and wary of efforts to posit some kind of authentic religious or liturgical experience. Such efforts imply that this experience is discontinuous or unique when compared with other life experiences. Although religious or liturgical experience is indeed irre- ducibly individual and distinctive for each particular person, it is also "conditioned by historical, cultural, and linguistic particularity."[42] Such experience may be regarded as a response involving the whole person, marked by a peculiar sort of intensity, and leading to action.[43]

In the Lutheran tradition, we know that the theme of experience received renewed attention during the time of the Reformation.[44] In differing and sometimes contradictory statements, Luther himself sought to sketch a new definition of the experience of faith that is indebted to his basic understanding of the doctrine of justification. This new definition drew first on the mystical tradition that he knew. Here Luther noted that the experience of faith is experience in the midst of life. Moreover, it is an experience of liberating perplexity brought about by the gospel. Although it is marked by trial and tribulation (or *Anfechtung*), it is also a permanent reminder of the word that enables daily remorse and penitence as well as full and trustful turning toward God. In addition, the experience of faith is a wholistic event—an event of perceiving, discovering, feeling—that grasps a human being and gives him or her an existential access to the discovery of God in Jesus Christ, and that, in turn, allows access to an understanding of scripture and certainty. Finally, experience is a connection to the word of promise that has been given to human beings. Yet this is a word that goes beyond all experience. This experience of faith is gift. It cannot be influenced or generated by the believer in any way.

Beginning with this threefold delineation of the experience of faith, Luther opposes the diminishing of experience in the mystical tradition as well as its understanding of experience as an unmediated source of faith and theology. He also opposes a late-medieval Roman Catholic approach to experience that has been tied both to tradition and to church as institution. And he opposes the left wing of the Reformation, which emphasized the relationship between experience and the Holy Spirit without the *verbum externum*—the external word.

Yet even in these differing and sometimes contradictory statements about what the experience of faith is, Luther still makes a salient point. Faith is not something that floats in thin air. It is a reality: *I believe*. We can only speak of faith in this subjective fashion. Hence, Luther will note that experience is a particular kind of feeling. It is possible to experience and feel faith. The grace of God "can be felt and experienced" and can produce "a most sweet stirring of the heart."[45]

RITUAL
PRACTICE:
INTO THE
WORLD,
INTO EACH
HUMAN
HEART

Another point to remember about experience in early Lutheran thinking is that experience is called "the school of the Holy Spirit."

> No one can correctly understand God or his Word unless he has received such understanding immediately from the Holy Spirit. But no one can receive it from the Holy Spirit without experiencing, proving, and feeling it. In such experience, the Holy Spirit instructs us as in His own school, outside of which nothing is learned but empty words and prattle.[46]

Here Luther is emphasizing experience over against those who would assert that faith is only a concern of the mind. He wants to underscore how the whole person is affected by the experience of faith. This experience is a legitimate way of getting to know God and along with such knowledge is brought affection, an experiential knowledge that orients a person to others, to the world, and to God. What one has come to know is God's goodness and power.

Though Luther will also speak of a faith that dwells in the deepest darkness, he wants to emphasize something that is positive, not a negation. In his Galatians commentary, for example, he will assert that faith is not "an idle quality or an empty husk." It is something that one has. At this juncture, we find a consideration of the experience of faith moving in the direction of trust. A warmer note is sounded, as von Loewenich has observed.[47] Moreover, we begin to

> sense the warmth of experience coming through. The subjective reference of faith finds beautiful expression especially in the idea of trust. While through the critical delimitation of the concept of faith the main emphasis was...placed on faith as that which is believed (fides quae creditur), here faith as an activity (fides qua creditur) is given its full due. The subjective element of faith demonstrates itself as trust...it assumes the concrete form of trust.[48]

Luther's view of faith as trust is well known. The explanation of the first commandment in the Large Catechism speaks of clinging to God "with all our heart" as being "nothing else than to entrust ourselves to him completely."[49] Similarly in the Small Catechism, we hear, "We should fear, love, and trust in God above all things."[50]

At the same time, however, faith has a specific content. It is even a possession—an intellectual possession: "If I define Christ this way [as one who gave himself for our sins], I define him correctly, grasp the authentic Christ, and truly make him my own."[51] Faith as possession, moreover—when it enters into our experience—also manifests itself as a power of a peculiar sort. It is a power that comes from the outside and that dwells in believers, moves them, changes them and gives them life—life in Christ and with others. As such, faith can be regarded as a basic stance out of which expressions of Christian piety proceed—expressions that are to be essentially social because it is with others that we meet God in the venture of trust and obedience as we respond to the forgiving and liberating work of Christ in faith.

We catch something of this understanding of faith as trust in Evelyn Underhill's description of the mood and tone of Lutheran worship. In her now classic study, *Worship*, she wrote about how Luther's insight into faith was the result of seeing the mystery of the Divine Charity from a fresh angle "and therefore seeming, to those who perceived it, a fresh thing and a fresh incentive to worship and love."[52] Moreover, according to Underhill, the view that faith involves both *fides* and *fiducia*, that childlike trust in God's mercy and grace, gives to Lutheran worship a "subjective tone" and "special colour." Both Underhill and subsequent writers have commented on this tone and color as reflective of a touching simplicity and a deep, tender piety—and that such simplicity and piety have given to Lutheranism that particular characteristic of "warmth." In fact, one historian has noted that "the real hidden strength of Lutheranism lay in its ways of worship and its warm piety."[53] This can be seen in Underhill's assertion that the essential mood of Lutheran worship is "loving confidence in the Divine generosity."[54]

A Lutheran take on experience, then, is an interpretation of something that happens or can happen in the church's worship. It is conditioned by historical, cultural, and linguistic particularity. Yet such an interpretation intends to offer more than mere explanation. It also intends to offer promise—that "loving confidence in the Divine generosity" will continue to be disclosed as the church celebrates word and sacrament. Here is all the more reason to recognize that the experience of worship that a particular interpretation seeks to articulate is crucial. We also need to consider how that recognition can be fostered. If the experience of worship itself is the testing ground for what we have been claiming, we must ask what is required of the liturgical event for it to be a vehicle of *fides* and *fiducia*. We must also ask what is required of those who take part so that they might be able to recognize what is indeed occurring.

Such questions bring us to the often vexing matters of ritual practice and design (or structure) as well as the style and tone of

RITUAL
PRACTICE:
INTO THE
WORLD,
INTO EACH
HUMAN
HEART

liturgical expression. In the background of our considerations is the realization of the dangers of manipulation and of imputing to worshipers the experience they "should" be having. Yet if we can move forward in a rather general fashion and say something about practice/practices, then we can proceed to flesh these out in a more particular way.

Dorothy Bass, a historian of American religion, has edited a recent book of essays, *Practicing Our Faith: A Way of Life for a Searching People*. In the introduction to this collection, she and coauthor Craig Dykstra consider the spiritual hunger of our day and suggest that thinking about Christian practices can help people living at the close of this century envision a vital and faithful way of life. To illustrate how older traditions can sustain ways of life that shelter and nourish people, they tell two stories.

> A Catholic priest recently told a gathering of friends about a time when he arrived in Israel late on a Friday afternoon, just as everything was about to shut down for the Sabbath. Public transportation was no longer available, and the house where people were expecting him was fifteen miles away. So he picked up his suitcase and started to walk. He did not get far before a family saw him and invited him to spend the Sabbath with them. He accepted their invitation, and they all had a wonderful time. When Saturday evening came, he found his bus and went on his way.
>
> After the priest finished his story, a Jewish friend said that he had a similar story to tell. As a longhaired college student in the late 1960s, he was travelling through Spain. One night, he got off a train in a village that was already asleep. A little frightened, he approached the only lighted place. It turned out to be a monastery, and the monks received him gladly. After his departure, he discovered that they had quietly slipped some coins into his pocket as he slept.[55]

We seem to be unaware of the rich insights and strong help a Christian tradition of practices can bring to our current concerns. Through these practices, we seek to respond to God's active presence, and the practices serve as our response, which we offer together over time for the life of the world. Such responses, or practices, range from keeping the Sabbath and honoring the body to singing the faith and forgiving one another. Woven together, these practices suggest the patterns of a faithful Christian way of life for our time.

Bass and Dykstra go on to spell out what they mean by "practices" and to offer their understanding of a shared way of life in order to help us think in new ways. Practices have four general

characteristics and purposes. First, they address fundamental
human needs and conditions through concrete human acts. So when someone is traveling alone, she or he does not need to be greeted with a sermon on hospitality but to be invited inside, given something to eat and a place to sleep. Those who do the inviting and are showing hospitality may or may not be able to articulate why they do these things, though in fact they are carrying on traditions rooted in the Bible. They are simply practicing hospitality. Other practices similarly provide concrete help for human flourishing. Practices have practical purpose, therefore, to heal, to shape communities, to discern.

A second feature of practices is that they are done together over time. Bass and Dykstra note:

> Enter a Christian practice, and you will find that you are part of a community that has been doing this thing for centuries—not doing it as well as it should, to be sure, but doing it steadily, in conscious continuity with stories of the Bible and in frequent conversation about how to do it better. You join by jumping in where you are: learn the hymns, volunteer to welcome the homeless, seek companions who will support you in prayer as you say yes to God and no to the destructive forces in your life. Once in, you find that a practice has a certain internal feel and momentum. It is ancient and larger than you are; it weaves you together with other people in doing things none of us could do alone.[56]

This perspective is reminiscent of a nineteenth-century Lutheran theology's emphasis on experience as the Christian experience—that is, a communal experience, to the degree that one is personally adapted to the community of God through Christ. To say that Christian experience is communal experience is also to say that it has a historical and biblical nature. Bible and history, however, are more than a past, once-upon-a-time set of teachings to be conveyed to a group of knowers. They have a present in the experience of the believers.

Third, practices possess standards of excellence. They are ways not just to add a warm glow to what we do but to consider how the light of God shines on our work or how we spend our money, so that we can shape our practices in response to God's activities of creating and providing for the care of the earth and all its inhabitants. "The challenge," note Bass and Dykstra, "lies in figuring out what this means with enough specificity to make a difference. Part of the figuring out requires soul-stretching theological conversations with others."[57]

RITUAL
PRACTICE:
INTO THE
WORLD,
INTO EACH
HUMAN
HEART

Finally, Bass and Dykstra assert that when we can see how some of our ordinary activities are Christian practices, we come to perceive how our daily lives are all tangled up with the things God is doing in the world, which is what the missio Dei really is. The task, then, is one of patterning our practices after what we believe God is doing—and in patterning, perhaps we can be moved to understand our own deepest hopes and longings as belonging to God's reconciling love for the world, a love that is at the very heart of this earthly world.

Bass's and Dykstra's understanding of the role of practices can provide a refreshingly different context in which to discuss the vexing matters of ritual practice and design (or structure) as well as the style and tone of liturgical expression. First, some comments on the design of our ritual practice. Even after twenty-plus years of using a resource such as *Lutheran Book of Worship*, many still think of worship as the repetition of set forms rather than as a textured dialogue on multiple levels—with our ancestors in the faith, with an inherited liturgical tradition, with the present, and with God. Why is this mind-set potentially problematic? Because, according to some scholars, it can obscure the so-called essentials of this activity—whether we name them word and sacrament, baptism, preaching, or the supper. And what makes these essentials "essential" is the dynamic expressed therein—namely, that "in, with, and under" these essentials, who Jesus is and what he does are encountered anew and in our own time and place. Indeed, they mirror an ongoing pattern of communication between God and humanity, that of God's continually coming to us and our faithful response to God.

Although essentials are emphasized to remind us that worship is more than just our good idea, when we use them uncritically we run the risk of dismissing the particularities and subjectivities of worshipers, their mind and heart, in which finally thoughts and feeling meet and mingle, thereby helping worshipers to make sense of things. For example, the recent effort to clarify structurally the central elements of the Holy Communion liturgy in *With One Voice* runs the risk of trying to lay down in advance what the experience of worship should be. It is claimed that the gathering, word proclaimed, and supper shared sends the community forth "to speak the words of the good news they have heard, to care for those in need, and to share what they have received with the poor and the hungry."[58] This sounds fine, but most likely once the liturgy has ended, we go downstairs to the coffee hour instead. The greater problem, however, is the confusion that such claims can engender, with the potential result that the missio Dei, what God is doing in the world, has been subsumed under our own agendas—whether of peace and justice concerns or the like. There is also the theoretical problem of repeating the consequentialist error noted earlier—that ritualizing is problem solving or immediately transformative.

Similarly, the style and tone of worship can also overshadow the missio Dei. Ceremony, body language, movement, or other things can often call attention to something other than the fundamental question of what God is doing in the world. But if the actions of worship leaders and worshipers are to dramatize or bring out the significance of the encounter that is said to be taking place, then it would seem that such actions would occur with considerable care and attention—not for the sake of exhibiting some flawless ritual/izing technique, but for the sake of evoking an ongoing recognition of God's presence and activity in the world.

Attention to ritual activity's design, style, and tone are, then, for a larger purpose—to remind us of what God is up to in the world and how this can affect and shape experience, and likely make a difference to our mind and heart. For example, although we might come to worship to be calmed in some way, we also want to get outside of ourselves, to be freed momentarily from self-preoccupation. After so doing, we find that we are strengthened in faith toward God and in fervent love toward one another. We also hear, following our eating and drinking in the supper, that the body and blood of the Lord Jesus Christ strengthens and keeps us in God's grace. And we wonder if God's grace is not something like our experience in worship.

A little introspection on this experience of grace might, in turn, move us toward a larger awareness that God's own self dwells with and within us. If we reflect on God's presence within us, then we might wonder whether this encounter and relationship between God and us—this communion—also reflects the divine nature's real self-communication in the person of Jesus and the activity of the Spirit: a doctrine of the Trinity.

> God who dwells in inaccessible light and eternal glory comes to us in the face of Christ and the activity of the Holy Spirit. Because of God's outreach to the creature, God is said to be essentially relational, ecstatic, fecund, alive as passionate love.... The heart of the Christian life is to be united with the God of Jesus Christ by means of communion with one another. The doctrine of the Trinity is ultimately therefore...a teaching about God's life with us and our life with each other. Trinitarian theology could be described as par excellence a theology of relationship, which explores the mysteries of love, relationship, personhood and communion within the framework of God's self-revelation in the person of Christ and the activity of the Spirit.[59]

RITUAL
PRACTICE:
INTO THE
WORLD,
INTO EACH
HUMAN
HEART

Yet as we continue our reflection, we come face to face with the ambiguities of our own human experience, including sin, alienation, and death. Can we discern even there the presence of God? Yes, we can. God's presence even in these ambiguities has been made known in the life, death, and resurrection of Jesus of Nazareth. It is in this one that the connectedness of God and the world we live in is permanently fixed, for "God has risen up and has already spoken his final word in the drama of history, no matter how much clamor the world keeps up."[60]

This meeting of God and an embodied self is an experience of grace. Hence, what we can find as a result of reflecting on the ritual dynamics of what we have experienced has a christological center and a trinitarian shape. That is, God's self-disclosure in our experience, God's self-communication to human beings, is a covenant relationship of love made possible by Jesus Christ in the power of the Holy Spirit. Our finite experience, shaped as it is by body, language, and society, is also an experience of trinitarian faith.

At this juncture, however, we need to ask whether these reflections are simply another way to an approach to worship in terms of the thoughts worshipers have while doing it. Also, as we noted earlier, it seems that whenever liturgical theologians manifest an interest in the meaning of this activity, *meaning* appears to be restricted to intellectual content. But is it possible to stretch our definition of meaning somewhat and to see how it derives from connection in its simplest sense ("dark clouds mean rain")?[61] If so, are we then able to speak of worship being meaningful to those who take part without trying to determine what the intellectual content of this meaning might be?

Yes, we are able, once we consider that meaning is as much an activity of "composing and being composed by the connections among things."[62] Then, when we return to our earlier reports of how and why worshipers find their participation to be meaningful (the rite imparted feelings and reinforced relationships), we might begin to see how these responses are made possible and shaped by intellectual, social, religious, psychological, cultural, and aesthetic structures and dynamics. Moreover, we see that this experience of insight and connection to others and to the world enables worshipers to have some sense of reality by virtue of which they can live in communication and relationship with others and with God.

Continuing to move in this direction can bring us to the realization (not always but perhaps sometimes) that if God's own self has been given to the world, it follows that what we have traditionally called doctrine constitutes an invitation to entrust ourselves to this world's ongoing history with God and our experience of it. Doctrine is much more than a list of items to be believed. It is an activity, an historical and communal process of interpretation and transmission of the ongoing experience of God's redeeming presence in Christ. Surprisingly, this experience will not mean that we will be protected or shut off from the baffling diversity and otherness of experience. Rather, we will be held open to them. And by so doing, we will begin to realize that what we have experienced—ourselves and God—is an experience of other people as well.

Here, Karl Rahner reminds us:

> Life in its full sense is in the concrete achieved in knowledge and freedom in which the "I" is always related to a "Thou," arising at the same moment in the "Thou" as in the "I," experiencing itself in all cases only in its encounter with the other person by recognizing itself to be different from that other person, and at the same time by identifying itself with that other person. The original objectivity of the experience of self necessarily takes place in the subjectivity of its encounters with other persons in dialogue, in trustful and loving encounter.... Thus the concrete relationship of the subject to himself is inextricably dependent upon the factor of how a subject encounters other human beings.[63]

Rahner goes on to emphasize that the experience of God and the experience of self are a unity, and that the experience of self and the encounter with our neighbor are a unity as well.[64] Here, perhaps, is the link between ritual practice and the missio Dei. In fact, love of God and love of neighbor are only conceivable because the experience of self and the experience of God are one. The self that is realized in the worship of the church is therefore radically different from the self posited by certain cultural, religious, and psychological sensibilities. It is a self with God and with the neighbor, a self who reaches out to that neighbor in unconditional love.

Although such an understanding of the relationship between our ritual practice and the missio Dei may appear to be rather modest (at least rhetorically), nevertheless the relationship seems to be something like a realization that loving confidence in the divine generosity is possible because of God's own loving generosity to us—because this missio Dei is the mode of God's presence in the world. "Therefore, we cannot remain indifferent to the earth, or try somehow to leave it behind. Indeed, God's very life dwells in it and our very life dwells in it as well."[65]

RITUAL
PRACTICE:
INTO THE
WORLD,
INTO EACH
HUMAN
HEART

Some concluding remarks

If ritual theory and a theological reconsideration of some of the salient emphases of our own Lutheran tradition about the purpose and power of worship have taught us anything, it is a lesson in rhetorical modesty as much as a challenge to think differently about the relationship between what we do in church and the missio Dei in the world. Let us return, for instance, to a statement such as *The Use of the Means of Grace*. We find lyrically elegant prose, a lovely poetic reflection about assembly as an open invitation to all peoples, about proclamation as telling us the truth about life and death in the world and calling us to faith in the life-giving God, equipping us for witness and service, awakening our care for the hungry ones of the earth, and sending us in service to God's beloved world.

Yet is not something missing in these words? Yes, we are missing the recognition of the heart of the worshiper and the hearts of the community to which the individual belongs. In the desire to claim that ritual practice and Christian mission are inextricably connected, what is overlooked is what the missio Dei really is. It is not primarily these good things—being open to all people, caring for the hungry, being equipped for witness and service. Rather, as this chapter has sought to emphasize, the missio Dei is God's revelation of God's self as irrevocably bound to this world. It is about God's own passionate desire, which will not be frustrated, to move more and more into the world and more and more into each human heart.

Is this to suggest, then, that there is no relationship whatsoever between what occurs in church and what we do in the world? Not at all! But there is a more foundational task: to assist worshipers to believe once again that they can be confident in the divine generosity toward us and toward the world. Such an experience of trust, as we have argued, is an experience of God that reminds us that God is at work with/in the realities we know as the world. An experience of trust can mean, also,

> that the world in its everydayness and its ongoing history (both natural and human) *is* the event of divine self-communication, that is, the way in which God's self-communication (not facts, but presence) takes place. Divine self-communication occurs in, with, and under the conditions of this world and in no other way.[66]

Moreover, this world, which really is the event of God's self-communicative generosity is still a history that seems to human beings a growing chaos—an impenetrable mix of sin and holiness, light and darkness; a history of simultaneous ascents and downfalls, of blood and tears, of noble achievements and rash presumption; a history that is appalling and magnificent, an ooze of endless trivia and yet a high drama; a history in which the individual is freed from the degradation of self-alienation and is reduced to the status of total insignificance among the billions of his brothers and sisters; a history of arrogant might and the inexorable demands of "planning," yet increasingly unpredictable, with a growing pluralism of cultures, economic systems, political systems; an even more variegated human consciousness, and trend toward society of the masses; so that this pluralism, with all the schizophrenia it begets in the consciousness of the individual, is compressed into a highly inflammable density by a human history ever more closely knit, ever more one.[67]

Although the world, with its wonder, horror, and ordinariness, might be the cause for despair and remind us too much of "the incurable ambivalence of all that is human,"[68] it is still the event of God's self-communication. Perhaps the modesty required of our gatherings for word and sacrament is this: to believe the truth of God's tremendous love and, in so doing, to receive "the improbable courage" that this indeed happens even in our own appalling, humdrum lives, "where nothing seems to happen but birth and death, and in between, amid emptiness, and the guilt no one is spared, a little longing and a little faithfulness."[69]

In the end, it would seem that Kathleen Norris is right. In her comments about worship, cited at the outset of this chapter, she wrote: "[W]e let loose with music, and the words of hymns, the psalms, canticles, and prayers. We cast the Word of God out into the world, into each human heart" because that is where "it needs to go to fulfill God's purpose." Is this not the missio Dei?

NOTES

1. Kathleen Norris, *Amazing Grace: A Vocabulary of Faith* (New York: Riverhead Books, 1998), 246–47.

2. *Ritualizing* seems to be the preferred term in current scholarship, because it better captures the embodied, enacted quality of a particular kind of human behavior that is undertaken for different reasons. *Ritual*, on the other hand, is a scholarly category that is used for the study and interpretation of this sort of behavior. *Rites* are the distinctive forms of a culture's or community's embodiments or enactments that are differentiated from other, usually more daily activities. Even with these distinctions, scholars tend to speak of "ritual." In the paper, I will use "ritual/izing" as a way of calling attention to its embodied, enacted character and dynamic. See Ronald L. Grimes, *Ritual Criticism: Case Studies in Its Practice, Essays on Its Theory* (Columbia, S.C.: University of

RITUAL
PRACTICE:
INTO THE
WORLD,
INTO EACH
HUMAN
HEART

South Carolina Press, 1990), 13ff; and Catherine Bell, *Ritual Theory, Ritual Practice* (Oxford: Oxford University Press, 1992), 69–74.

3. We should not forget, however, that ritual/izing can be undertaken to abuse, traumatize, terrorize, and dominate others. See Joseph D. Driskill, "The Significance of Ritual in the Case of Joanne: Insights from Depth Psychology," *Religious and Social Ritual: Interdisciplinary Explorations*, ed. Michael B. Aune and Valerie DeMarinis (Albany, N.Y.: SUNY Press, 1996), 267–91.

4. Bell, *Ritual: Perspectives and Dimensions* (New York: Oxford University Press, 1997), 264–65.

5. Aidan Kavanagh, *On Liturgical Theology* (New York: Pueblo Publishing, 1984), 96, 100–102.

6. Although David Fagerberg asserts in his *What Is Liturgical Theology? A Study in Methodology* (Collegeville, Minn.: Liturgical Press, 1992) that liturgical theology "actually happens in liturgies and not on paper" (12), one looks in vain for a consideration of any liturgies in this book. Similarly, we can examine Kavanagh's *On Liturgical Theology* or Gordon W. Lathrop's *Holy Things: A Liturgical Theology* (Minneapolis: Fortress Press, 1993) and not find a theological examination of a particular liturgy at all.

7. Clifford Geertz, "Making Experiences, Authoring Selves," *The Anthropology of Experience*, ed. Victor W. Turner and Edward M. Bruner (Urbana, Ill.: University of Illinois Press, 1986), 373.

8. John Cheever, *The Journals of John Cheever* (New York: Knopf, 1991), 62.

9. Marjorie Procter-Smith, *In Her Own Rite: Constructing Feminist Liturgical Tradition* (Nashville: Abingdon Press, 1990), 13.

10. *The Use of the Means of Grace: A Statement on the Practice of Word and Sacrament* (Evangelical Lutheran Church in America, 1997), application 51B.

11. Donna Lynne Seamone, "The Proclamation of the Obvious: An Investigation of Performance Studies in Relation to Liturgical Enactment" (Ph.D. comprehensive examination paper, Graduate Theological Union, May 1995), 11.

12. See n. 6.

13. Michelle Rosaldo, *Knowledge and Passion* (Cambridge: Cambridge University Press, 1980), 25.

14. Anthropologists and cultural theorists operate with particular definitions of both *emotion* and *affect*. In sharp contrast to our regnant notions that equate emotion and affect with passivity and irrationality, they underscore their interpretive, interactive, and cognitive dimensions for the purpose of showing how human beings are aware of and engaged with the world and with others. These contemporary definitions are strikingly similar to an older rhetorical tradition's emphasis on being moved—where one is empowered to feel as well as to know more deeply. Philip Melanchthon, for example, employed *movere* to interpret how faith is a matter of the intellect as well as of the heart and will. See Michael B. Aune, "'A Heart Moved': Philip Melanchthon's Forgotten Truth About Worship," *Lutheran Quarterly* 12, no. 4 (winter 1998): 395–418. For a discussion of how emotion and affect are understood in contemporary scholarship, see *Culture Theory: Essays on Mind, Self, and Emotion*, ed. Richard A. Shweder and Robert A. LeVine (Cambridge: Cambridge University Press, 1984).

15. Bell, "Performance," *Critical Terms for Religious Studies*, ed. Mark C. Taylor (Chicago: University of Chicago Press, 1998), 205.

16. Bell, *Ritual: Perspectives and Dimensions*, 258.

17. Ibid.

18. Joyce Ann Zimmerman, *Liturgy as Language of Faith: A Liturgical Methodology in the Mode of Paul Ricoeur's Textual Hermeneutics* (Washington, D.C.:

University Press of America, 1988), 194.

19. Bell, "The Authority of Ritual Experts," *Studia Liturgica* 23, no. 1 (1993): 120.

20. F. Allan Hanson, "The Semiotics of Ritual," *Semiotica* 33, no. 1/2 (1981): 169–78.

21. Lawrence A. Hoffman, "How Ritual Means: Ritual Circumcision in Rabbinic Culture and Today," *Studia Liturgica* 23, no. 1 (1993): 82.

22. Sally F. Moore and Barbara Myerhoff, "Sacred Ritual: Forms and Meanings," in *Secular Ritual* (Assen, The Netherlands: Van Gorcum, 1977), 10–15.

23. See Ninian Smart, *Worldviews: Crosscultural Explorations of Human Beliefs* (New York: Charles Scribner's Sons, 1983), 131.

24. Peter Stromberg, *Symbols of Community: The Cultural System of a Swedish Church* (Tucson, Ariz.: University of Arizona Press, 1986), 66.

25. John D. Kelly and Martha Kaplan, "History, Structure, and Ritual," *Annual Review of Anthropology* 19 (1990): 119.

26. Fred Clothey, "Toward a Comprehensive Interpretation of Ritual," *Journal of Ritual Studies* 2, no. 2 (summer 1988): 156.

27. Eugene L. Brand, "A Lutheran Agenda for Worship after Dar-Es-Salaam," *A Lutheran Agenda for Worship* (Geneva: Department of Studies, Lutheran World Federation, 1979), 16.

28. One thinks here, for example, of the gradual "victory of restorationism" in matters liturgical and hymnic among Lutherans in this country. That such a development belonged to a larger set of cultural dynamics leading American Lutherans to "a middle-of-the-road consensus modernity" is rarely considered. (For an exception, see Leigh D. Jordahl, "American Lutheranism: Ethos, Style, and Polity," *The Lutheran Church in North American Life: 1776–1976 1580–1980*, ed. John E. Groh and Robert H. Smith [St. Louis: Clayton Publishing House, 1979], 33–57.) Moreover, the loss of older forms of worship has also meant the loss of an older piety that some observers have noted "may deepen, strengthen, and even correct the life of the Lutheran churches today" (Leonard R. Klein, "Remembrance and Renewal," *Lutheran Forum* 15 [Reformation 1981]: 13).

29. Carlos Eire, *War Against the Idols: The Reformation of Worship from Erasmus to Calvin* (Cambridge: Cambridge University Press, 1986), 1. Such wonders, states Eire, included the absolving of adulterers and murderers, the blessing of fields and cattle, preaching to the birds and fish, and hastening a soul's release from purgatory. Eire continues: "The map of Europe bristled with holy places; life pulsated with the expectation of the miraculous. In the popular mind and in much of the official teaching of the Church, almost anything was possible. One could even eat the flesh of the risen Christ in a consecrated wafer."

30. Steven Ozment, "Luther and the Late Middle Ages: The Formation of Reformation Thought," in *Transition and Revolution: Problems and Issues of European Renaissance and Reformation History*, ed. Robert M. Kingdon (Minneapolis: Burgess Publishing, 1974), 128.

31. "The German Mass and Order of Service, 1526," in *Luther's Works*, ed. Helmut T. Lehmann (Philadelphia: Fortress Press, 1965), 53:84.

32. Bell, *Ritual Theory, Ritual Practice*, 197.

33. "The Sacrament of the Body and Blood of Christ—Against the Fanatics, 1526," in *Luther's Works*, ed. Helmut T. Lehmann (Philadelphia: Fortress Press, 1960), 36:352, emphasis mine.

34. Robert J. Goeser, "Whither Lutheranism?" *Lutheran Quarterly*, new series 1, no. 1 (spring 1987): 45–46, 47–48.

35. *The Use of the Means of Grace*, application 51B.

RITUAL
PRACTICE:
INTO THE
WORLD,
INTO EACH
HUMAN
HEART

36. Ibid., background 51A.

37. Karl Rahner, "Reflections on the Experience of Grace," *Theological Investigations: Theology of the Spiritual Life*, vol. 3, trans. Karl-H. and Boniface Kruger (London: Darton, Longman & Todd, 1974), 86.

38. Grimes, *Ritual Criticism*, 40–41.

39. Ibid., 42.

40. Ibid.

41. Helpful here is Luke Timothy Johnson's *Religious Experience in Earliest Christianity* (Minneapolis: Fortress Press, 1998).

42. Ibid., 54.

43. Ibid., 60ff.

44. Informing the discussion here is Joachim Track, "Erfahrung III," in *Theologische Realenzyklopädie*, vol. 11, ed. Gerhard Krause and Gerhard Muller (Berlin: de Gruyter, 1976), 118ff.

45. The discussion here follows Walther von Loewenich, *Luther's Theology of the Cross*, trans. Herbert J.A. Bouman (Minneapolis: Augsburg Publishing House, 1976), 93ff.

46. Ibid., 94. Von Loewenich is citing Luther's explanation of the Magnificat here.

47. Ibid. 95.

48. Ibid.

49. The Large Catechism 1, 15, in *The Book of Concord: The Confessions of the Evangelical Lutheran Church*, trans. and ed. Theodore G. Tappert et al. (Philadelphia: Fortress Press, 1959), 366.

50. The Small Catechism 1, 2, in *The Book of Concord*, 342.

51. "Lectures on Galatians, 1535," in *Luther's Works*, ed. Jaroslav Pelikan (St. Louis: Concordia Publishing House, 1963), 26:39.

52. Evelyn Underhill, *Worship* (New York: Harper, 1936), 277.

53. D. Parker, "Protestantism and Confessional Strife," *The New Cambridge Modern History*, vol. 3, *The Counter-Reformation and Price Revolution 1559–1610*, ed. R.B. Wernham (Cambridge: Cambridge University Press, 1968), 89.

54. Underhill, *Worship*, 286.

55. Craig Dykstra and Dorothy C. Bass, "Times of Yearning, Practices of Faith," in *Practicing Our Faith: A Way of Life for a Searching People*, ed. Dorothy C. Bass (San Francisco: Jossey-Bass, 1997), 2–3.

56. Ibid., 7.

57. Ibid.

58. "Holy Communion: The Shape of the Rite," in *With One Voice: A Lutheran Resource for Worship* (Minneapolis: Augsburg Fortress, 1995), 9.

59. Catherine Mowry LaCugna, *God for Us: The Trinity and Christian Life* (San Francisco: HarperSanFrancisco, 1991), 1.

60. Rahner, *Prayers and Meditations: An Anthology of the Spiritual Writings by Karl Rahner*, ed. John Griffiths (New York: Crossroad, 1981), 14–15. See also Carol Ruth Jacobson, "For God So Loved the World: Constructing a Worldly Understanding of the Work of Christ," (Ph.D. dissertation, Graduate Theological Union, 1998), 188.

61. See S. Michael Price, "Ritual, meaning, and subjectivity: Studying ritual as human religious expression," *Epoche: UCLA Journal for the History of Religion* 16 (1988): 29.

62. Sharon Daloz Parks, "Communication, Ritual as," *The New Dictionary of Sacramental Worship*, ed. Peter E. Fink, S.J. (Collegeville, Minn.: Michael Glazier, 1991), 236.

63. Rahner, "Experience of Self and Experience of God," *The Content of Faith: The*

Best of Karl Rahner's Theological Writings, ed. Karl Lehmann and Albert Raffelt, trans. and ed. Harvey D. Egan, S.J. (New York: Crossroad, 1994), 225 (originally published in *Theological Investigations: Theology, Anthropology, Christology*, vol. 13, trans. David Bourke [New York: Crossroad, 1983], 127–28).

64. It needs to be pointed out here that Rahner does not mean that the experience of God and the experience of self are exactly the same. Rather, they constitute a unity, and the unity between the experience of God and the experience of self makes it possible to achieve that unity between love of God and love of neighbor.

65. Jacobson, "For God So Loved the World," 217.

66. Ibid., 126.

67. Rahner, "The World and History as the Event of God's Self-Communication," in *Servants of the Lord*, trans. Richard Strachan (New York: Herder & Herder, 1968), reprinted in Rahner, *The Content of Faith*, 195; cited in Jacobson, "For God So Loved the World," 127.

68. Rahner, "The World and History," 195.

69. Ibid., 195–96.

Occasional Services: Border Crossings

Robert D. Hawkins

THE CONVERGENCE of ecumenical liturgical thinking, particularly since the 1963 promulgation of the *Constitution on the Sacred Liturgy*, has come to identify the eucharist as the central action of the church, the fount as well as summit of the church's life.[1] Since 1963, studies have explicitly pointed to the gathering of God's baptized, holy people as the appropriate context for the meal.[2] Most recently, serious scholarship has focused on the relationship between the eucharistic community and unchurched people,[3] and indeed, all of creation.[4]

There is a danger, however, in fixating on the essentials of the eucharistic gathering, for such action can suggest that the church has no official liturgical life apart from the eucharist. The *Constitution on the Sacred Liturgy* even warns of such reductionist thinking.[5] Our focus here is on a diverse constellation of rites called the occasional services, which cluster around the central activities of the church. They are the liturgical events of the church's cradle-to-grave ministry, the day-to-day, seasonal, and life cycle occasions that provide the necessary counterpoint to the church gathered weekly around the word, the holy bath, and Christ's holy meal. Although some of the occasional services may be celebrated during the eucharistic gathering, others occur outside the normal Sunday liturgy in homes, hospitals, schools, and places of business—in short, wherever God's people venture. The occasional services take the church to the very borders of faith, to the places where belief confronts and converses with unbelief, to the places the Bible calls "the ends of the earth." The occasional services' ability to embody God's healing and empowering word even at the borders reveals their missional character.

~

OCCASIONAL MINISTRIES OF THE CHURCH

The church is the gathered community of those called out to be Christ's body active in this world. Christ's body the church, however, is not static; it is constantly in flux, growing and declining, reflecting the cycles of life manifest in community. This growth and decline is reflected in the rites and rituals that comprise the occasional services. The occasional services address various themes, including invitation; God's household and people; nourishment, enabling, and sustaining; affirmation and equipping for the future; and healing, forgiveness, and being commended to God. As the church lives out its calling ecclesially (intentionally as "church") and familially (in the day-to-day events of God's people as "family" or within other meaningful associations), some occasions will demand ritual observance. Family systems theory and recent ritual studies recognize the operative communities that affect the lives of people[6] and also the ritual interactions that establish and deepen relationships as well as frustrate or destroy them.[7] These events are part of the life cycle and must be ritually acknowledged or celebrated for the health and well-being of both individuals and community.

Communal interrelatedness is the hallmark of these rites, which are shaped not only by Jesus' own formative words to his disciples but the emerging ecclesiologies apparent in Paul's and other biblical and post-testamental writings.[8] We are at heart people called, healed, nourished, and sent by God's word. The occasional rites form concentric rings around that formative core of faith—word, bath, meal, and mission. This core constitutes the traditional "marks of the church,"[9] from which the church's life flows, expressed most succinctly in the Sunday eucharistic gathering but also in daily life. The Pauline corporal and communal imagery of the church as "royal priesthood," "God's stewards and household," "a spiritual temple," and "Christ's own body"[10] suggests the essential unity of purpose in the occasional services, despite their widely divergent content and ordering of details. Some of the occasional services reflect more than one aspect of the core. Some of the services may be encountered during the communion liturgy itself.

It is helpful when talking about the occasional services, such as the various rites in *Ocassional Services* (1982),[11] to begin with some schema, to develop clusters of rites that share similar characteristics. We could focus primarily on how each relates to the marks of the church—word, baptism, eucharist, and mission. We could also look at the primary purpose of each rite, attending to rites of invitation, nourishment, healing, and so forth. Given the topic of this volume, liturgy and *mission,* however, we will examine the rites in each of several venues for mission: the faith community itself; the family in its daily life apart from the faith community's eucharistic gathering; and the wider community, beyond the borders of these first two communities. Within each venue, we will notice, some rites are more closely related to the church's ministry of the word and others to baptism, eucharist, or mission.

~

CARING FOR THE FAITH COMMUNITY

We speak of baptism as a rite of initiation, and it makes sense that many of the occasional services that help us to care for one another as members of a faith community are related to this beginning point, our incorporation into the community. The number of rites associated with baptism has substantially expanded, thanks to widespread revival of the adult catechumenate and baptism in traditions that heretofore primarily baptized infants.[12] The church has had to relearn Paul's missional work "in the marketplace with those who happened to be there" (Acts 17:17). Thus, rites of welcoming and for the journey of discernment speak to the adult and embrace the longing and searching, crisis and resolution that have always been part of conversion.

Individual and corporate confession are connected theologically to baptism.[13] It is through confession that the whole church and its individual members are enabled to walk daily in baptism. Rites of confession acknowledge our constant need for God's presence and action to fill us with truth and peace, purify, direct, reform, provide for, and establish the body of Christ in unity.[14] A faith community as a whole is also susceptible to dissension; the ravages of sin are seen in the life of Christ's own body the church. That Luther refers to confession as "the third sacrament" reflects the historical practice of subsuming the cradle-to-grave ministries with individuals under the church's sacramental system. (It is helpful to remember that discussions about occasional services by Orthodox and Roman Catholic theologians are likely to be couched in sacramental terms.)

The rites that cluster around the service of Christian burial are explicit extensions of the baptismal rites.[15] The Commendation of the Dying announces baptism as the grounding event for the Christian's entire life; the readings for Comforting of the Bereaved echo this grounding. The funeral rite itself invokes central Pauline imagery about baptism, death, and resurrection, and the Committal offers prayers "in sure and certain hope of the resurrection...," echoing the sixth chapter of Romans.[16] All these rites have great impact on the life of the community, not just for the immediate family. The commendation of a brother or sister in Christ, a "fellow member" and "worker in the kingdom"[17] is part of life's experience and a purpose of the funeral.

Although most of the liturgical action associated with holy communion pertains to the actual celebration of the meal within the context of the gathered community, congregations are recovering the ancient practice of taking the eucharistic elements from the communion liturgy to those who are sick or homebound. Far preferable to the current practice of "private communion"—a woeful contradiction in terms—is the extension of the community's meal to those who are absent but no less members of the faith community, a powerful witness not only to apostolic practice but to vital pastoral care in a culture that isolates individuals one from another. Rites of blessing for those who carry communion to the homebound as well as rites for distribution exist.

Rites for the establishment and blessing of those responsible for proclamation, teaching, and sacramental oversight[18] of the word include ordination, consecration, installation, setting apart, induction, and commissioning, as well as the blessing of lectors.[19] The church is indeed called to steward the ministry of the word, and such stewardship is essential to the church's well-being. Such ministries, however, are "instituted and appointed in order that God's Word may exert its power publically."[20] The impact of these word-centered rites, therefore, is seen not only within the faith community but in the wider community as well.

One of the most crucial questions currently facing the church, a question with significant implications for the viability of its mission and ministries, is about the nature of the various offices of ministry—ordered, rostered, and lay. At this time there is no consensus among traditions about ministry. Witness recent, painful debate over ecumenical dialogues among Lutherans, Episcopalians, and various Reformed traditions. Even within the Evangelical Lutheran Church in America, we cannot point to a clear consensus on ministry.[21] Thus, we should note with care the language and actions employed to communicate what the church believes is happening in the various occasional rites used for ritually setting apart individuals for service.

Some rites help Christian communities recognize the stages in the life cycle of their own institutions. Rites for the opening of a congregation or mission, a school or seminary academic year, or an assembly or church conference remind us why these institutions exist, what God has called the church to do through these earthen vessels. Ecclesial rites of ending—when a congregation is closing, or a pastor or staff member leaves or retires—bring closure and are important for the life of the church. The same dynamic encountered at the time of death is to some extent present when a congregation or individual ends a particular ministry and is thus reflected in such rites. Usually far less emotional in impact, a rite for the closing of an academic year or assembly nevertheless lifts up both the accomplishments and hopes as well as the disappointments and sorrows of such gatherings. Importantly, God's presence and blessing are invoked not only on what has happened, but for the ongoing faith journey. The same is true for the rite of Farewell and Godspeed.[22]

Blessings and dedications of people and things constitute another dimension of occasional services. Whether the purpose of the rite is to recognize the ministry of lectors, youth, or elders (perhaps using the rites provided in the African American resource for worship, *This Far by Faith*[23]), or to dedicate a church building, its furnishings, or cemetery, such blessings announce that we stand on holy ground and that God's people are at work.

∿

Caring for the Family

Obviously individuals and families may be deeply affected by the events recognized through the rites of their faith community. When a baptism or funeral is celebrated, someone confesses wrong doing and receives pardon, or a homebound loved one becomes part of the congregation's eucharistic celebration, it is not only the congregation that is affected. Individual members and the families of which they are a part are changed. Paul understands the Christian family[24] as a microcosm of the church; what is true of the interrelatedness in Christ of the church in general is true as well for the specific family.[25] Therefore, rites that solemnize a family's significant occasions are part of the constellation of occasional services and logical extensions of the church's ministry.

The cluster of events that ritualize marriage, formally and informally, establish new beginnings for the people involved as well as their extended circle of family and friends. A new family is formed; relationships adjust and shift accordingly. Banns may be formally read or posted. Prayers of blessing may accompany the couple. In rites of affirmation and blessing on an anniversary, we remember how God has worked through these people and pray for God's ongoing providence.

A significant development within the family-related rites is the recovery of the house blessing, important for married and single individuals alike in times of transition. Pastoral theology has helped the church articulate the holiness of the dwelling, even a dormitory room, a reality long recognized, for example, by the Jewish community.[26] Case studies demonstrate how simple prayers of blessing within the gathering of one's friends aid those who have moved to become settled and established at a time normally marked by crisis and turmoil.[27]

An extension of the house blessing is the blessing of one's office or workplace, an event that invites the church to be present in the marketplace. Such rites provide strong witness to God's healing and energizing presence. In a culture that often expects people to keep work separate from the discipline of faith, a rite of blessing can begin to break down the artificial barriers.

There are familial rites for closure. The rite Farewell and Godspeed, adjusted to bless a child leaving for college, for example, explicitly extends God's constant benediction into the home. The rites associated with death announce God's providential care of and presence for the dead as well as ourselves, even when we confront the "last enemy" (1 Cor. 15:26).

~

CARING FOR THE WIDER COMMUNITY

Baptism and the ministry of the laity is the starting point for the ministry of the church to the wider community. Although ordained ministries have historically received greater attention, the ministry of all the baptized, sometimes called the ministry of the laity, is now the subject of widespread recognition.[28] Importantly, newer occasional rites associated with baptism also include rites of blessing for the vocations of all the baptized,[29] the ever-present and perennially overlooked compliment to ordained ministry. Such attention to the ministry of the laity is crucial, for it is in the daily encounter of Christians with non-Christians, in life at the border, that significant missional activity occurs.

Living day to day as God's baptized children finds us more often outside the church's building than in the pew. Our lives are punctuated by the events of birth, growth, and dying, of change and transition, of becoming and letting go, of beginnings and endings. These events place us, with Paul, in the marketplace, with the *hoi polloi* who "know not the Lord Jesus."[30] For many Christians, a simple roll call of family members will reveal people who

are unchurched, disaffected, searching, or even openly hostile to
the church. Whether or not they are members of a faith community, consider themselves freelance Christians, or believe themselves to be spiritual in some fashion, they are nevertheless in relationship with the faithful and will likely be included in family or church functions such as weddings, baptisms, funerals, or even ordinations. Some Christians feel embarrassed or uncomfortable when non-Christians are present for Christian rites, but such occasions are opportunities to embody God's always gracious invitation to draw near.

Just as the rites through which a faith community cares for itself affect the families connected with a congregation, the rites used to nurture both the faith community and the family have implications for the wider community. To some extent, then, all the occasional services could be said to serve the wider community. The occasional ministries of the church extend outward in mission from the church's life-giving engagement with the sacramental and proclaimed Word, Jesus Christ. The church lives out the relationship God has established in Christ through the power of the Spirit by entering into mission and service in the world. The church carries its godly mission into all the world in witness to God's intense and personal involvement in all of the rhythms of life. The occasional services provide a liturgical and pastoral bridge from the proclamatory and sacramental center of the church's life in worship to its borders and beyond.

The church lives from the center with its eyes on the borders, to the places and times when God's presence causes the stranger and unbeliever to stop, turn aside to notice, and ponder life's meaning. Such godly activity at the borders is easily overlooked, particularly by the church itself. The church interprets the world from its proclamatory and sacramental perspective. *Church* conjures up for Christians liturgical scenarios involving altars and pulpits, open hymnals and people singing, a vocabulary of faith, and catechized patterns of action. In these contexts God's people more or less know what to do. Strangers, however, have no experience with the proclamatory and sacramental core of faith. Liturgical celebrations may appear vaguely familiar, although often unintelligible, incidental, and even threatening.[31] Nevertheless, the church welcomes the stranger into a faith community's attempt to wrestle with life-and-death issues. Whether a crisis is spurred by a birth, marriage, divorce, move, change or loss of occupation, death, or nagging questions about self-worth and life's meaning, strangers embark on a sometimes frantic, sometimes systematic search for answers that may lead them to the church or its members. It is at these moments, when strangers tread on holy ground, that the church can and ought to speak God's welcome to them.

In the church's ministries and rites, God's Word of life and love for all creation is made incarnate.[32] What does the church say and do about the establishment of families, birth and growth, maturity and decline, dying and death? What does the church say and do about the need for human community, for God's presence in that community, and our culture's fixation on individualism? What does the church, itself compromised by internal strife, say and model to a world broken by suspicion and hatred? What does the church say and do in the face of isolation and despair, sickness and suffering? The church is privileged to bear God's invitation to be healed, restored, reconciled, and recreated. It can speak God's welcome clearly, ambiguously, or not at all, depending on how it orders its life and ministry.

The occasional services and ministries bring order to the church's inner life and public witness. Although the eucharistic gathering of the church is the meeting and meal of the baptized, the occasional ministries and their rites intentionally reach out to include those whom Paul addresses as strangers and unbelievers, individuals and groups who live at the church's borders and are not part of the eucharistic community. These people are very likely to be included among the interlocking circles of members' family and friends, associates and colleagues, neighbors and acquaintances who play important roles in Christians' lives. Thus, whenever marriages or funerals, ordinations or commissionings, house blessings and dedications occur, the church invites outsiders to the events, for they too are a part of the lives of the faithful and are affected by what happens among the faithful. The church's intention is not merely to be nice to the outsider, nor should such events be seen as opportunities to "win souls for Christ," to boost the numbers tallied by eager evangelism teams. Rather, the occasional services offer opportunities to embody God's hospitality to the stranger. Within life-cycle celebrations, strangers are invited to become acquainted with the church and its people, thereby seeing how their own family members, relatives, and friends live as a part of the church. Importantly, occasional services and ministries become the opportunities for the church to assure strangers that they, too, are cared about and prayed for.

Christians encounter strangers and unbelievers at every turn in life. Some of these people beyond the border simply never have had the opportunity to hear about or witness God's love for humankind embodied in community. Others may have been a part of a church at one time but have fallen away through boredom, crisis, or misunderstanding. Some people are distracted by and addicted to societal and cultural lures. Not a few simply have difficulty committing to any relationship in an era that has drifted into isolation and individualism. Still others have been profoundly hurt by the church's misunderstanding of its own mission and calling, alienated by the church's arrogance and hypocrisy, real or imagined. When such is the case, lines are drawn and enemies declared. Depending on the perspective, either the church or the stranger has become the hostile adversary.

The occasional ministries of the church demonstrate that God is not willing to allow creation's hostility to alienate it from God and the church. This divine will drives the church to develop ministries that struggle "to convert the *hostis* into a *hospes*, the enemy into a guest and to create the free and fearless space where brotherhood and sisterhood can be formed and fully experienced."[33] It is God's fundamental desire for unity and peace, for health and wholeness[34] that impels occasional ministry. This becomes the context and commentary on life from the cradle to the grave, the church's traditional designation for such pastoral care. Whether by establishing a new congregation, setting apart a missionary or consecrating a deaconess, blessing the vocation of all the baptized, or through the rites of healing and forgiveness, the church demonstrates and incarnates God's desire for health and salvation, reconciliation and wholeness, relationship and community. Occasional ministries bring the faithful and any in their company full circle. Life and relationship, occasional ministries remind us, are gifts of God that can be treasured but ultimately never possessed and hoarded. Regardless of the myriad ecclesiastical and ministerial patterns that have been evolving throughout history, the biblical hallmark of authentic ministry is its God-gifted ability to still the world's hostility. The ability to still hostility is possible when the church opens itself to become an instrument of God's reconciling work—sometimes in spite of itself—and discovers itself to be in need of reconciliation, healing, and forgiveness.

> God-in-Christ enters "enemy territory," a society of people so immersed in rebellion and delusion that they no longer recognize or acknowledge him. Into such an estranged world, the Holy One can only come as stranger—one unrecognized, unsought, and unloved by most of those to whom he came.[35]

The missional church is seared by the memory of all that has divided it from the love of God and neighbor, rendering even the church enemy territory (Eph. 2:13-16). Thus, old hostilities need to be reconciled and walls of sin broken down. A new creation emerges or is more clearly perceived. Through the church's gracious actions, outsiders should be able to hear, see, and respond to God's call of reconciliation and welcome. Moreover, substantive mission is not the result of Christians becoming savvy marketers of religious goods or feelings. Nor does it arise because we change the source and summit of worship, the holy ingathering of God's people who celebrate the life-giving, healing, forgiving, sustaining, merciful, and just community God makes possible. In essence, mission remains the sometimes intentional, often subtle, and seemingly insignificant process of embodying God's incredible work on behalf of creation for those who either do not know this God or have been alienated from or bored by God's people. The church's mission also becomes more credible when God's presence is found to have meaning in the day-to-day experiences of living and dying. This is the stuff of the occasional services.

∽

THE ROLE OF THE RITES IN THE WIDER COMMUNITY
Strangers who cross faith's borders are being drawn near to the center of the church's life: the eucharistic gathering of the baptized. The Spirit blows where it wills, guiding and nudging strangers in surprising and unexpected ways. The paths are many and varied; the trip is slower than card-carrying Christians might think proper, for it entails a reorienting of life itself. Strangers need time to investigate and question, to come to some understanding of the deep yearning they sense.[36] At first, the faithful might not notice the stranger's presence—across an office desk, at the gym, in the neighborhood—and openness to the ever-beckoning Spirit dwelling within God's faithful. Certainly the stranger is unlikely to be in the position to assess what is happening, at least in theological terms. Whether because of spiritual hunger, a longing, or mere curiosity, the stranger may choose to draw near, to accept an invitation to a wedding or neighbor's consecration, or simply to show up at the congregation that seems so important to a friend or acquaintance.

The church itself needs to engage in some serious cleansing of the heart, mind, and ears in order to expect strangers in its midst, as well as listen to them. Too quickly the faithful's senses are numbed to their own and others' yearning. Renowned preacher Barbara Brown Taylor observes:

My secret fear about churchgoing is that it works like a vaccine: a couple of drops under the tongue each week and pretty soon we are immune to the whole thing. The God-beseeching language requires no extraordinary effort. The summoning of the Holy Spirit expects no untoward response. Even the sacrament, when it comes, tastes more like breakfast than sacrifice.[37]

Family systems theory suggests that transitional events in life—and these are what the occasional services ritualize—constitute major upheavals and crises that can threaten destruction for the ones experiencing the events, particularly for individuals or groups who have no structured faith or for whom faith has become a major struggle. On these occasions, questions about ultimate meaning and purposefulness arise. At such critical moments, the stranger and Christian alike, out of fear, anger, despair, or hope, ask where God is in the midst of the turmoil.

Far from being nicely domesticated rituals for the initiated, the occasional services demand to be celebrated for what they are: ministry at the borders, the occasions of life full of glory and gore, joy and suffering, unvarnished and unadorned. Even the "churchy" rites such as ordination and consecration cannot afford to be tamed into pious submission, for Christ promises to send his disciples out "like lambs into the midst of wolves" (Luke 10:3). Thus it is that the church prays for laity committed to serve in the world as well as to have "courage, patience, and vision."[38] Ordinands also submit to pointed vows.[39] Taylor offers some sage advice:

> One good way to get some perspective on this is to leave church more often—not permanently, but regularly—to vacate the holy premises and mingle with people whose lives do not include church. Ask them why not and listen to what they say without trying to convince them they are wrong. Find out what really matters to them, and stay open to the possibility that they too know something about the truth. Then head back to church with them in tow, if only in your heart, and let them nag you while you are doing whatever you do there.[40]

THE SHAPE OF THE RITES

The occasional services display a clear unity of purpose despite the myriad differences of detail and specific, ritual purpose.[41] The table of contents of *Occasional Services* or other similar resources lists rites, prayers, and liturgical resources that at first glance seem to be related to one another only insofar as they are religious observances for a particular tradition. What is not as readily apparent is the sheer force of the faith community's life required to integrate these various ritual acts.[42] What holds the occasional services together is an implicit pattern of meaning and movement operative in all such rites. This pattern functions, crudely put, in the same way and for the same purpose as notes posted on the family's refrigerator: the schedules and reminders keep the whole family mindful of individuals' and groups' appointments, obligations, and important events.

The occasional services' implicit patterns all serve to remind individuals and communities that we do not live in isolation. When the family dashes from the dinner table and the church is dismissed into the world to serve, life conspires to isolate and fragment. The professional juggles family and work demands; soccer and PTA compete with family dinner and intimacy; individualism and indifference ravage the faith community into which God calls people. Thus, for the church, the occasional services celebrate and solemnize the occasions in a faith community that bind together God's people throughout all time and ages. The intentional remembering and celebrating of these widely varying events form the rhythm of the church's life together. To ignore, forget, or avoid these occasions in the midst of business-as-usual can inflict pain and suffering. The birthday or anniversary forgotten, the promotion uncelebrated, or the farewell assiduously avoided can haunt and cripple. Ignoring a parishioner's gift to the church, failing to recognize new and veteran Sunday school teachers, or forgetting the pastor's or congregation's significant anniversary all strike at the heart of the faith community's ministry and mission.

Gathering and Invitation

Each occasional service has as its context Christ's body the church, the called-out, baptized, and eucharistic community, whether or not the entire community has gathered for the particular occasion. Even when the rite involves, for example, only a pastor and penitent or family and friends gathered for a house blessing, the church is by definition represented and present. When occasional services do occur within the congregation's Sunday liturgy, the congregation has the opportunity to focus on an individual's or group's specific gifts. God's Spirit gifts people variously (1 Cor. 12:4-11, 27-31). Gathered from the midst of God's people are groups or individuals who will be specifically addressed in the rite, whether they be ordinands, confirmands, or seekers who desire closer connection with the church. They will be for a time or forever set apart for the sake of the community. Significant life-cycle events or our discerning God's invitation into varied ministries results in a transformed understanding of a people's future mission.

The occasional services signal relational shifts—radical shifts through marriage or death—both for individuals and the entire parish. The occasional services may even be said to mark crisis moments—those times and events that make it impossible to think and react as one heretofore has. In such cases, perspective alters; one's vision undergoes transformation. Importantly, the gathering for the occasional rites names and situates those specifically involved. The time of gathering may require statements of intent or vows to be spoken that give shape and content to the transitional event. Witnesses or sponsors provide further testimony that the individuals or groups involved are in a position to undertake what the church celebrates.

The Word

Once gathered, appropriate passages of scripture are read that speak of God's fidelity and presence in the events of life, God's desire for all creation to be healed and restored to relationship with God, God's sorrow in moments of tragedy, and God's rejoicing with the church in the joyful events of life and ministry. As the story of God's own unfathomable, limitless love for the cosmos is told, strangers and the faithful alike, no matter what the circumstances, hear their own stories addressed by God's love. Basic gestures such as anointing; imposition of hands; an embrace, holy kiss, or welcoming handshake often are paired in scripture with a description of God's and the church's activity. The occasional services include these ritual embodiments of the word because of their accessibility even to the stranger.[43] In some occasional services, objects or symbols are given as reminders of the word's creative power—a ring, a stole, or a book.

Preaching may be a part of the occasional services, particularly for the great life-cycle events for church, family, and individual: marriage, funeral, ordination, or consecration, for example. Here the gospel is made concrete for the particular community. Here the gospel breaks through the fragility of human existence and declares God's radical, saving work on our behalf throughout all our lives, whether or not strangers and unbelievers are yet able to perceive salvation. Preaching can more fully welcome into the life of God's people even strangers who now can only muster curiosity or a dull hunger. Ultimately, God's story proclaimed and preached in its fullness provides the missional alternative, allowing the despondent to "give up, abandon, and renounce other stories that have shaped their lives in false or distorting ways."[44]

Theologically, prayer is closely associated with the word.

Prayer, the daily conversation of the faithful living in response to the word,[45] is the Spirit's gift to humankind and all creation, a yearning and desire for health and wholeness, for relationship with God, even when creation has lost its capacity to pray (Rom. 8:22-25). The prayers of the occasional services articulate the hopes of the faith community about the given occasion. The prayers are not mere texts to be rushed through; they form hearts and minds to what is indeed possible in Christ (James 5:16).

Reintegrating into the Eucharistic Community

The process of reintegrating members and friends of a faith community into that community, moving beyond the occasion and becoming again a part of the whole, is essential if Christian ministry is to serve God's desire for wholeness and health, reconciliation and unity.[46] Ministry does not end with an incident or occasion such as death, marriage, an anniversary, sickness, or dissension. Always, we need to move beyond that singular event. The occasional services are brief opportunities to step aside and discover that life is changing and the ground is holy. But such journeys are made in order to return to the community with hope restored and to serve God's people. The Spirit moves us inexorably toward community, wholeness, and healing, because life is found in unity; brokenness and death, in disunity and isolation.

The occasional services describe ministry and mission, a moving out and returning, a pattern of living and being that God constantly renews. Vision is transformed and gives rise to a heightened sense of mission in the saving encounter with the word. New possibilities for living are seen and new hopes voiced. The lowly are lifted up and the puffed-up confounded in their self-sufficiency. Those who sat in darkness begin to be bathed in the light of God's presence. Strangers are brought near; masks of anonymity and hostility are dropped. A bath refreshes, restores, recreates; the holy conversation continues. Finally, the table is set and all is prepared. "[W]e had to celebrate and rejoice, because this brother of yours was dead and has come to life; he was lost and has been found" (Luke 15:32).

The occasional ministries of the church and the associated rites make the gospel concrete in the midst of living and dying, voicing God's cosmic love for a creation still largely ignorant of or hostile to that love. The invitation of this good news must be as good in the marketplace and in the midst of the wilderness as in the liturgy. The gospel is not a carping attack on the world in general, an attack that cuts off strangers before they can draw near. It must be perceived

even by strangers to be "good," a compelling word to "turn around
and notice" (the root meaning of *conversion*). Only then can the
gospel begin to reveal God's presence in the midst of a stranger's
own troubled life. Strangers are invited to draw near—to cross the
borders and be welcomed into the midst of God's holy people.

$\sim$

The right rite when there is no rite: a case study
A careful survey of the present occasional services continually
reveals opportunities and occasions in the lives of Christians in the
world that sometimes cry out for ritual observance. Cultural taboos
and misguided care can silence the church when it should speak and
act. The changing and always evolving vagaries of life surface new
occasions for ministry. But what is the church to do when it encounters occasions for which there seem to be no appropriate
prayers or accepted ways to ritualize the events? All too often individuals plunge in with good intention but remain ill informed.

For example, a perennial issue seminarians and pastors face in
hospital obstetrics units is the care of stillborn or miscarried infants.
The scenario is a pastoral nightmare: the caregiver encounters dis-
traught and grieving parents, or sometimes only a grieving mother
if no father has been named. The parent's thoughts are haunted by
what-ifs. Did poor self-care or a traumatic experience precipitate
the miscarriage? Did the fetus die as the result of some genetic
defect that will reappear if the couple conceives again? Is the mother
physically capable of carrying a fetus to term? The caregiver feels
impotent to speak of God's desire for life when life itself perhaps
never had a chance. Hospital staff members, some superbly trained
to minister to people reeling from shock, nevertheless are compelled
to bring the event to some sort of closure. Misguided friends and
family may try to comfort by suggesting that the couple can always
have another child. In effect, the parents are urged to forget that the
stillborn or miscarried child ever existed. Someone might suggest,
"God had more need of the little angel and called it home." God, by
default, becomes the perpetrator of a cruel hoax, particularly if the
parents have experienced previous miscarriages.

Frequently, the caregiver, wishing to be "pastoral," accedes to
the request or suggests that the stillborn or miscarried infant be
baptized, particularly if the caregiver or the parents are members of
a tradition that baptizes infants. The desperate logic is clear: the
church baptizes babies. A baby is present, albeit miscarried or stillborn. The parents are grieving not only for their child but for their

own dashed hopes; they hunger for God's presence in this time of terrible loneliness. Therefore, the baby shall be baptized, because the church has no other rites specifically for infants. Moreover, the act will be a harmless albeit well-intentioned source of comfort for the parents.

Unfortunately, this scenario is invariably played out in a matter of minutes, allowing no time for serious reflection on the ramifications of any decisions made. It is often in the heat of the moment, when pastoral demands loom large and the caregiver does not have the leisure to work out biblical, theological, and long-term pastoral implications, that knee-jerk ritualizing can play havoc with the church's life and mission embodied as word and sacrament.

Although one in three pregnancies ends in a miscarriage, other painful experiences are not encountered as frequently. No matter how common the event, however, when caregivers, pastors, or church workers sense that uncharted territory has been entered and there are no appropriate rites for the occasion, through conversation and reflection they might consider whether at least a provisional rite should be prepared. First, reflection on their own ministry and conversations with colleagues in the field can help them to ascertain whether they are facing an isolated incident or a common, though perhaps unrecognized, life experience.

In the case of stillborn and miscarried infants, a provisional rite was prepared by Pastor Janet S. Peterman in 1988 to care better for grieving parents as well as to acknowledge the loss of relationship.[47] Peterman's reflection and research on miscarriage, the absence of any such rite, our societal tendency to be silent about such deaths, the sublimated grief that results, and the discussion and widespread acceptance the rite engendered after publication provide a general pattern for addressing similar situations.

Reflecting on her research and pastoral experience, Peterman concludes that it is possible to identify the "shape" of a rite dealing with stillborn and miscarried infants. Peterman senses the context to be God's providential care and love for all of creation: God calls life into being and receives all who have died into eternal welcome of God's presence. A rite is drawn up that recognizes three "burning bushes": (1) we acknowledge the integrity and identity of the child; (2) we recognize God's knowledge of human grief and that God has already embraced the child in mercy; and (3) we provide closure, so that life may go on for family and friends. Peterman provides a way to respond to grieving parents who assume that baptism is the only possible option for the child. Instead, the church is able to respond neither with a denial nor by capitulating to grief and compromising the place and meaning of sacraments, but with a positive and solid alternative.

All the occasional services, whether already available or as yet undiscovered, serve as commentary and guidance through the significant and often troublesome events of living and dying. They strengthen the faith community's bonds of relationship, assist the community to welcome the stranger, incorporate individuals within the community, and reiterate at every stage of life God's constant presence and protection.

Occasional services that speak good news can begin to shape the stranger's entrance and participation in the church. These services make the gospel word specific in the midst of life and death. They voice God's cosmic love for a creation still largely ignorant of that love, intentionally inviting strangers to cross the borders into the midst of God's holy people.

NOTES

1. *Constitution on the Sacred Liturgy* (Second Vatican Council: 4 December 1963), par. 2, 7–10. See also *Baptism, Eucharist and Ministry* (Geneva: World Council of Churches, 1982), viii, 16:28–31.

2. Gordon W. Lathrop, ed., *What Are the Essentials of Christian Worship?* Open Questions in Worship, vol. 1 (Minneapolis: Augsburg Fortress, 1994), 7. More recently, *Holy People: A Liturgical Ecclesiology* (Minneapolis: Fortress Press, 1999).

3. Darrell L. Guder, ed., *Missional Church: A Vision for the Sending of the Church in North America* (Grand Rapids, Mich.: Wm. B. Eerdmans, 1998).

4. Frank C. Senn, "The Care of the Earth as a Paradigm for the Treatment of the Eucharistic Elements," *A Stewardship of the Mysteries* (New York: Paulist Press, 1999), 175–90.

5. *Constitution on the Sacred Liturgy*, par. 5.

6. Representative examples are: Herbert Anderson and Edward Foley, *Mighty Stories—Dangerous Rituals: Weaving Together the Human and the Divine* (San Francisco: Jossey-Bass, 1998); Dorothy C. Bass, ed., *Practicing Our Faith: A Way of Life for Searching People* (San Francisco: Jossey-Bass, 1997); Edwin H. Friedman, *Generation to Generation: Family Process in Church and Synagogue* (New York: Guilford, 1985); Evan Imber-Black and Janine Roberts, *Rituals for Our Times: Celebrating, Healing, and Changing Our Lives and Our Relationships* (New York: HarperPerennial, 1992).

7. Imber-Black and Roberts, "Holiday Rituals: Celebrating with Merriment, Memory, and Meaning"; "Life Cycle Rituals: Living Life's Changes"; and "Keeping Your Rituals Alive," in *Rituals for Our Times*, 229–306.

8. For example, Raymond E. Brown, *The Churches the Apostles Left Behind* (New York: Paulist Press, 1984); Bonnie Thurston, *Spiritual Life in the Early Church: The Witness of Acts and Ephesians* (Minneapolis: Fortress Press, 1993); as well as numerous studies of the church orders that address the liturgical life of the early church.

9. The Large Catechism preface, 4–27, in *The Book of Concord: The Confessions*

of the Evangelical Lutheran Church, trans. and ed. Theodore G. Tappert et al. (Philadelphia: Fortress Press, 1959), 362–64; and Carl E. Braaten and Robert W. Jenson, eds., *Marks of the Body of Christ* (Grand Rapids, Mich.: Wm. B. Eerdmans, 1999).

10. Rom. 12:5; 1 Cor. 3:16f; 4:1-2; 6:19; 10:16f; 12:27; Eph. 2:19, 21; 4:4-13; 5:23; Col. 1:18; 1 Peter 2:5, 9.

11. *Occasional Services* (Minneapolis: Augsburg Publishing House; Philadelphia: Board of Publication, Lutheran Church in America, 1982).

12. Following the Roman Catholic promulgation of the *Rite of Christian Initiation of Adults* (RCIA) in 1974, Episcopal, Lutheran, United Methodist, and Reformed rites related to holy baptism for adults and affirmation of baptism have been published.

13. Martin Dudley and Geoffrey Rowell, eds., *Confession and Absolution* (Collegeville, Minn.: Liturgical Press, 1990), 23–24, as well as The Large Catechism, 4, 74–75, in *The Book of Concord,* 445.

14. Petitions, Intercessions, and Thanksgivings, *Lutheran Book of Worship* (Minneapolis: Augsburg Publishing House; Philadelphia: Board of Publication, Lutheran Church in America, 1978), 45.

15. Geoffrey Rowell, *The Liturgy of Christian Burial: An Introductory Survey of the Historical Development of Christian Burial Rites* (London: Alcuin, 1977); and Richard Rutherford, *The Death of a Christian: The Order of Christian Funerals* (Collegeville, Minn.: Pueblo Books, 1990).

16. *LBW,* 213.

17. Holy Baptism, Ibid., 125.

18. The Augsburg Confession 5.1–4, in *The Book of Concord,* 31.

19. Blessings of Lectors, *This Far by Faith: An African American Resource for Worship* (Minneapolis: Augsburg Fortress, 1999), 77.

20. The Large Catechism 1, 94, in *The Book of Concord,* 378.

21. *Together for Ministry: Final Report and Recommendations Task Force on The Study of Ministry 1988–1993* (Minneapolis: Augsburg Fortress, 1993), par. 98–101; "Officially Recognized Ministries," par. 30–31. See also Braaten and Jenson, eds., "Ordination: The Special Ministry of the Ordained," *Marks of the Body of Christ,* 123–36.

22. *Occasional Services,* 151–52.

23. Blessings of Lectors, Young People Coming to Adulthood, Blessing of Women and Men, and Blessing of Elders, *This Far by Faith,* 77–79, 104–106, 110–11, 112.

24. *Family* in this study is understood to include not only multigenerational, related people but also to a large extent unmarried individuals, their immediate relatives, and their closest friends.

25. Eph. 5:32. Despite what often is skewed to support male dominance in relationships, Paul's referent for relationship, individual and communal, is that of Christ's relationship to humankind (not of male to female!) marked by a mutual forbearance and self-offering for the other, motivated out of a fundamental love and respect of the other's being and well-being.

26. Hayim H. Donin, *To Be a Jew: A Guide to Jewish Observance in Contemporary Life* (New York: Basic, 1972), 8–12, 36–38.

27. Elaine Ramshaw, *Ritual and Pastoral Care* (Philadelphia: Fortress Press, 1987), 13.

28. For example, David N. Power, *Gifts That Differ: Lay Ministries Established and Unestablished* (New York: Pueblo Publishing, 1985).

29. Representative Lutheran and United Methodist rites are: Affirmation of the Vocation of the Baptized in the World, *Welcome to Christ: Lutheran Rites for*

the Catechumenate (Minneapolis: Augsburg Fortress, 1997), 59–61; A Service for Affirmation of Ministry in Daily Life, *Come to the Waters* (Nashville: Discipleship Resources, 1996), 120–21.

30. From "A Bidding Prayer (Traditional)" in Advent Festival of Lessons and Music. *The Book of Occasional Services—1994* (New York: Church Hymnal Corp., 1995), 32.

31. Author Kathleen Norris remembers that she felt "bombarded by the vocabulary of the Christian Church." In her most recent work she explores the "scariest" words of this vocabulary in order to "inhabit it, to claim it" as hers. *Amazing Grace: A Vocabulary of Faith* (New York: Riverhead Books, 1998), 2f.

32. The familiar passage from John's gospel is blunted in English translation. God's love is described in the Greek to extend to the entire cosmos, not just the "world." See John 3:16, "For God so loved [τὸν κόσμον]."

33. Henri Nouwen, *Reaching Out: The Three Movements of the Spiritual Life* (Garden City, N.Y.: Doubleday, 1975), 46.

34. This is the basic meaning of *salvation*, rather than a quest for souls or a snatching from the jaws of hell. Werner Foerster, σώζω, *Theological Dictionary of the New Testament*, ed. Gerhard Friedrich and trans. Geoffrey Bromiley (Grand Rapids, Mich.: Wm. B. Eerdmans, 1971), 7:990–98.

35. Marjorie J. Thompson, *Soul Feast: An Invitation to the Christian Spiritual Life* (Louisville, Ky.: Westminster/John Knox, 1995), 124.

36. See, for example, Douglas John Hall, *Why Christian? For Those on the Edge of Faith* (Minneapolis: Fortress Press, 1998) or the various essays in *Welcome to Christ: A Lutheran Introduction to the Catechumenate* (Minneapolis: Augsburg Fortress, 1997).

37. Barbara Brown Taylor, "Leaving the Church," *The Christian Century* 116, no. 18 (June 16–23, 1999): 655.

38. Affirmation of the Vocation of Christians in the World, *Occasional Services*, 148.

39. Ordination, *Occasional Services*, 193–94.

40. Taylor, "Leaving the Church," 655.

41. It is not the purpose of this essay to chart the unique development of each rite, to discuss, for example, differences in understanding of ordained ministry within one faith tradition, nor to offer a comparative study of specific rites of several traditions. Rather, the purpose of this study suggests ways that the constellation of occasional services in conjunction with the central things of faith serve together "for building up of the body of Christ, until all of us come to the unity of the faith...." See Eph. 4:1-16.

42. Friedman, "A Family Approach to Life Cycle Ceremonies," 162–90; "The Extended Family: Its Potential for Salvation," *Generation to Generation*, 294–309.

43. *Missional Church*, 181.

44. Walter Brueggemann, *Biblical Perspectives on Evangelism* (Nashville: Abingdon Press, 1993), 10.

45. "Sermon at the Dedication of the Castle Church at Torgau: Luke 14:1-11, October 5, 1544," in *Luther's Works*, ed. Helmut T. Lehmann (Philadelphia: Fortress Press, 1959), 51:333.

46. This is why, for example, Lutheran theology has a difficult time with "absolute" ordination, that is, ordaining those whose calling is not clearly related to some viable expression of a faith community.

47. It was subsequently published in *Lutheran Partners* 4, no. 4 (July/August 1988): 21–24.

Liturgy and Mission in the North American Context

Gordon W. Lathrop

THE ASSEMBLY for worship is itself a gift from God. We may give thanks that we can go to such a place of truth telling and refuge, sing such songs, tell such stories, eat such a meal of grace, enact and remember such a bathing in grace, celebrate such a great forgiveness. These central marks of the faithful Christian assembly—word and sacrament amid a singing, participating people—overwhelm us with mercy. In a certain sense, their very existence is itself enough. The meeting for worship is its own end. Indeed, whenever we try to turn that meeting to some particular purpose of our own—to build up our numbers, increase our income, shore up our children's or our neighbor's morality—we find that we diminish the honest truth and the rich mercy of the meeting itself. Authentic reform invites us simply to receive the great central gifts of the faithful meeting in their clarity and strength and let them be. They are astonishing gifts and they are enough.

And yet, like every gift of God, the gift of the assembly for worship also keeps on giving more widely and more surprisingly than we had expected. It turns inside out. It reaches out to give meaning and mercy not only to those of us who are gathered—those who call this assembly "our church"—but to anyone who would come near our gathering, to all people around our gathering, to the world itself. These stories and songs, this bath and this meal are for everyone, especially for those who are hungry, little, lost, regarded as unclean by the others. Such is the surprising mission of God that is always planted in the heart of our liturgy.

LITURGY
AND MISSION
IN THE
NORTH
AMERICAN
CONTEXT

Worship, then, is not just for us. Lines of connection and meaning run out from the worship gathering to the very contours of ordinary daily life, to the structures of our societies, to the commerce and communication between peoples, to the earth itself and all its animate and inanimate inhabitants. The stories of Christian worship tell of the hope and life, passion and loss, sin, need, and death that all people know. And they narrate the judgment and passion of God amid this universal need, proclaiming God's still unfrustrated, continuing creation of all things and God's triumphant, all-covering mercy.

Furthermore, the meal of Christian worship promises a time when there will be food for all. And the bath, which has introduced each of us to participation in Christian worship, identifies the baptized with Jesus Christ, who identifies with all. Even in its most personal moments—my baptism, a Bible story I love, the body and blood of Christ given and shed for me—Christian worship always refers to the wider world. Baptism makes me brother or sister of a multitude. The Bible story draws the earth itself into its saving narrative. The food of communion is always "given and shed" for a plural "you" and is passed on and on to the hungry world. The gifts at the heart of worship all turn inside out.

There are several ways we may articulate this continual surprise of worship. We may make a simple, powerful assertion, such as that made by the great Lutheran preacher Alvin Rogness: If you are accustomed to pray using something like the words of the old Sunday school song—"Into my heart, into my heart, come into my heart, Lord Jesus; come in today; come in to stay; come into my heart, Lord Jesus"—be careful. He will come, as he promises. But when he comes, he will bring with him all those who belong to him. That is a great crowd. If it is truly Christ who comes, your heart will be filled with all the little and needy ones of the earth. Such is always the outward turn of Christian worship.

Another such assertion was made by Martin Luther concerning participation in holy communion. At that supper, where each of us is quite personally given mercy and relief by Christ, we too are inserted into a community of such mercy and relief:

> When you have partaken of this sacrament, therefore, or desire to partake of it, you must in turn share the misfortunes of the fellowship.... Here your heart must go out in love and learn that this is a sacrament of love. As love and support are given to you, you in turn must render love and support to Christ in his needy ones. You must feel with sorrow all the dishonor done to Christ in his holy Word, all the misery of Christendom, all the unjust suffering of the innocent,

with which the world is everywhere filled to overflowing. You must fight, work, pray, and—if you cannot do more—have heartfelt sympathy. See, this is what it means to bear in your turn the misfortune and adversity of Christ and his saints. Here the saying of Paul is fulfilled, "Bear one another's burdens, and so fulfill the law of Christ." See, as you uphold all of them, so they all in turn uphold you; and all things are in common, both good and evil. Then all things become easy, and the evil spirit cannot stand up against this fellowship.[1]

Authentic worship—worship in word and sacrament, even very personal participation in word and sacrament—turns inside out.

But how do these lines of meaning run out from the Christian assembly to the specific North American context in which our assemblies find themselves? Or, to ask the question in the other direction, how does Christ bring North America as well as the rest of the world when he comes into the hearts of assembled Christians? And how, in that assembly, may we be formed to give love and support to Christ in his needy ones in North America?

∿

CHRISTIAN ASSEMBLY IN THE NORTH AMERICAN CULTURAL CONTEXT

The assembly that is turned inside out, if it is faithful, is related to the culture of North Americans in several ways. Culture is found, after all, not just in museums. Current culture is made up of the ways we actually live in interdependence with each other and with the land where we dwell. Culture is the sum of those patterns—in language, symbol making, food sharing, social organization, and much more—which we reinforce in ourselves and pass on to our children, patterns that both provide and reflect the shape and values of such common life. A Christian assembly in North America will inevitably—both subtly and not so subtly!—be marked by the cultures of these lands where we live. Indeed, trusting that God is the creator of both land and people, such an assembly will treasure much that belongs to our human life here: our languages, our ways of gathering and making music, our widespread democratic values. But if it is a Christian assembly, it will not just be a gathering centered around our North American values. The assembly in word and sacrament, the assembly gathered in the name of the triune God, will call us to a way of living on the land that comes from standing before that God, under the mercy of that God. The assembly may even invite us to resist certain characteristics of the pervasive North American cultures. In any case, it will certainly invite us to see ourselves as a people in

LITURGY
AND MISSION
IN THE
NORTH
AMERICAN
CONTEXT

communion with other peoples of many other cultures, many other ways of living on the lands of the earth, many other patterns of inter-dependence from throughout the world.

Culture is thus a term referring to the ways people live. If our Christian worship turns inside out, then it also turns toward the cultures of the people who live near our worship assemblies. Indeed, it turns toward our own ways of daily living, since we are part of those people.

When thinking about this relationship of worship and culture, we are helped by a statement crafted by Christians from around the world who met in Nairobi, Kenya, in 1996 as part of the Lutheran World Federation Study of Worship and Culture. This "Nairobi Statement" asserts:

> Christian worship relates dynamically to culture in at least four ways. First, it is *transcultural*, the same substance for everyone everywhere, beyond culture. Second, it is *contextual*, varying according to the local situation (both nature and culture). Third, it is *counter-cultural*, challenging what is contrary to the Gospel in a given culture. Fourth, it is *cross-cultural*, making possible sharing between different local cultures. In all four dynamics, there are helpful principles which can be identified.[2]

We can make use of these categories when thinking about Christian worship in our own cultural contexts.

Here in North America, too, faithful Christian worship will need to have a transcultural heart. After all, what we have seen is that it is God's gift of word and sacrament, at the center of a participating assembly, that turns inside out. Lutherans believe that the practice of baptism, the reading and preaching of the scriptures, and the celebration of the holy communion are all given to us by God. The central use of these things marks and defines any given gathering as indeed being Christ's church, no matter in what cultural context it occurs. The absence or insignificance of these things in our gatherings, on the other hand, leaves us prey to making our own culture into the center of the meeting and leaves us doubtful about whether this meeting—no matter whether we call it a "worship service" or not—is really Christ's church. Word and sacrament need to be at the center of our gatherings and need to be seen there in order for those gatherings to relate in authentic Christian dialogue with our cultures.

But here in North America, these gatherings for word and sacrament take place among us and our ways of living in the land, our cultures. Our ways of being together, our manners of communicating, gathering, leading will inevitably provide a context for the meeting. Indeed, they will come into the meeting. This is a good thing, rather like the old Christian image of all the treasures of the nations being carried into the city of God (Rev. 21:26), as all the people of earth are finally brought to gather around the throne of God and of the Lamb. What are the North American treasures? Of course, they are our ways of making music, doing art, erecting buildings. They are our ways of speaking English as well as the many other languages that are alive in our midst. All these are very welcome in the assembly, as long as they come in to serve God's gospel in Christ and God's people gathered in word and sacrament.

But there is also much more. For whatever historical reasons, North Americans have come to treasure the importance of individual life, though we also sometimes ignore and suppress it. North American life has also come to be marked by a deep resistance to inappropriate authority and a deep belief in the value of democracy. And North Americans have slowly learned to abandon the old idea that the "melting pot" would make one single people out of us, instead accepting the idea that we are many—both diverse First Peoples and also relatively "new" Americans from European, African, Asian, and Oceanic origins—and our oneness will have to come in the midst of our continued diversity. These cultural values can also be welcome in the Christian assembly. Christian worship, centered in word and sacrament, can best be celebrated in North America in a personal-communal way, one in which each individual is treasured, addressed, and honored amid the continuing importance of the whole assembly. And Christian worship will be appropriately contextualized in North America when its gathering for word and sacrament has many leaders—choirs and musicians and readers and leaders of prayer and ministers of communion—drawn from among the whole people, and when its principal presiding minister has a sense of serving the assembly, building a climate of mutual trust. Furthermore, a diversity of peoples gathered together in one body belongs to the very gospel of Christ, not just to our own cultural moment. If we will receive God's gift, our familiar cultural longing for unity amid diversity may find its fulfillment in Christ.

But the very gifts we may bring into the Christian assembly also have their shadow side. Our individualism can become the overwhelming interest of each individual in the well-being of his or her self. Indeed, the fulfillment and success of the self can become our major religion, no matter what other name we give this all-consuming value. Furthermore, our despair of the melting pot can become simply racism or classism, straight-out. And democratic

LITURGY
AND MISSION
IN THE
NORTH
AMERICAN
CONTEXT

values can lead us to refuse even legitimate authority, even the authority of one who speaks the word of God, if that authority challenges the autonomy of the self. Paradoxically, our distrust of authority can yield to an idolization of celebrities when these charismatic figures promise happiness—or at least, entertainment and diversion. Even our music, art, and languages can be used in ways essentially intended to serve only the self. The music I like, for example—whether this is Baroque or Romantic or folk or gospel or Christian rock—can be disguised with sacred terminology and then used exclusively, as if it were the only really holy music.

Thus, in North America, Christian worship must also sometimes be marked by the countercultural dynamic. This dynamic will be present as the Christian assembly seeks to make sure that word and sacrament—not the self, not the charisma of the leader, not any race or class, not any musician or music group or particular music—are at the center of the meeting. But the countercultural dynamic will be even more active in our midst as the Christian assembly sees the astonishing surprise: God's purpose to include in our meeting the wounded and marginalized people that our culture intentionally excludes as unsuccessful themselves and as irrelevant to the success of our own self. God will show this purpose by saving us with a word that always includes the little and the wounded ones. God has washed each of us with a bath that identifies us with Jesus Christ, who identifies himself with the unclean, the marginalized, the sinners, and the dying. God feeds us with a meal meant only for the hungry and thus meant profoundly for all. Thus, God calls these forgotten ones to our minds, placing them in our prayers, identifying us with them, sending us toward them. Faithful Christian worship, with its word and bath and meal intended for everyone, will not allow a hegemony by any one culture. Faithful worship, with word and sacrament at its center, turns inside out, often in a countercultural way.

This very relativization of our own culture can be further served by the cross-cultural dynamic. The Christian assembly through history has often engaged in a cross-cultural exchange of gifts with other assemblies from other times and other places. If, for example, a community of African Christians is willing to share with us a song that was born in their midst as their own cultural patterns were brought into the assembly in praise of the triune God, we may receive that gift while receiving with the song at least three other gifts as well. Singing that song, we will be able to see that no one music—nor any other single cultural phenomenon—is "holy" by itself. We will see that culture comes into the meeting best as it serves the center of the meeting, not as it tries to become the center of the meeting. And we will find our own worship service in tangible communion with other Christians in another place. Contemporary Christian assemblies for worship in North America are rightly receiving such diverse gifts from other places, as long as they make sure that these are genuinely gifts, not stolen goods used without the consent of the places from which they come.

When Christ comes into the assembly, he brings with him those who belong to him in North America. They come with their democratic and multicultural values, their songs and languages. But the wounded and forgotten ones, the culturally damaged ones, also come. So do other peoples from other places. Our worship turns inside out, inviting our own hearts to open, sending us with love and support into the world.

But how shall we actually do this in North America? These characterizations of our worship—that it should be transcultural, contextual, countercultural, and cross-cultural—sound abstract, perhaps unclear. What shall we actually do? And will this practice actually express God's inside-out-turning mission?

~

ORGANIZING THE ASSEMBLY FOR MISSION

The first clear answer to these questions arises from the center of our assembly itself. We should do word and sacrament in strength. This book has demonstrated the missional importance of these central things and has examined their practice. But the point bears repeating. We will be faithfully present in North America as we continue to hold assemblies—on Sunday, first, but also on other days—in which the scriptures are read and preached so that in the power of the Spirit, the death and resurrection of Jesus Christ are known as God's action for the life of the world. We will be at the heart of God's mission in North America as, right beside the reading and preaching, we eat and drink that very same word, made present in the gift of Christ's body and blood in the holy supper, and do so at least every Sunday. And we will begin to be formed into North American witnesses to this God's life-giving mercy as we respond to the preached and tasted word with prayers for all the needy world, with gifts of food, money, and support that can be given away to those who are hungry for food and for dignity, and with a way to welcome others into our witnessing community by bringing them to that washing with water and the word we call baptism.

It matters for mission that each of our congregations should do word and sacrament in strength. Scripture, preaching, prayers of

LITURGY
AND MISSION
IN THE
NORTH
AMERICAN
CONTEXT

intercession, the meal of thanksgiving in Christ, and a collection for mission and for the poor—these make up that transcultural center of Christian liturgy to which the Nairobi Statement calls us. These are the things that by God's gift turn our meetings for worship inside out. These are the things that are to be done in this context. These are the gifts that bear witness to who the triune God really is and to what the triune God is actually doing. There is much talk about God and about Jesus in North America. In many ways, our cultures are soaked in religion and spirituality. But without the stories of the scriptures, without "this is my body, given for you," without the living water of baptism, this talk can be hazy, unhelpful, perhaps gnostic, often simply code words for the self. The life-giving presence of God is actually given in word and sacrament.

So these are urgent matters for the renewal of our congregations in mission:

- that the scriptures be read in fullness, as proposed in the three-year lectionary, and that they be read with clarity and strength and beauty;
- that preaching open up these scriptural texts to hold our needs and our hopes in the death and resurrection of Christ, and so to bring us to faith in the life-giving mercy of the triune God;
- that the assembly then pray for the real needs of the world and of the churches in mission in the world;
- that the Lord's supper be held as the principal service of every congregation, every Sunday, and that the assembly eat and drink Christ's gift;
- that many people participate in leading this assembly and that all the leaders understand their roles as marked by serving love;
- that a collection be taken, of which a large part is given away to people in need;
- and that each congregation surround those adults and children who are coming to join the assembly through the waters of baptism with communal support, prayer, and mutual faith sharing.

The continually recovered strength of word and sacrament in the congregations matters for mission. But the astonishing truth about these central matters of liturgy and mission is that, allowed their strength, they are not really very religious. The central actions of the Christian assembly are not obscure and arcane rituals nor rare and magical substances. At the heart of faithful Christian worship there live stories, a meal, and a great bath. We are given by the risen Christ the use of a book, bread and wine, water. If we use these gifts in such a way as to let them stand in clarity, undiminished and unobscured, they will show us the remarkable connections that exist between our worship and daily life, between the center of worship and its cultural context.

So, for example, let the Lord's supper be practiced as a meal. That is: let us use real and beautiful bread and a real drink from a great cup of good wine. Let the altar be seen as a table, a great and important and yet utterly simple table, around which we gather, with the one who presides facing us and with the food of our meal on the table. Let the prayer be the great thanksgiving prayer of a meal. Let many people help to serve the meal. We will not receive a belly-filling menu here, but only the bread and cup of the meal, the old Jewish beginning and end of a meal, the food to which Jesus gave his promise. Still, let us bring much more food than that—and money to buy food—and then let us give away all these gifts to the hungry—directly, through food pantries in our own churches or communities, and more indirectly, through relief agencies that build up the dignity and mutually caring life of those they help.

Then our celebration will be seen to cast a light over our daily life. All of our meals will be drawn into a reflection of the meaning of the holy supper. At our daily tables we may see these things: Food is a marvelous gift of God. It is not to be wasted but shared. Hospitality is a high Christian virtue. Meals are to be taken with thanksgiving. And thanksgiving to God, the triune God known in Jesus Christ, inevitably brings with it the prayer for the hungry beyond our table and the witnessing gesture of sending such food as we can to those who have none. As long as a meal remains the primary act of Christian worship and as long Christian believers see the connection between that meal and our daily tables, issues of world hunger and of the distribution of resources that people need to live will not disappear from the agenda of Christian daily life. In North America, with its rich agricultural resources and its plentiful and relatively inexpensive food, that ordering of our meals, with the meal of the eucharist at the center, is a missional priority. Yet in North America, with its tendency to individualism, we need to recover ordinary communal or familial meals full of hospitality and joy and shared meaning. This need also remains in Christian communities.

Similar connections to the patterns of daily living can be drawn from the other central matters of the assembly when these matters are practiced in ways that are generous and strong. The great book of the assembly, for example, carried and read and preached in the service as if we were gathered around the very Book of life itself, invites us to pay attention to all the stories by which we live, for our daily lives are accompanied and shaped by stories. In North America, these stories

LITURGY
AND MISSION
IN THE
NORTH
AMERICAN
CONTEXT

include the brief dramas of television advertisements as well as the patterns of sitcoms and soap operas. There are also movies, newspaper reports, the virtual identities crafted by participants in electronic chatrooms, and the personal and familial stories that are told and retold as the sources of identity. All of these stories carry values and shape the ways we live. But they are not all life-giving. And they do not all form us to live in mercy and love in the world. The truth-telling stories of the scripture, when they are read in strength and opened up in ways that are not trivializing, when their strong images are seen to witness to the Holy Trinity, are life-giving. And they may resonate in our lives, giving us strength to refuse some stories—to turn off those television programs that demean humanity, cease to do impersonations on the Internet, avoid some films—and to encourage others. The lectionary—its readings, its psalms, its primary images—can provide us with materials to read and recite and on which to meditate in important moments of each day. A book such as *Between Sundays,*[3] with its scripture readings echoing and supporting the Sunday lectionary, can give us ways to hear yet more of the Bible and ultimately to learn how to hear all our important stories in the light of God's judgment and grace.

But the word-tradition, the story-tradition, of the scriptures does yet more. It gives us a gift to give our neighbor. Our neighbors in North America are also living by stories, some of these stories being poisonous. "Let me tell you what gives life and hope to me," we may offer. Or, "Come and listen with me," we may say, as we invite them to the assembly. The great way to baptism being recovered in the churches, the catechumenate, is mostly made up of the sharing of stories, our life stories and God's life-giving story.

And then there are the prayers. The Christian community, when it is faithful in worship, genuinely stands before God as priests for the world, crying out to God for all those throughout the world and in our near neighborhood whose wretchedness is their only prayer. Worship renewal must always be about the recovery of the seriousness and importance of this intercessory prayer. The temptations to pray only for ourselves, for our congregation, even only for our own sick must be resisted. But if we pray as a priestly people before God for the sake of the world, we will be formed to walk in the world in a different way—to listen, respond, love, rejoice in signs of the life-giving mercy of God. Indeed, the gifts of money and food that we give in church will then not be our solution to the problems we name in the prayers nor some demonstration of how benevolent we are. Rather, these gifts will be part of the prayers themselves, witness-tokens that we believe that God has made the world for life and mutual support, demonstrations of our own neediness before

God, signs that mercy and support have been shown to us and this
love and support can only be shared.

Stories in the church, prayers of intercession, and the celebration of the holy supper turn inside out. But without a strong practice of the word, of intercessions and the eucharist in our liturgies, these things would be unavailable for the reinterpretation of our daily lives.

In North America, there are diverse political practices and diverse economic theories. Too often the politics is a politics of rage, and the economics is whatever garnering and dispersal of money will benefit the self. The Christian liturgy has its own politics and its own economy. Its politics is established by baptism in which each of us is given our identity in Jesus Christ. That identity unites us with a community in mission, identifies us with all those little and needy ones who belong to Christ, makes us resistant to the boundaries between people that the politics of rage would throw up. In Christ, there is neither male nor female, Jew nor Greek, insider nor outsider, black nor white, but Christ is all and in all. The economics of the liturgy is found in the Lord's supper: there is some for all, given in mercy, welcoming to life. It is a matter of mission that Christian congregations set out this politics and this economics in North America.

Or say it this way, with the Evangelical Lutheran Church in America:

> In every celebration of the means of grace, God acts to show forth both the need of the world and the truth of the Gospel. In every gathering of Christians around the proclaimed Word and the holy sacraments, God acts to empower the Church for mission. Jesus Christ, who is God's living bread come down from heaven, has given his flesh to be the life of the world. This very flesh, given for the life of all, is encountered in the Word and sacraments.
>
> Baptism and baptismal catechesis join the baptized to the mission of Christ. Confession and absolution continually reconcile the baptized to the mission of Christ. Assembly itself, when that assembly is an open invitation to all peoples to gather around the truth and presence of Jesus Christ, is a witness in the world. The regular proclamation of both Law and Gospel, in Scripture reading and in preaching, tells the truth about life and death in all the world, calls us to faith in the life-giving God, and equips the believers for witness and service. Intercessory prayer makes mention of the needs of all the world and of all the Church in mission. When a collection is received, it is intended for the support of mission and for the concrete needs of our neighbors who are sick, hurt, and hungry. The holy Supper both feeds us with the body and blood of Christ and awakens our care for the hungry ones of the earth. The dismissal from the service sends us in thanksgiving from what we have seen in God's holy gifts to service in God's beloved world.[4]

LITURGY
AND MISSION
IN THE
NORTH
AMERICAN
CONTEXT

So by God's grace, the liturgical assembly is itself mission in North America. It is also continually forming us for mission in North America. Such assembly around word and sacrament, strongly practiced, is an astonishing gift, a gift that is always turning inside out.

NOTES

1. "The Blessed Sacrament of the Holy and True Body of Christ, and the Brother-hoods, 1519," in *Luther's Works*, ed. Helmut T. Lehmann (Philadelphia: Fortress Press, 1960), 35:54.

2. S. Anita Stauffer, ed., *Christian Worship: Unity in Cultural Diversity* (Geneva: Lutheran World Federation, 1996), 24.

3. Gail Ramshaw, *Between Sundays* (Minneapolis: Augsburg Fortress, 1997).

4. *The Use of the Means of Grace: A Statement on the Practice of Word and Sacrament* (Evangelical Lutheran Church in America, 1997), principle 51, background 51A.

CONTRIBUTORS

MICHAEL B. AUNE is academic dean and professor of liturgical and historical studies at Pacific Lutheran Theological Seminary, Berkeley, California.

MARK P. BANGERT is Christ Seminary-Seminex Professor of Worship and Music at Lutheran School of Theology at Chicago, Illinois.

JANN E. BOYD FULLENWIEDER is assistant professor of worship and homiletics and dean of the chapel at Lutheran Theological Seminary at Saskatoon, Saskatchewan.

ROBERT D. HAWKINS is professor of worship and music at Lutheran Theological Southern Seminary, Columbia, South Carolina.

WALTER C. HUFFMAN is professor of worship and dean of the chapel at Trinity Lutheran Seminary, Columbus, Ohio.

GORDON W. LATHROP is Charles A. Schieren Professor of Liturgy and chaplain at Lutheran Theological Seminary at Philadelphia, Pennsylvania.

MARK W. OLDENBURG is associate professor of liturgics at Lutheran Theological Seminary at Gettysburg, Pennsylvania.

THOMAS H. SCHATTAUER is associate professor of liturgics and dean of the chapel at Wartburg Theological Seminary, Dubuque, Iowa.

MONS A. TEIG is professor of worship at Luther Seminary, St. Paul, Minnesota.

PAUL WESTERMEYER is professor of church music at Luther Seminary, St. Paul, Minnesota.

BIBLIOGRAPHY

GENERAL

Baptism, Eucharist and Ministry. Faith and Order Paper 111. Geneva: World Council of Churches, 1982.

Braaten, Carl E., and Robert W. Jenson. *Christian Dogmatics.* Philadelphia: Fortress Press, 1984.

Constitution on the Sacred Liturgy. Second Vatican Council: 4 December 1963.

Jenson, Robert W. *Invisible Word: The Interpretation and Practice of Christian Sacraments.* Philadelphia: Fortress Press, 1978.

Johnson, Luke Timothy. *Religious Experience in Earliest Christianity.* Minneapolis: Fortress Press, 1998.

Senn, Frank C. *Christian Liturgy: Catholic and Evangelical.* Minneapolis: Fortress Press, 1997.

Statement on Sacramental Practices. Evangelical Lutheran Church in Canada, 1991.

The Use of the Means of Grace: A Statement on the Practice of Word and Sacrament. Evangelical Lutheran Church in America, 1997.

Wainwright, Geoffrey. *Doxology: The Praise of God in Worship, Doctrine and Life, a Systematic Theology.* New York: Oxford University Press, 1980.

White, James F. *Sacraments as God's Self Giving: Sacramental Practice and Faith.* Nashville: Abingdon Press, 1983.

LITURGY, CHURCH, AND MISSION

Anderson, E. Byron, and Bruce T. Morrill, eds. *Liturgy and the Moral Self: Humanity at Full Stretch before God.* Collegeville, Minn.: Liturgical Press, 1998.

Clapp, Rodney. *A Peculiar People: The Church as Culture in a Post-Christian Society.* Downers Grove, Ill.: InterVarsity Press, 1996.

Davies, J. G. *Worship and Mission.* London: SCM Press, 1966.

Dawn, Marva. *Reaching Out without Dumbing Down: A Theology of Worship for the Turn-of-the-Century Culture.* Grand Rapids, Mich.: Wm. B. Eerdmans, 1995.

Guder, Darrell L., ed. *Missional Church: A Vision for the Sending of the Church in North America.* Grand Rapids, Mich.: Wm. B. Eerdmans, 1998.

Kavanagh, Aidan. *On Liturgical Theology.* New York: Pueblo Publishing, 1984.

Lathrop, Gordon W. *Holy People: A Liturgical Ecclesiology.* Minneapolis: Fortress Press, 1999.

———. *Holy Things: A Liturgical Theology.* Minneapolis: Fortress Press, 1993.

———, ed. Open Questions in Worship. 8 vols. Minneapolis: Augsburg Fortress, 1994–96.

  1. *What Are the Essentials of Christian Worship?*
  2. *What Is "Contemporary" Worship?*
  3. *How Does Worship Evangelize?*
  4. *What Is Changing in Baptismal Practice?*
  5. *What Is Changing in Eucharistic Practice?*
  6. *What Are the Ethical Implications of Worship?*
  7. *What Does "Multicultural" Worship Look Like?*
  8. *How Does the Liturgy Speak of God?*

Nessan, Craig L. *Beyond Maintenance to Mission: A Theology of the Congregation.*
  Minneapolis: Fortress Press, 1999.
Pannenberg, Wolfhart. *Christian Spirituality.* Philadelphia: Westminster Press,
  1983.
Saliers, Don E. *Worship as Theology: Foretaste of Glory Divine.* Nashville: Abing-
  don Press, 1994.
———. *Worship Come to Its Senses.* Nashville: Abingdon Press, 1996.
Schmemann, Alexander. *For the Life of the World: Sacraments and Orthodoxy.*
  Crestwood, N.Y.: St. Vladimir's Seminary Press, 1973.
Senn, Frank C. *The Witness of the Worshiping Community: Liturgy and the Practice
  of Evangelism.* New York: Paulist Press, 1993.
Stauffer, S. Anita, ed. *Baptism, Rites of Passage, and Culture.* Geneva: Lutheran
  World Federation, 1999.
———. *Christian Worship: Unity in Cultural Diversity.* Geneva: Lutheran World
  Federation, 1996.
———. *Worship and Culture in Dialogue.* Geneva: Lutheran World Federation,
  1994.
Zizioulas, John D. *Being as Communion: Studies in Personhood and the Church.*
  Crestwood, N.Y.: St. Vladimir's Press, 1985.

PROCLAMATION OF THE WORD

Bonneau, Normand. *The Sunday Lectionary: Ritual Word, Paschal Shape.* College-
  ville, Minn.: Liturgical Press, 1998.
Brueggemann, Walter. *Cadences of Home: Preaching among Exiles.* Louisville, Ky.:
  Westminster/John Knox, 1997.
Buttrick, David. *The Mystery and the Passion.* Minneapolis: Fortress Press, 1992.
Foley, Edward. *Preaching Basics: A Model and a Method.* Chicago: Liturgy Training
  Publications, 1998.
Long, Thomas G. *The Witness of Preaching.* Louisville, Ky.: Westminster/John Knox,
  1989.
Ramshaw, Gail. *God beyond Gender.* Minneapolis: Fortress Press, 1995.
West, Fritz. *Scripture and Memory: The Ecumenical Hermeneutic of the Three-Year
  Lectionaries.* Collegeville, Minn.: Pueblo Books, 1997.

HOLY BAPTISM

Johnson, Maxwell. *The Rites of Christian Initiation: Their Evolution and Interpre-
  tation.* Collegeville, Minn.: Pueblo Books, 1999.
Kavanagh, Aidan. *The Shape of Baptism: The Rite of Christian Initiation.* New
  York: Pueblo Publishing, 1978. Reprint, Collegeville, Minn.: Pueblo Books,
  1991.
Rite of Christian Initiation of Adults. Chicago: Liturgy Training Publications,
  1988.
Schlink, Edmund. *The Doctrine of Baptism.* Trans. Herbert J.A. Bouman. St. Louis:
  Concordia Publishing House, 1972.
Schmemann, Alexander. *Of Water and the Spirit.* New York: St. Vladimir's Seminary
  Press, 1974.
Welcome to Christ: A Lutheran Introduction to the Catechumenate; *Welcome to
  Christ: Lutheran Rites for the Catechumenate*; *Welcome to Christ: A Lutheran
  Catechetical Guide.* Minneapolis: Augsburg Fortress, 1997.
White, James F. *Sacraments as God's Self Giving: Sacramental Practice and Faith.*
  Nashville: Abingdon Press, 1983.
Yarnold, Edward. *The Awe-inspiring Rites of Initiation: Baptismal Homilies of the
  Fourth Century.* 2nd ed. Collegeville, Minn.: Liturgical Press, 1994.

HOLY COMMUNION

Davies, Horton. *Bread of Life and Cup of Joy: Newer Ecumenical Perspectives on the Eucharist*. Grand Rapids, Mich.: Wm. B. Eerdmans, 1993.

Foley, Edward. *From Age to Age: How Christians Celebrated the Eucharist*. Chicago: Liturgy Training Publications, 1991.

Just, Arthur A. *The Ongoing Feast: Table Fellowship and Eschatology at Emmaus*. Collegeville, Minn.: Pueblo Books, 1993.

LaVerdiere, Eugene. *Dining in the Kingdom of God: The Origins of the Eucharist according to Luke*. Chicago: Liturgy Training Publications, 1994.

Reumann, John. *The New Testament, Ecumenical Dialogues, and Faith and Order on Eucharist*. Philadelphia: Fortress Press, 1985.

Schmemann, Alexander. *The Eucharist: Sacrament of the Kingdom*. Trans. Paul Kachur. Crestwood, N.Y.: St. Vladimir's Seminary Press, 1988.

Wainwright, Geoffrey. *Eucharist and Eschatology*. New York: Oxford University Press, 1981.

TIME AND CALENDAR

Adam, Adolf. *The Liturgical Year: Its History and Its Meaning after the Reform of the Liturgy*. Trans. Matthew J. O'Connell. New York: Pueblo Publishing, 1981.

Alexander, J. Neil. *Wait for the Coming: The Liturgical Meaning of Advent, Christmas, Epiphany*. Washington, D.C.: Pastoral Press, 1993.

Cantalamessa, Raniero. *The Mystery of Easter*. Trans. Alan Neame. Collegeville, Minn.: Liturgical Press, 1993.

Porter, H. Boone. *The Day of Light: The Biblical and Liturgical Meaning of Sunday*. Washington, D.C.: Pastoral Press, 1987.

Stevenson, Kenneth. *Jerusalem Revisited: The Liturgical Meaning of Holy Week*. Washington, D.C.: Pastoral Press, 1988.

Stookey, Laurence Hull. *Calendar: Christ's Time for the Church*. Nashville: Abingdon Press, 1996.

Talley, Thomas J. *The Origins of the Liturgical Year*. 2nd ed. Collegeville, Minn.: Pueblo Books, 1991.

LITURGY AND ARCHITECTURE

Adams, William Seth. *Moving the Furniture: Liturgical Theory, Practice and Environment*. New York: Church Publishing, 1999.

Environment and Art in Catholic Worship. Washington, D.C.: United States Catholic Conference, 1978.

The Environment for Worship: A Reader. Washington, D.C.: National Conference of Bishops, 1980.

Giles, Richard. *Re-pitching the Tent: Reordering the Church Building for Worship and Mission*. Collegeville, Minn.: Liturgical Press, 1999.

Huffman, Walter C., and Ralph R. Van Loon, *Where We Worship* Process and Leader Guide, ed. S. Anita Stauffer. Philadelphia: Board of Publication, Lutheran Church in America, 1987.

Kuehn, Regina. *A Place for Baptism*. Chicago: Liturgy Training Publications, 1992.

Mauck, Marchita. *Shaping a House for the Church*. Chicago: Liturgy Training Publications, 1990.

Schloeder, Steven J. *Architecture in Communion: Implementing the Second Vatican Council through Liturgy and Architecture*. San Francisco: Ignatius Press, 1998.

Sovik, Edward A. *Architecture for Worship*. Minneapolis: Augsburg Publishing House, 1973.

Turner, Harold W. *From Temple to Meeting House*. New York: Mouton Publishers, 1979.

Cherwien, David. *Let the People Sing*. St. Louis: Concordia Publishing House, 1997.

Farlee, Robert Buckley, ed. *Leading the Church's Song*. Minneapolis: Augsburg Fortress, 1998.

Leaver, Robin A., and Joyce Ann Zimmerman, eds. *Liturgy and Music*. Collegeville, Minn.: Liturgical Press, 1998.

Westermeyer, Paul. *The Church Musician*, rev. ed. Minneapolis: Augsburg Fortress, 1998.

————. *Te Deum: The Church and Music*. Minneapolis: Fortress Press, 1998.

Wilson-Dickson, Andrew. *The Story of Christian Music: From Gregorian Chant to Black Gospel*. Minneapolis: Fortress Press, 1996.

RITUAL

Bass, Dorothy, ed. *Practicing Our Faith: A Way of Life for a Searching People*. San Francisco: Jossey-Bass, 1997.

Bell, Catherine. *Ritual: Perspectives and Dimensions*. New York: Oxford University Press, 1997.

————. *Ritual Theory, Ritual Practice*. New York: Oxford University Press, 1992.

Grimes, Ronald. *Ritual Criticism: Case Studies in Its Practice, Essays on Its Theory*. Columbia, S.C.: University of South Carolina Press, 1990.

Hoffman, Lawrence. *Beyond the Text: A Holistic Approach to Liturgy*. Bloomington, Ind.: Indiana University Press, 1987.

Underhill, Evelyn. *Worship*. New York: Harper, 1937.

LITURGY AND PASTORAL CARE

Allen, Joseph J. *The Ministry of the Church: Image of Pastoral Care*. Crestwood, N.Y.: St. Vladimir's Seminary Press, 1986.

Anderson, Herbert, and Edward Foley. *Mighty Stories, Dangerous Rituals: Weaving Together the Human and the Divine*. San Francisco: Jossey-Bass, 1998.

Capps, Donald. *Life Cycle Theory and Pastoral Care*. Philadelphia: Fortress Press, 1983.

Jones, L. Gregory. *Embodying Forgiveness: A Theological Analysis*. Grand Rapids, Mich.: Wm. B. Eerdmans, 1995.

Mitchell, Leonel L. *Pastoral and Occasional Liturgies: A Ceremonial Guide*. Cambridge, Mass.: Cowley Publications, 1998.

Perham, Michael. *Liturgy Pastoral and Parochial*. London: SPCK, 1984.

Ramshaw, Elaine. *Ritual and Pastoral Care*. Philadelphia: Fortress Press, 1987.

Underwood, Ralph L. *Pastoral Care and the Means of Grace*. Minneapolis: Fortress Press, 1993.

INDEX